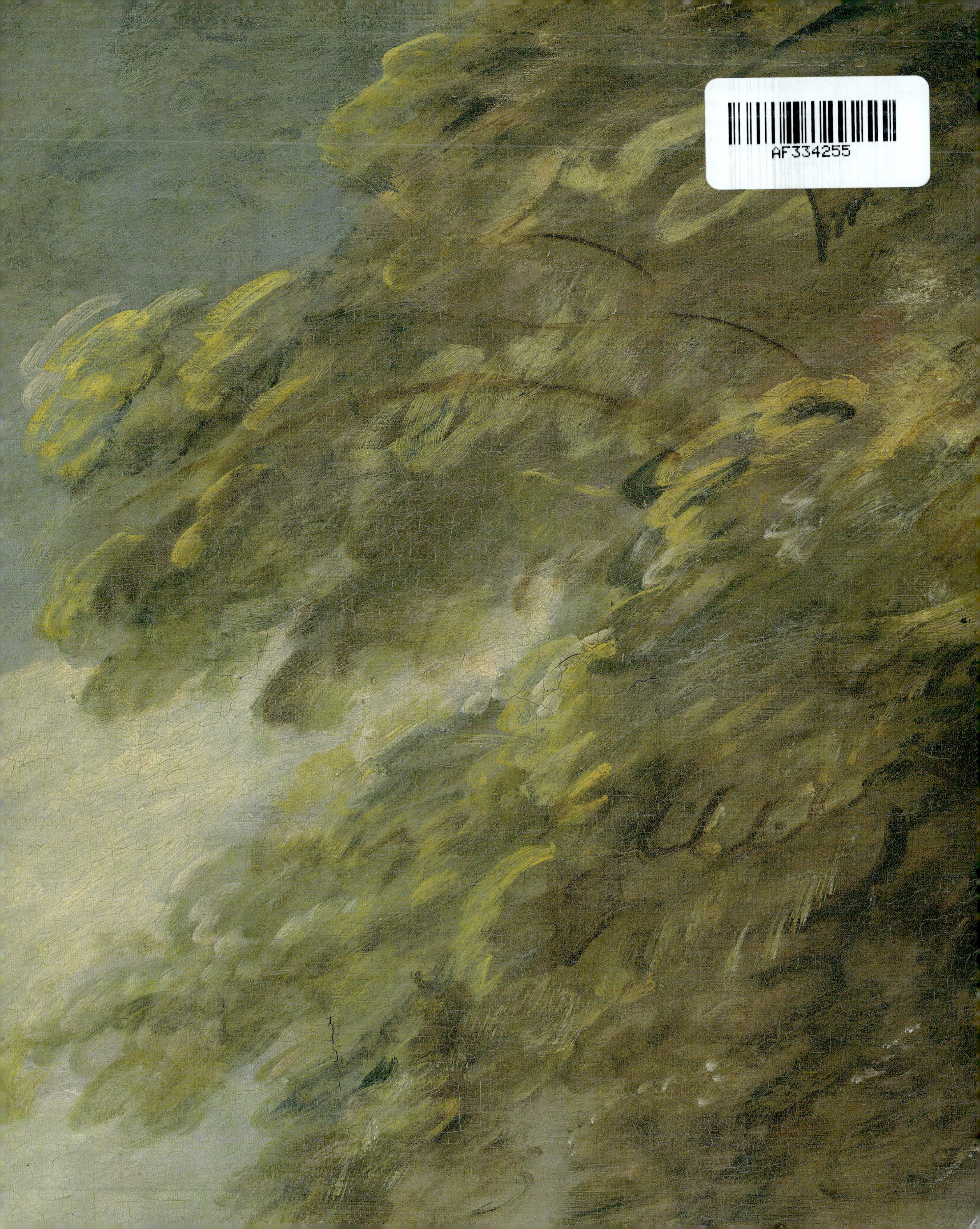
AF334255

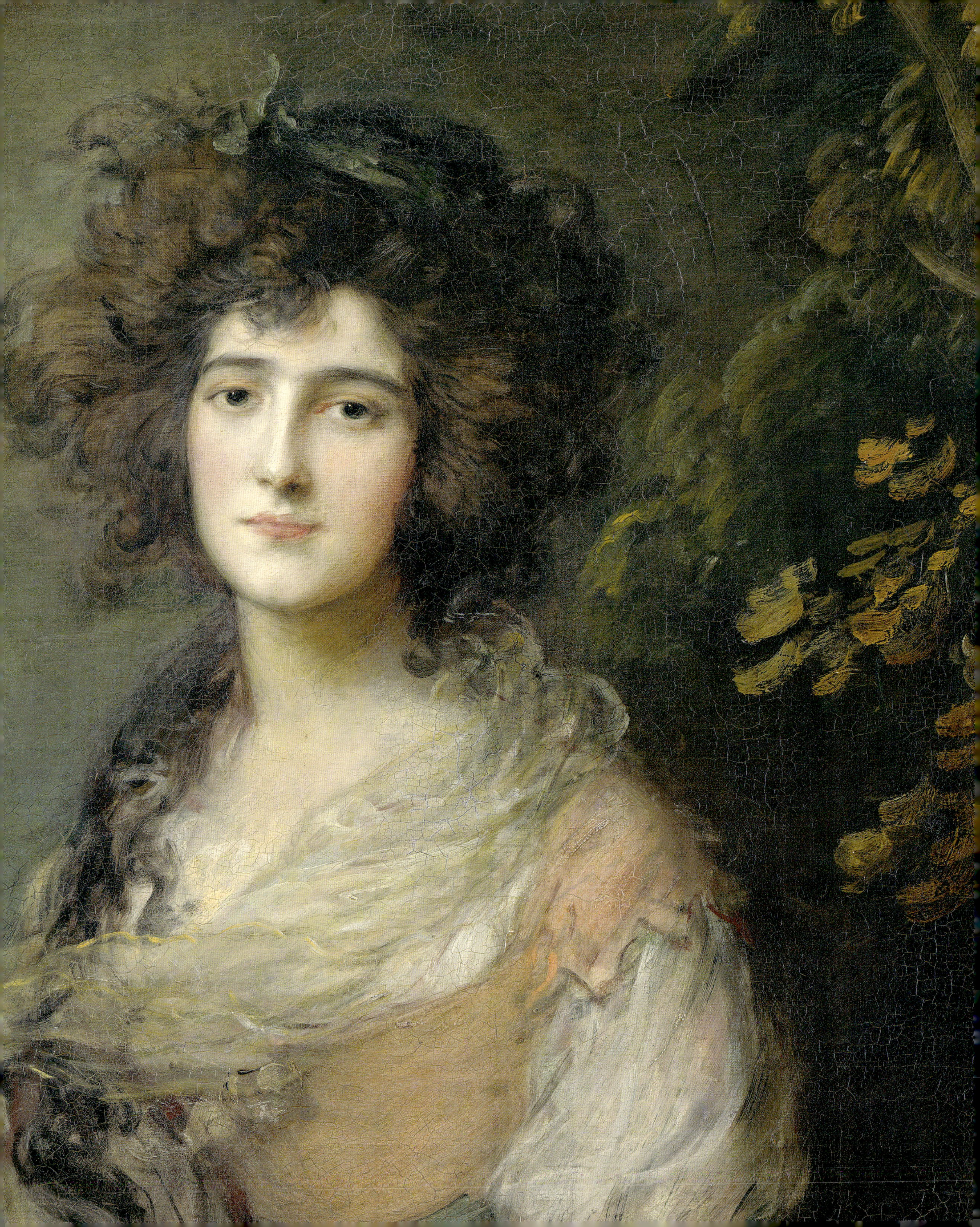

Thomas Gainsborough

AND THE

Modern Woman

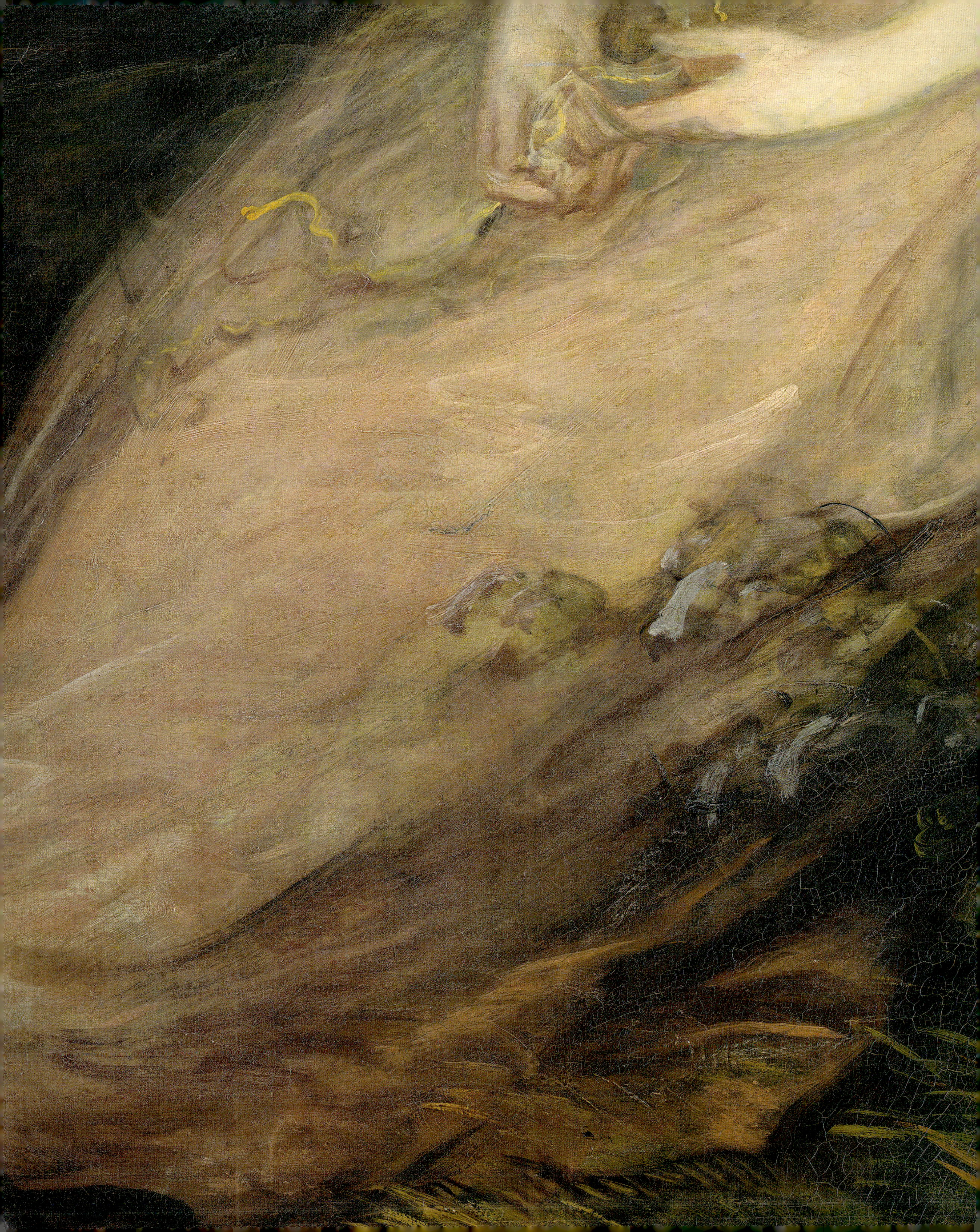

Thomas Gainsborough

AND THE

Modern Woman

ORGANIZED AND
EDITED BY

Benedict Leca

ESSAYS BY
Benedict Leca
Aileen Ribeiro
Amber Ludwig

This catalogue

ACCOMPANIES THE EXHIBITION

Thomas Gainsborough and the Modern Woman
AT THE Cincinnati Art Museum
September 18, 2010 — January 2, 2011
AND AT THE San Diego Museum OF Art
January 29, 2011 — May 1, 2011

First published jointly in 2010 by GILES

AN IMPRINT OF D GILES LIMITED

4 Crescent Stables, 139 Upper Richmond Road, London SW15 2TN, UK
www.gilesltd.com

For the Cincinnati Art Museum:

Organizer and editor:
BENEDICT LECA

Designer:
MARTIN VENEZKY'S
APPETITE ENGINEERS

Production editor:
ANNE BUENING

Photographic services:
SCOTT HISEY

Deputy director, presentation:
STEPHEN JAYCOX

For D Giles Limited:

Proofread by:
SARAH KANE

Produced by:
GILES, AN IMPRINT OF
D GILES LIMITED, LONDON

Printed and bound in
CHINA.

Library of Congress Cataloging-in-Publication Data

Thomas Gainsborough and the modern woman / organized and edited by Benedict Leca ; essays by Benedict Leca, Aileen Ribeiro, Amber Ludwig.
  p. cm.
  "This catalogue accompanies the exhibition ... at the Cincinnati Art Museum, September 18, 2010–January 2, 2011, and at the San Diego Museum of Art, January 29, 2011–May 1, 2011."
  Includes bibliographical references and index.
  ISBN 978-1-904832-85-0 (hardcover) — ISBN 978-0-931537-37-0 (pbk.)
  1. Gainsborough, Thomas, 1727–1788—Exhibitions. 2. Gainsborough, Thomas, 1727–1788—Criticism and interpretation. 3. Women—Great Britain—Portraits—Exhibitions. 4. Celebrities—Great Britain—Portraits—Exhibitions. 5. Women in art--Exhibitions. 6. Art and society—Great Britain—History—18th century—Exhibitions. I. Gainsborough, Thomas, 1727–1788. II. Leca, Benedict, 1963–. III. Ribeiro, Aileen, 1944–. IV. Ludwig, Amber, 1979–. V. Cincinnati Art Museum. VI. San Diego Museum of Art.
  ND1329.G34A4 2010
  759.2—dc22
2010027454

ISBN (hardcover): 978-1-904832-85-0

ISBN (softcover): 978-0-931537-37-0

All measurements are in inches and centimeters; height precedes width.
FRONT COVER: Thomas Gainsborough, *Ann Ford (later Mrs. Philip Thicknesse)*, detail, 1760, oil on canvas, 77-5/8 x 53-1/8 IN. (197.2 x 134.9 CM), Cincinnati Art Museum, Bequest of Mary M. Emery (1927.396)
FRONTISPIECE: Thomas Gainsborough, *Mrs. Richard Brinsley Sheridan*, detail, 1785–87, oil on canvas, 85-5/8 x 60-5/8 IN. (217.5 x 154 CM), The National Gallery of Art, Washington, Andrew W. Mellon Collection (1937.1.92)

Contents

Acknowledgments

THE Cincinnati Art Museum

AND

THE San Diego Museum OF Art

wish to thank the following for making the exhibition

Thomas Gainsborough and the Modern Woman

possible:

Sponsors

THE ALPAUGH FOUNDATION

THE ROBERT LEHMAN FOUNDATION

THE HAROLD C. SCHOTT FOUNDATION

THE SELZ FOUNDATION

A FRIEND OF THE CINCINNATI ART MUSEUM

PAUL F. MOSHER

Lending Institutions

FINE ARTS MUSEUMS OF SAN FRANCISCO

J. PAUL GETTY MUSEUM, *Los Angeles*

HUNTINGTON LIBRARY, ART COLLECTIONS, AND

BOTANICAL GARDENS, *San Marino, California*

KRANNERT ART MUSEUM AND KINKEAD PAVILION,

University of Illinois, Urbana-Champaign

METROPOLITAN MUSEUM OF ART, *New York*

NATIONAL GALLERY, *London*

NATIONAL GALLERY OF ART, *Washington*

PHILADELPHIA MUSEUM OF ART

TATE, *London*

WORCESTER ART MUSEUM, *Worcester, Massachusetts*

The Cincinnati Art Museum gratefully acknowledges the generous operating support provided by:

THE FINE ARTS FUND

THE OHIO ARTS COUNCIL

THE CITY OF CINCINNATI

THE CAROL ANN AND RALPH V. HAILE, JR./US BANK FOUNDATION

AND OUR MEMBERS.

THIS EXHIBITION IS SUPPORTED BY AN INDEMNITY FROM THE FEDERAL COUNCIL ON THE ARTS AND THE HUMANITIES.

Directors' Forewords

The Ladies' Reunion

By Aaron Betsky
Director
Cincinnati Art Museum

THE CINCINNATI ART MUSEUM, the oldest such institution west of the Alleghenies, holds a collection of over 60,000 works of art spanning six millennia of human history for its community. One of the greatest strengths of that wide-ranging assemblage of art objects is its British portraiture. Through the collecting acumen and subsequent generosity of Mary Emery and others, the Art Museum has acquired some of the greatest and grandest portraits of the late eighteenth and early nineteenth century by Thomas Gainsborough, Joshua Reynolds, and George Romney. This exhibition makes excellent use of that assemblage of pictures, while profiting from the generosity of lenders in both the United States and the United Kingdom.

What is always of special interest to me in our collections is how we can use these objects of art, both singularly and in groupings, to trace the development, maturation, and transformation of particular effective elites throughout history. These were, after all, in every culture the clients able to command the best art in order to make their achievements, aspirations, and fears real, immediate, and enduring. Our Art Museum can show the glory of British portraiture as the affirmation of that country's ruling class at the height of its power. It also displays the change from a land-based aristocracy showing itself on its country estates to the emergence of a new set of clients who gained power through trade and manufacturing. In this new world, one made a place for oneself in the world as much as one inherited a fixed position. Character became as important as parentage, and art conspired with economy to define how the new effective elite defined itself.

The portrait at the heart of this small exhibition is of signal importance in this development — as our curator, Dr. Benedict Leca, so brilliantly shows. The emergence of a group of both women and artists who made their way through their talents, and whose expressive modes stood out against the fixed and canonizing modes of some of their predecessors, paralleled the psychological portrait as it was then appearing in literature and theory both in England and on the Continent. In the portrait of Miss Ann Ford, and in that of the other "demireps" Dr. Leca has collected, we see indeed the face of the modern, powerful woman appearing. We hope that subsequent exhibitions will draw on other such signal moments in our collections to help us understand where our current definitions of self and its place in society came from.

This momentary collection could not have come about without the support and generosity of the lenders of this exhibition, who all agreed to part with their masterpieces for the duration of this exhibition. We realize how difficult it was to part with these beautiful ladies. We are very grateful to all of these lenders, and to the sponsors of the exhibition, including the Alpaugh Foundation, the Robert Lehman Foundation, the Harold C. Schott Foundation, the Selz Foundation, and a Friend of the Art Museum. And as always, the generous operating support provided by the Fine Arts Fund, the Ohio Arts Council, the City of Cincinnati, the Carol Ann and Ralph V. Haile, Jr./US Bank Foundation, and our members is deeply appreciated. We also thank Stephen Bonadies, the Art Museum's former chief conservator, for beginning the process of restoring Miss Ford to her proper glory. I am also deeply grateful to all those at the Art Museum who worked so diligently and creatively to bring this project to fruition.

Fashioning Women

By Julia Marciari-Alexander
Deputy Director for Curatorial Affairs
San Diego Museum of Art

THE SAN DIEGO MUSEUM OF ART is delighted to be the second venue for this groundbreaking show, especially as it complements this institution's remarkable collection of Old Masters, a collection notable for its group of portraits from the Renaissance to the eighteenth century, by such artists as Giorgione, Van Dyck, Goya, and Batoni. To bring this choice selection of Gainsborough's striking portraits of the most visible women of his day to San Diego augments our audiences' appreciation of the way portraiture not only contributed to but also shaped modern society. *Thomas Gainsborough and the Modern Woman* makes clear that twenty-first-century practices and notions of celebrity and self-fashioning, especially of women, share deep connections with — and arguably derive directly from — the modern Western society that took shape in the second half of the eighteenth century in London, Paris, and Rome. Beyond adding to our understanding of portraiture, moreover, the exhibition affords the opportunity to see the brilliant brushwork of Gainsborough, one of the supreme technicians in the history of putting oil paint to canvas.

We are deeply grateful to the many lenders to the exhibition, all major institutions in the United States and the United Kingdom, and we very much hope that this will be the marker of continued collaborations. For their untiring cooperation in securing major pictures for both venues, we would like to thank especially the trustees of and our colleagues at the National Gallery of Art, foremost among them Franklin Kelly, deputy director and chief curator, and at the Huntington Library, Art Collections, and Botanical Gardens: Steven Koblik, president; John Murdoch, the Hannah and Russel Kully Director of the Art Collections; and Catherine Hess, chief curator of European art. We have benefited greatly from the expert work of Benedict Leca, curator of European painting, sculpture, and drawings, and his colleague Susan Hudson, exhibition coordinator, at the Cincinnati Art Museum. In San Diego the installation and interpretation have been coordinated by John Marciari, curator of European art, and Scot Jaffe, associate director for exhibitions and collections. The San Diego Museum of Art extends its special thanks to Paul Mosher, the lead sponsor of this exhibition in San Diego. Finally, this exhibition could not have come to San Diego without the remarkable support of the Federal Council on the Arts and the Humanities, which generously provided indemnity for the loans.

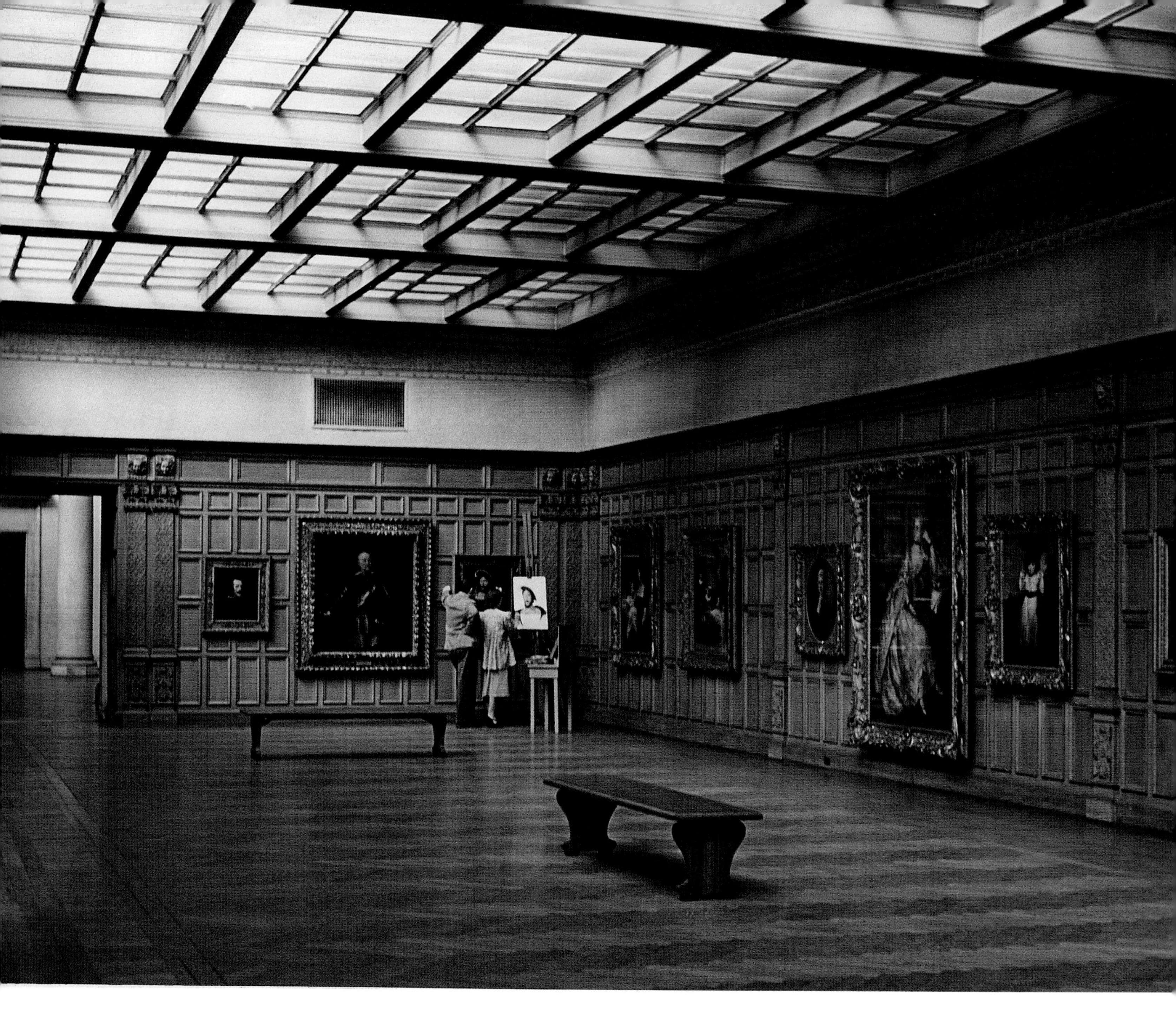

Introduction

By Benedict Leca
Curator of European Painting,
Sculpture, and Drawings
Cincinnati Art Museum

WHEN STROLLING THE GALLERIES of museums, we tend to forget that the canonical works we so revere today were often the subject of controversy in their original context. Old Master portraiture, in this light, is especially slippery. For even if we can discern period fashions, we rarely know the codes and mores that painter and sitter were engaging, if not repudiating, when creating a signal portrait. Standards of decency change, and what appears today as utterly benign might have been scandalous in another era. Often, conventional gallery installations of British eighteenth-century art have played, consciously or not, on stereotypes of tea-sipping elegance, further inflecting given pictures in ways more in step with enduring projections of feminine propriety than historical accuracy. Witness the Cincinnati Art Museum's pre-war installation of its Thomas Gainsborough masterpiece portrait *Ann Ford* (OPPOSITE), the painting at the heart of this exhibition. There, the onetime *enfant terrible* of musical life in 1760s London has been encased in a narrative of sanitized domestic life, flanked on one side by family portraits and an oval of a man (a "husband"), and on the other by a depiction of a robed infant by Gainsborough's later contemporary Hoppner.

It is indeed hard to imagine Ann Ford's portrait as a radical painterly statement or Thomas Gainsborough — he of the bucolic "landskips" and dashing society portrayals — as a fundamentally seditious artist. But without overstating the case, Gainsborough was oppositional in some of his artistic affinities compared to most of his peers. In his emphasis on the individuality of his touch, his attention to the material effects of paint, and his dissident posture toward academicism, Gainsborough was hardly just another amenable portraitist obediently plying the conventions of his genre. We can blame the dazzling beauty of his paintings, the sheer bravura of masterworks such as the National Gallery of Art's *Mrs. Richard Brinsley Sheridan* or the Metropolitan Museum of Art's *Grace Dalrymple*, for hindering our full appreciation of his achievement and its progressive bent. Whether one chooses to call him modernist or not, Gainsborough surely figures at bedrock as the primary British rejoinder to the Francocentric lineage of modernism.

It seems strange that a portrait and portraiture itself — in one sense that most retrograde of genres, given its responsibility to likeness — might function as the vehicle for proto-avant-garde painting. But this is a testament to the import assigned to portraits in the celebrity culture of Georgian England, a period that saw British portraitists establish their preeminence at the same time Britain was emerging as a modern commercial powerhouse. It isn't for nothing that the jurist Sir William Blackstone referred to his fellow citizens as "a polite and commercial people," just as it isn't surprising that portraits should be the site where portraitist and woman might affirm their progressive outlooks.[1] In a class-conscious yet upwardly mobile society, a female performer like Ann Ford was very much akin to a portraitist like Gainsborough: both were relatively marginalized professionals dependent on portraiture and image to negotiate new social positions that differed from those assigned to them by contemporary society. In the eighteenth century, portraits were part of an active negotiation of social and gender relations, and the argument here is that a special complicity between Gainsborough and women like Ann Ford formed the basis from which painter and sitter conspired to confound both traditional portraiture and calcified gender roles.

With fluidity of identity a hallmark of modernity, it behooves us therefore to attend not only to portraits and painting but also to norms of fashion and conduct, and how these might be implicated in the conventions of portrait painting. To this end, the differing but related emphases of the three essays in this catalogue aim to provide a fuller view of period perceptions — and representations — of famous women. My essay sets out first to establish Gainsborough's comparatively more permissive attitude toward women and how this was manifested in his compositions, in the attitudes he gave his feminine sitters, and in the general tenor of his feminine portraits. However, the crux of what I discuss centers on the very manner in which Gainsborough painted: a self-consciously painterly style that pushed the boundaries of decorum at the same time that it described and otherwise serviced progressive femininities. Indeed, what we are witness to in the present exhibition are provocative women provocatively painted. In the second essay, Aileen Ribeiro of London's Courtauld Institute, the world's foremost expert on early modern clothing and fashion, grapples anew with the subtleties of fashion and femininity invoked in the Art Museum's portrait of Ann Ford. Here we are reminded again of the subtlety with which Gainsborough navigated a complex of contemporary discourses

1
William Blackstone, *Commentaries on the Laws of England* (1765–69) 3:326.

on feminine fashion and visibility that had wide social and cultural implications. In the eighteenth century, even more than today, clothing assisted a woman's self-fashioning in significant ways: as a means to assert her individuality as well as to construct socially determined identities. In the final essay, Amber Ludwig, a Ph.D. candidate at Boston University and a specialist in British eighteenth-century portraiture, addresses what was the ever present requirement of an eighteenth-century woman's identity: virtue. Yet, as we learn, while the need for a woman to project virtue was a constant, the specifics surrounding any portrait — the sitter, the context of its creation, or the circumstances of its reception — were different and varied. In any case, painted portraits remained the most powerful means for women to fashion themselves as virtuous.

If Gainsborough was early on recognized by his contemporaries as a special talent, Cincinnatians, too, were precocious in their appreciation of the artist in America. Perhaps there is no better evidence of the special relationship between Gainsborough and the Cincinnati Art Museum than the episode recounted by *Cincinnati Post* reporter Eugene Segal in a special 1934 article devoted to Gainsborough's famous *Blue Boy*, now at the Huntington Library, Art Collections, and Botanical Gardens. Segal describes "the secrecy surrounding an exhibit of the [*Blue Boy*] at the Cincinnati Art Museum while it was on its way to California [in 1921]. Directors received a cryptic invitation telling them to be at the museum at a certain hour. After they had viewed it, the picture departed as stealthily as it had come."[2]

And yet this was hardly the most important or enduring of the Art Museum's initiatives regarding Gainsborough, since the Cincinnati Art Museum was the very first American museum to put on a large retrospective exhibition of his work, in May 1931. Featuring some fifty canvases — including no less than ten from Cincinnati collections — and a slew of rarely seen drawings from all over the United States and Britain, this exhibition was the only one devoted to the artist outside England fit to be listed in the eminent Ellis Waterhouse's still unsurpassed 1958 catalogue raisonné of Gainsborough's oeuvre. Indeed, one can venture that it remained unsurpassed in America in the breadth of the material presented until the National Gallery of Art's definitive retrospective of 2003. And what we might call the love affair between Cincinnati museum patrons and Gainsborough's portrait of Ann Ford continues unabated, as it remains one of the most recognized and sought-out pieces in the museum's collection and its reproductions an endur-ing hit in the gift shop (OVERLEAF). The present exhibition thus extends a long and rich history at the same time that it seeks to shed further light on one of the very great portraits of the Western tradition.

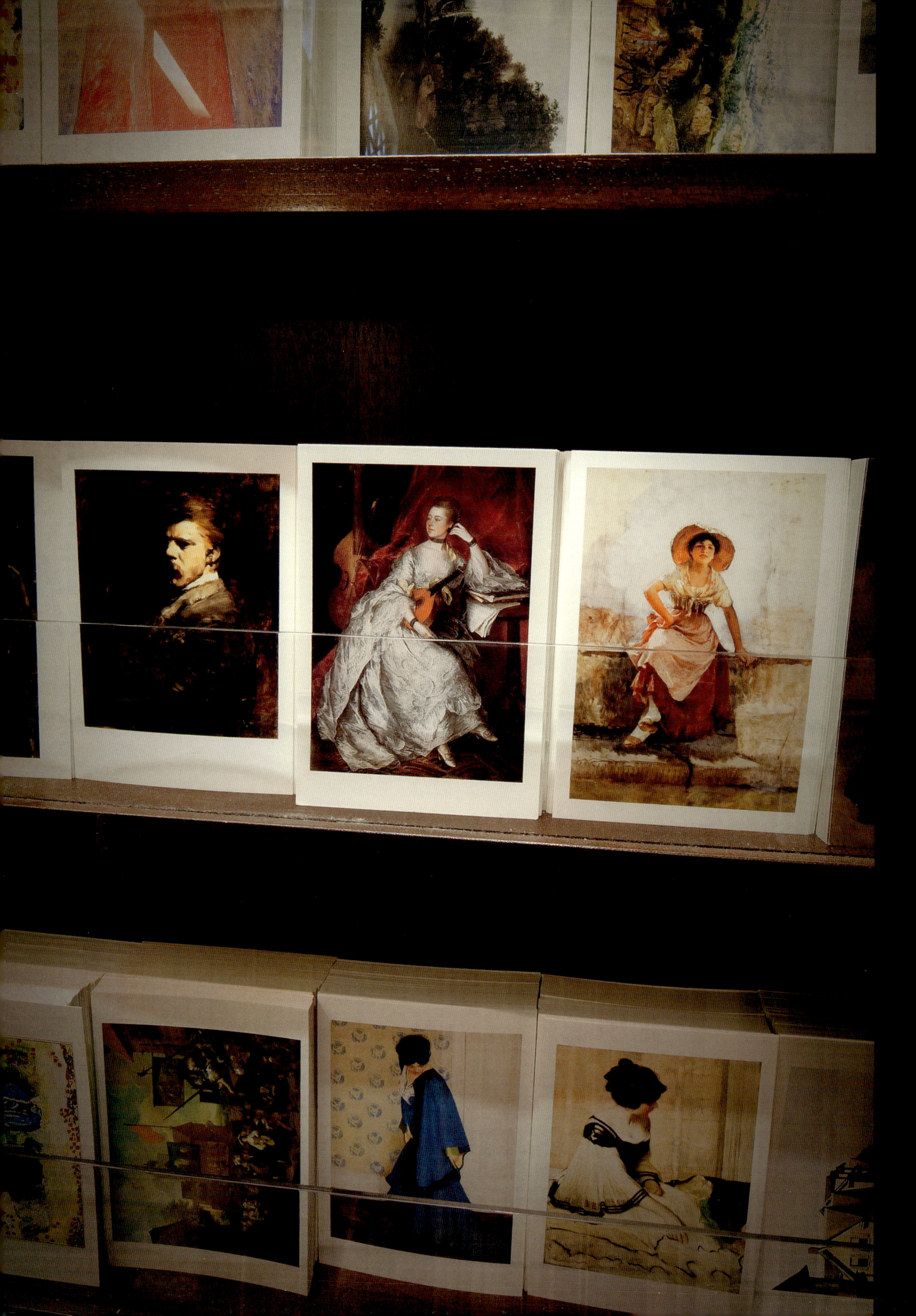

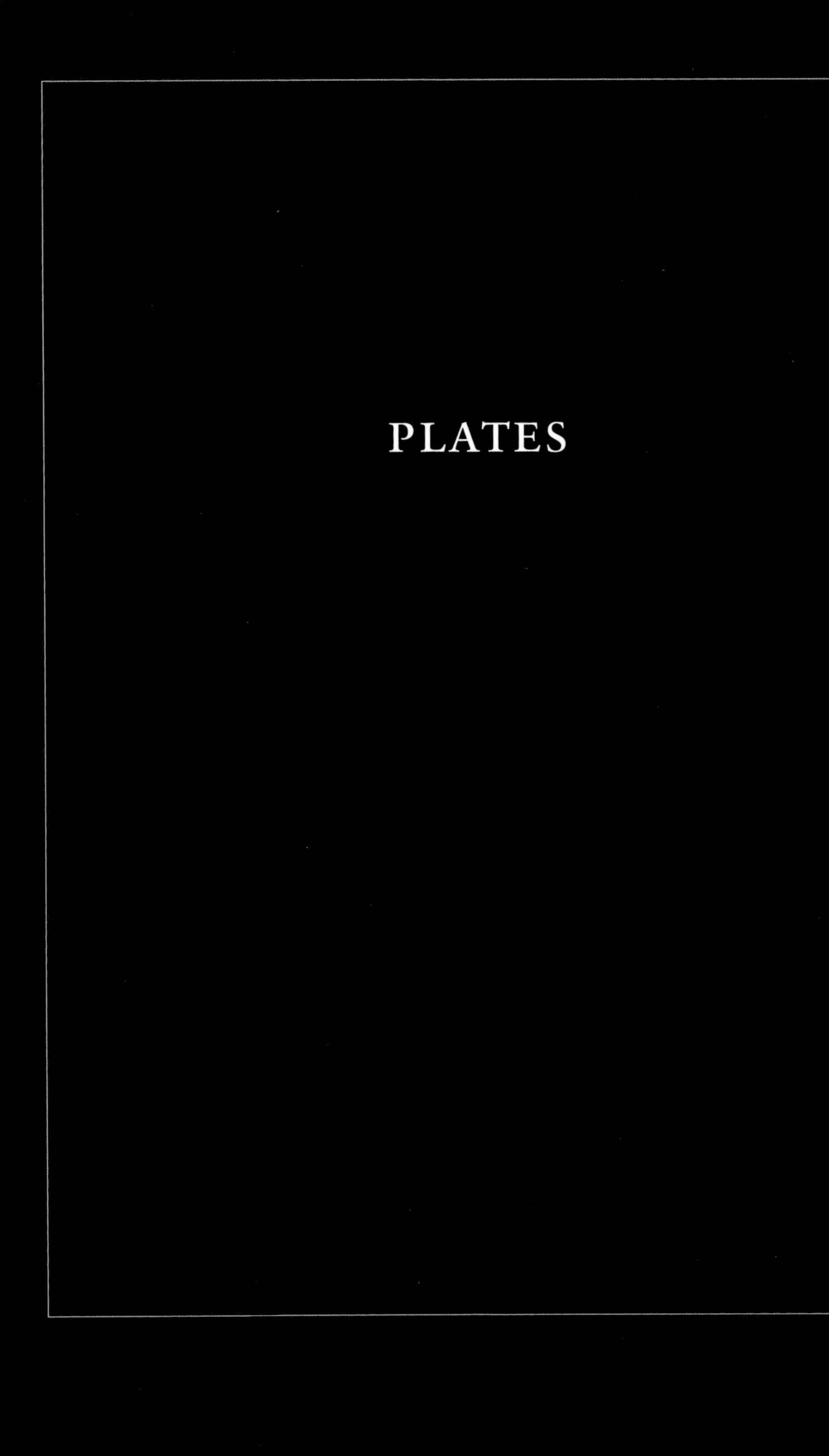

PLATES

PLATE

I

THOMAS GAINSBOROUGH
Ann Ford (later Mrs. Philip Thicknesse)
1760
OIL ON CANVAS
77-5/8 X 53-1/8 IN (197.2 X 134.9 CM)
CINCINNATI ART MUSEUM
BEQUEST OF MARY M. EMERY
(1927.396)

DETAILS APPEAR ON PAGES
41–42, 47, 59, 76, 108–110, 142–144

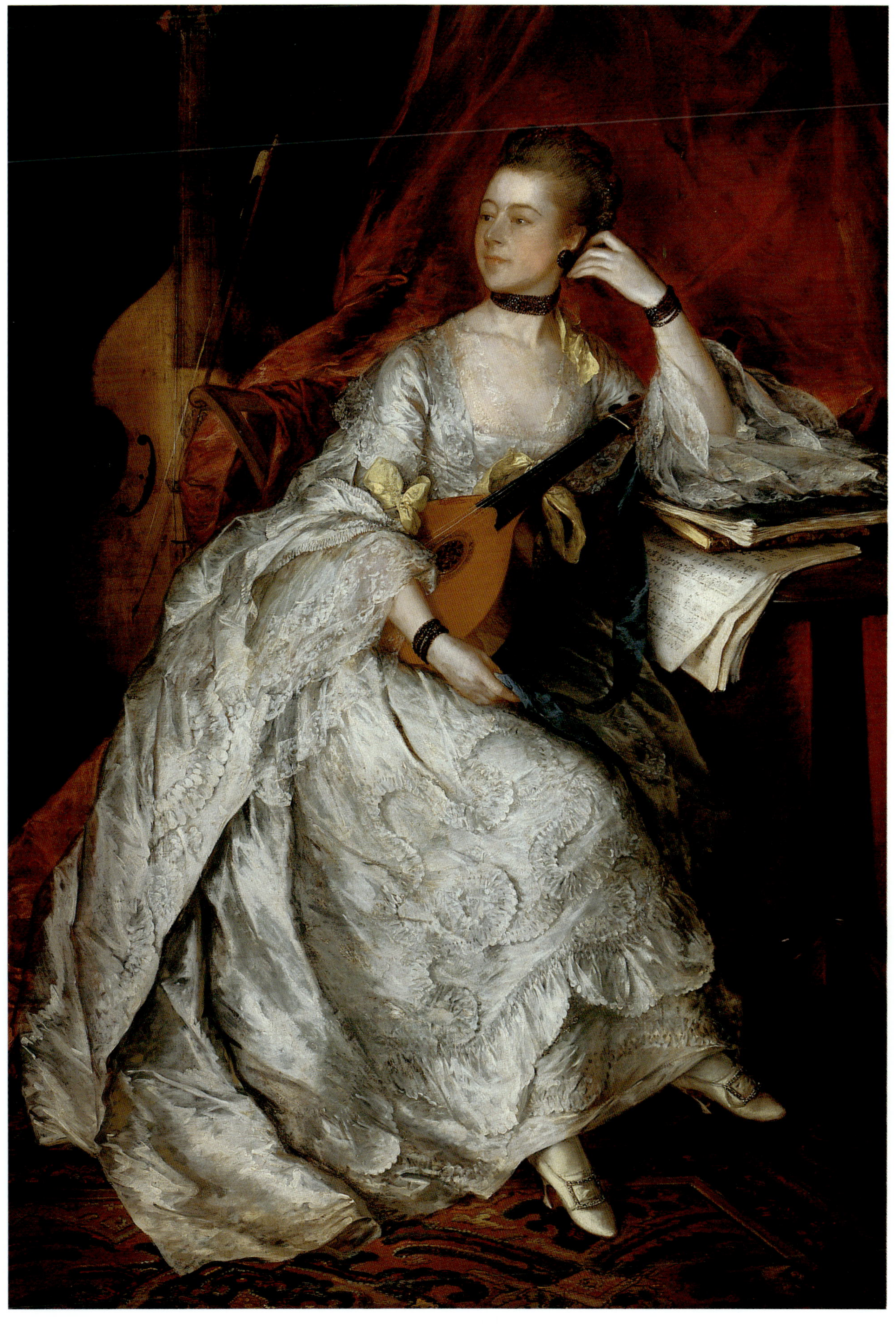

PLATE

2

THOMAS GAINSBOROUGH

Portrait of the Artist's Daughters

CA. 1763 – 64

OIL ON CANVAS

50-1/8 X 40-1/16 IN (127.3 X 101.7 CM)

WORCESTER ART MUSEUM

WORCESTER, MASSACHUSETTS

PURCHASE (1917.181)

DETAILS APPEAR ON PAGES
174–176

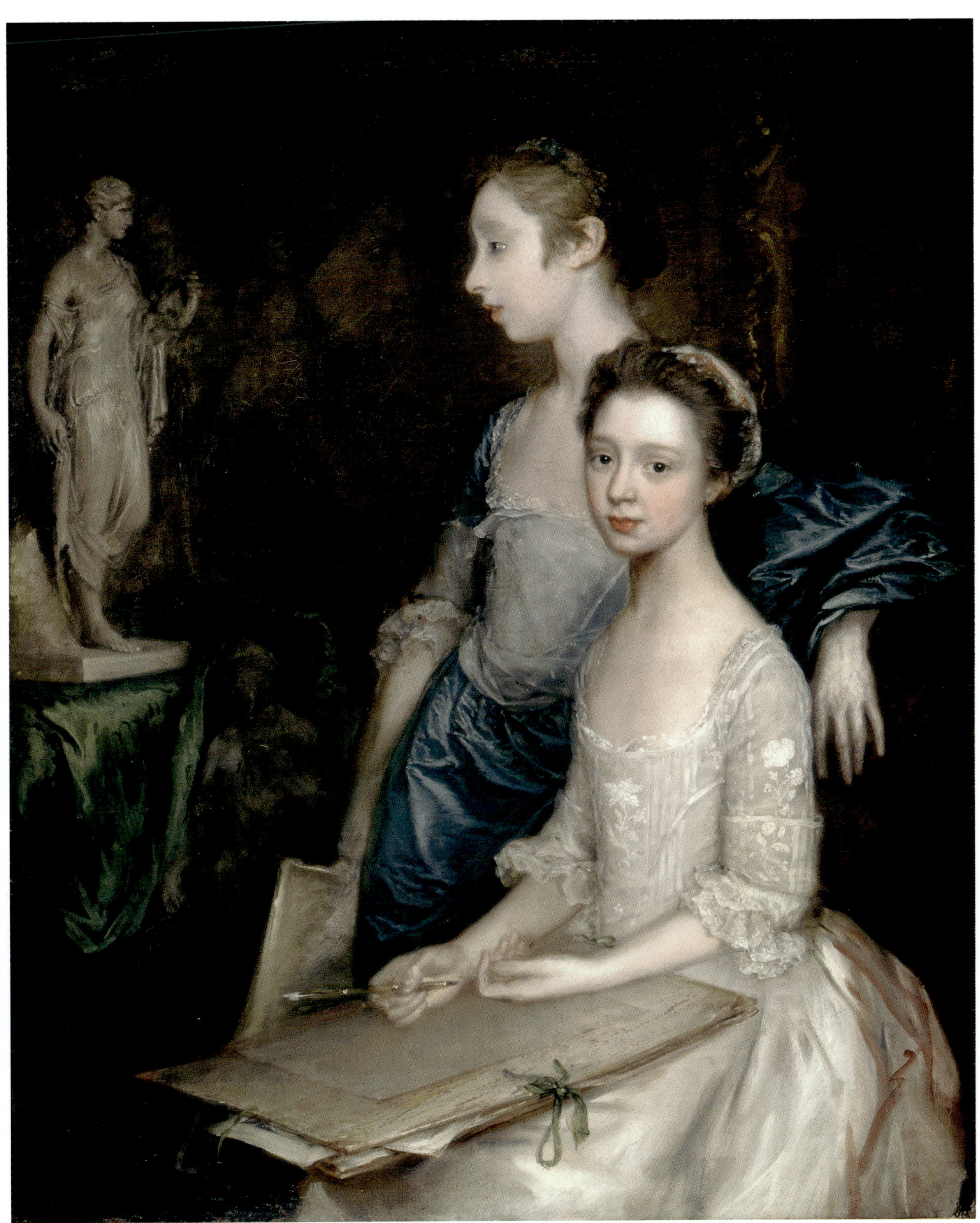

PLATE

3

THOMAS GAINSBOROUGH

Penelope, Viscountess Ligonier

1770

OIL ON CANVAS

94-1/2 X 61-3/4 IN (240 X 156.9 CM)

THE HUNTINGTON LIBRARY, ART COLLECTIONS,

AND BOTANICAL GARDENS

(11.29)

DETAILS APPEAR ON PAGES
194 – 196

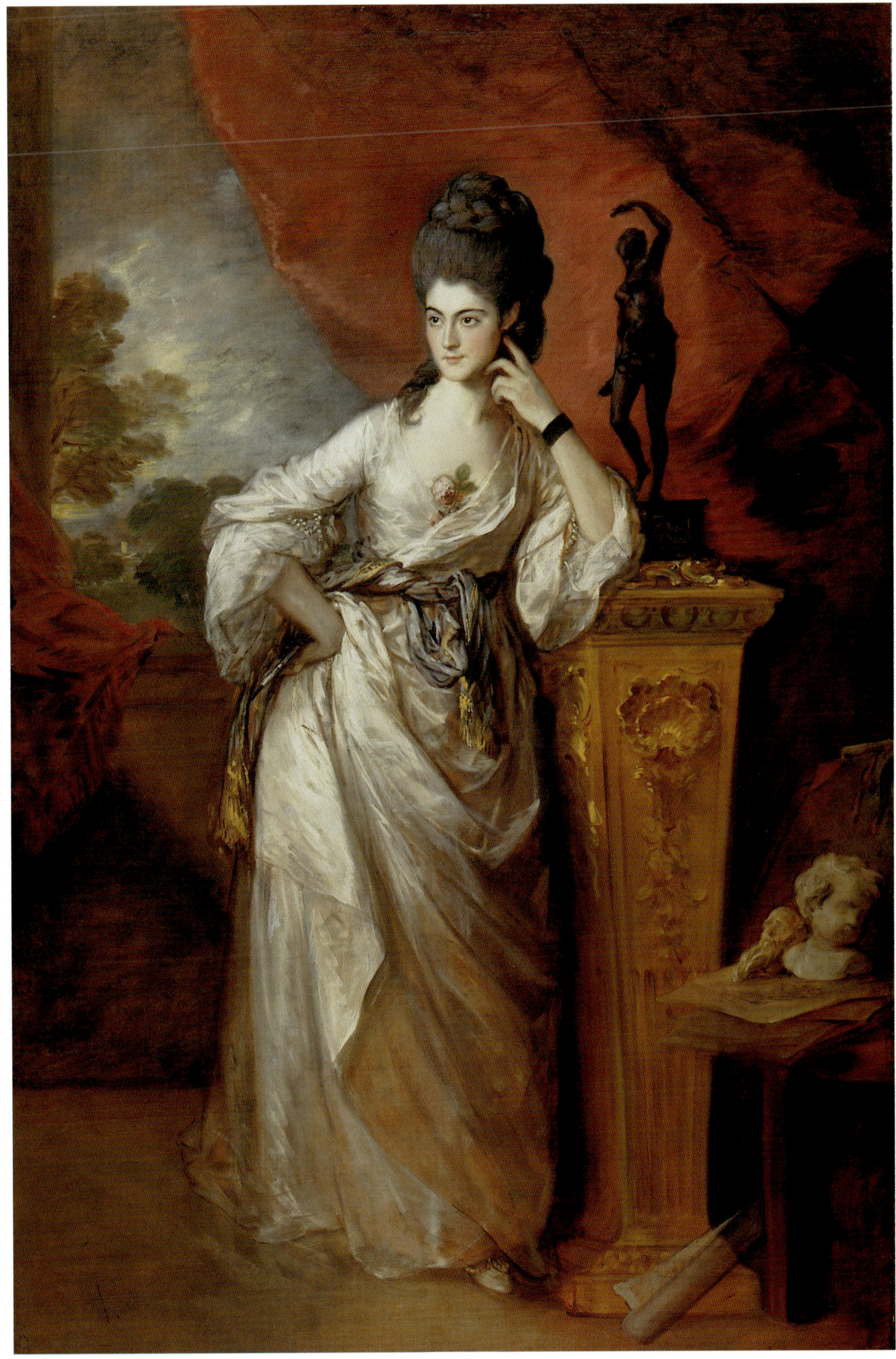

PLATE

4

THOMAS GAINSBOROUGH
Portrait of Miss Elizabeth Linley
(Later Mrs. Richard Brinsley Sheridan)
CA. 1775

OIL ON CANVAS

30 X 25 IN (76.2 X 63.5 CM)

PHILADELPHIA MUSEUM OF ART

THE GEORGE W. ELKINS COLLECTION, 1924

(E1924-4-13)

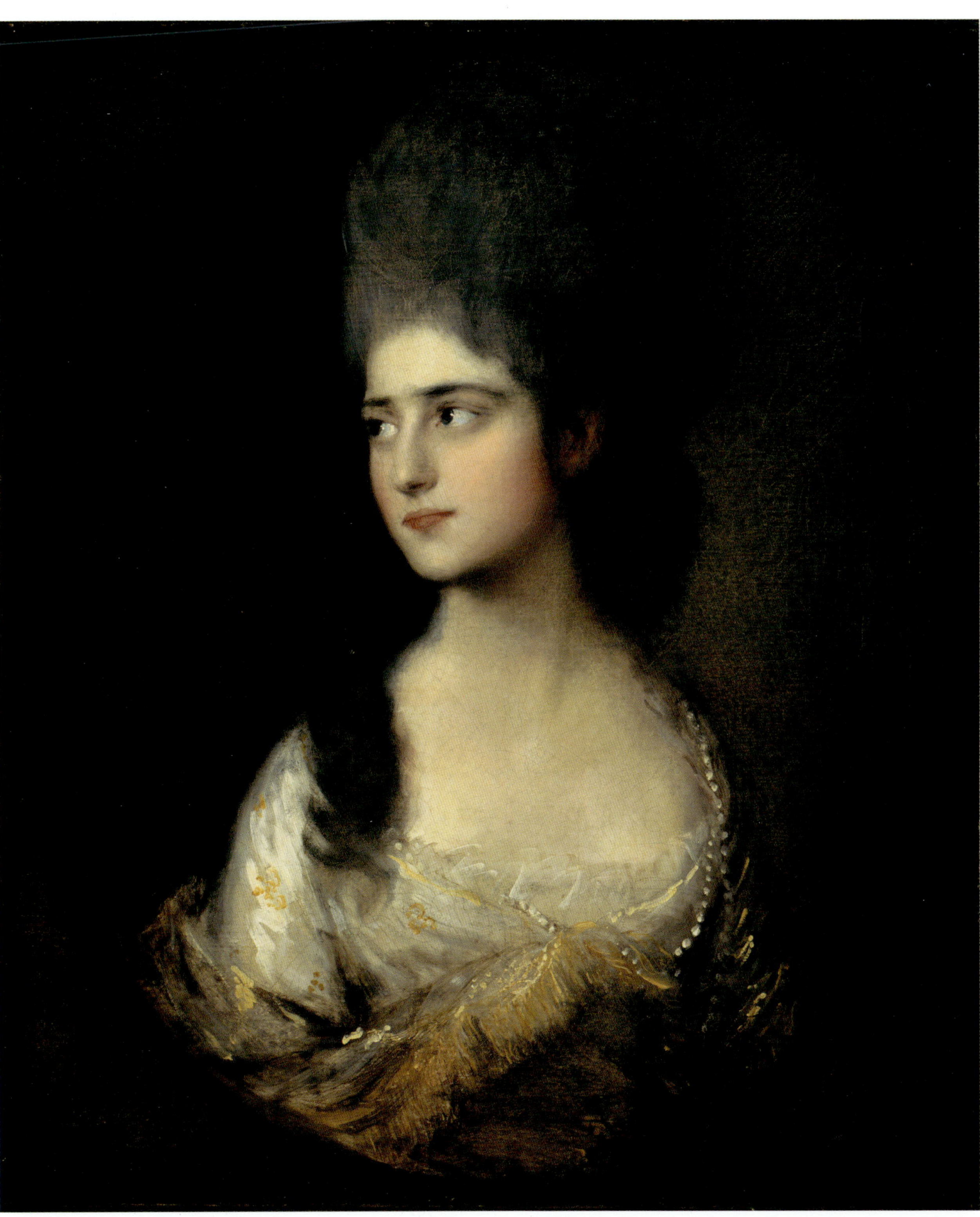

PLATE

5

THOMAS GAINSBOROUGH

Portrait of Anne, Countess of Chesterfield

1777 – 78

OIL ON CANVAS

86-1/2 X 61-1/2 IN (219.7 X 156.2 CM)

THE J. PAUL GETTY MUSEUM, LOS ANGELES

GIFT OF J. PAUL GETTY

(71.PA.8)

DETAILS APPEAR ON PAGES

101–103

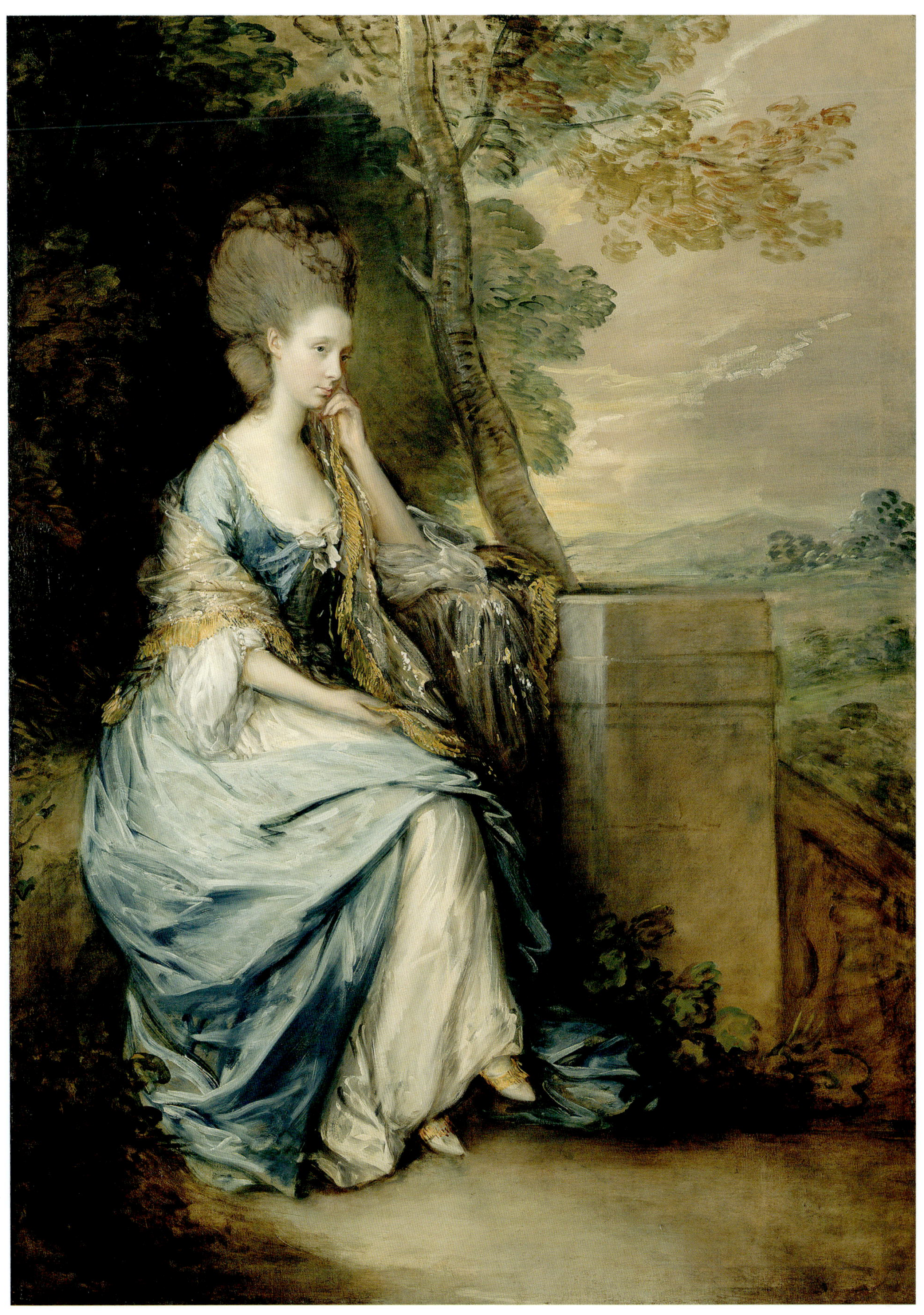

PLATE

6

THOMAS GAINSBOROUGH

Mrs. Grace Dalrymple Elliott (1754? – 1823)

1778

OIL ON CANVAS

92-1/4 X 60-1/2 IN (234.3 X 153.7 CM)

THE METROPOLITAN MUSEUM OF ART

BEQUEST OF WILLIAM K. VANDERBILT, 1920

(20.155.1)

DETAILS APPEAR ON PAGES
104, 106–107

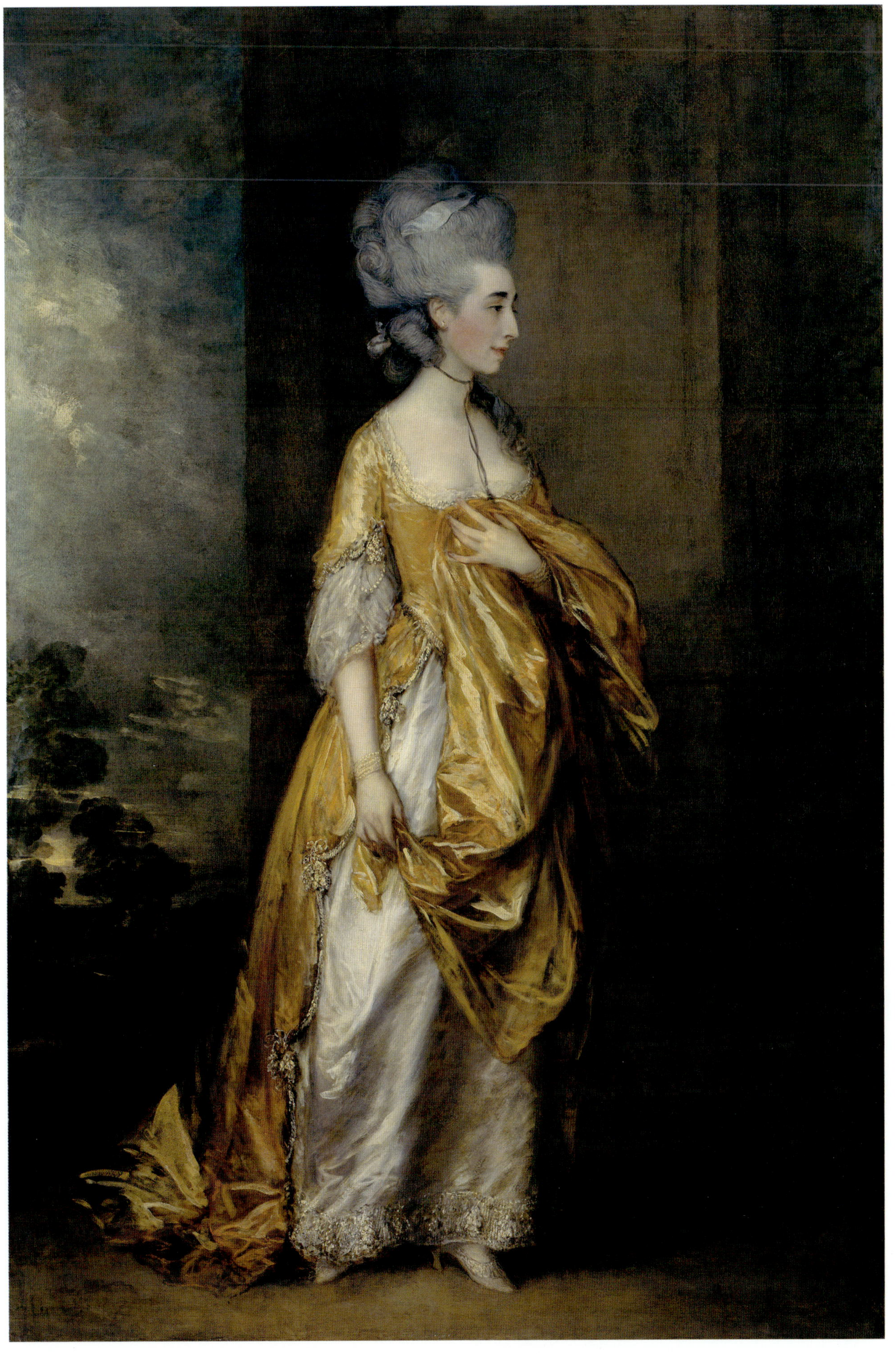

PLATE

7

THOMAS GAINSBOROUGH

Giovanna Baccelli

EXHIBITED 1782

OIL ON CANVAS

89-1/4 X 58-1/2 IN (226.7 X 148.6 CM)

TATE

PURCHASED WITH ASSISTANCE FROM

THE FRIENDS OF THE TATE GALLERY, 1975

(T02000)

DETAILS APPEAR ON PAGES
83–85, 87–90, 94–95

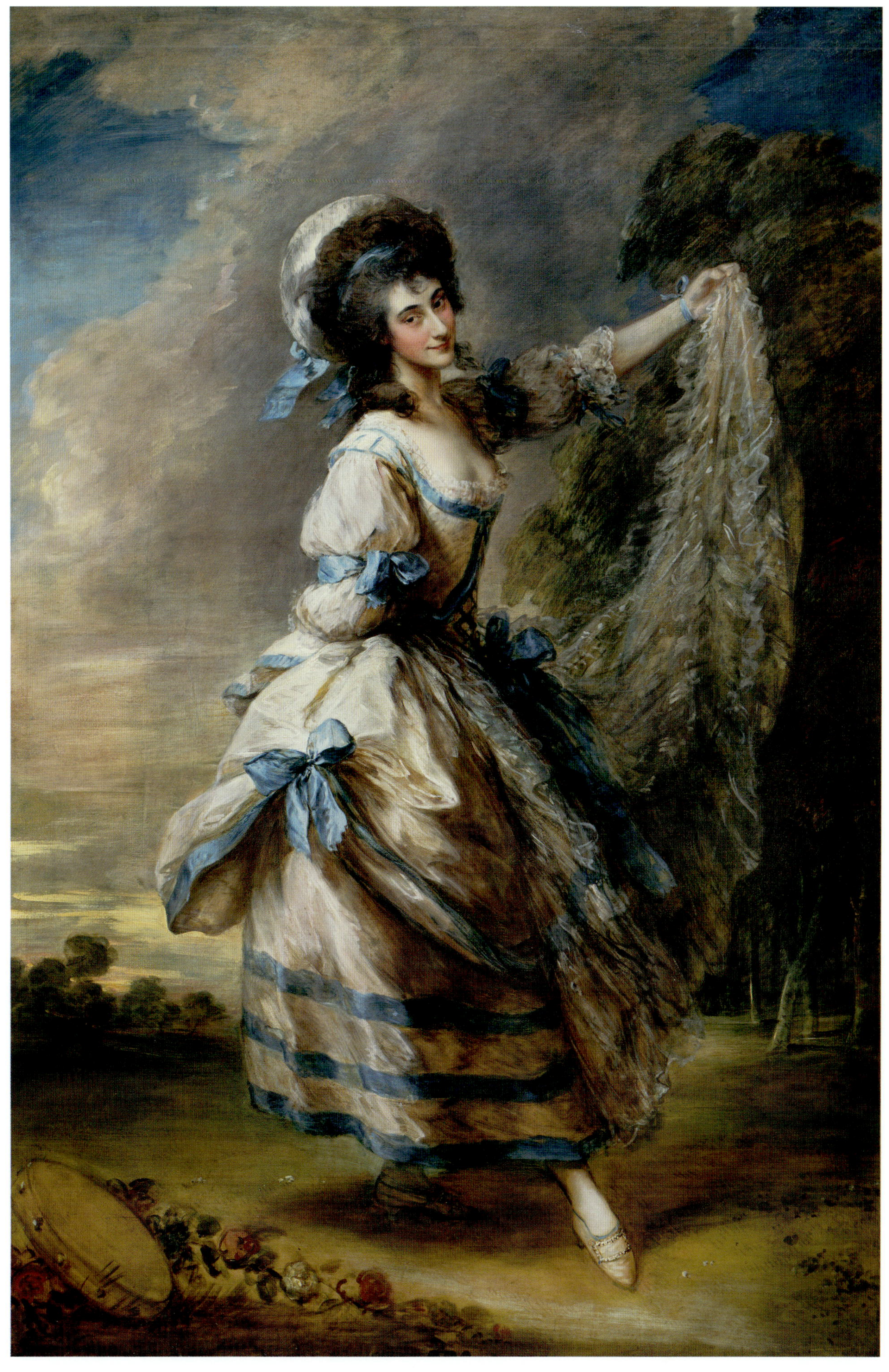

PLATE

8

THOMAS GAINSBOROUGH

Mrs. Maria Anne Fitzherbert

1784

OIL ON CANVAS

29-7/8 X 25 IN (75.9 X 63.5 CM)

FINE ARTS MUSEUMS OF SAN FRANCISCO

MUSEUM PURCHASE, MILDRED ANNA WILLIAMS COLLECTION

(1941.19)

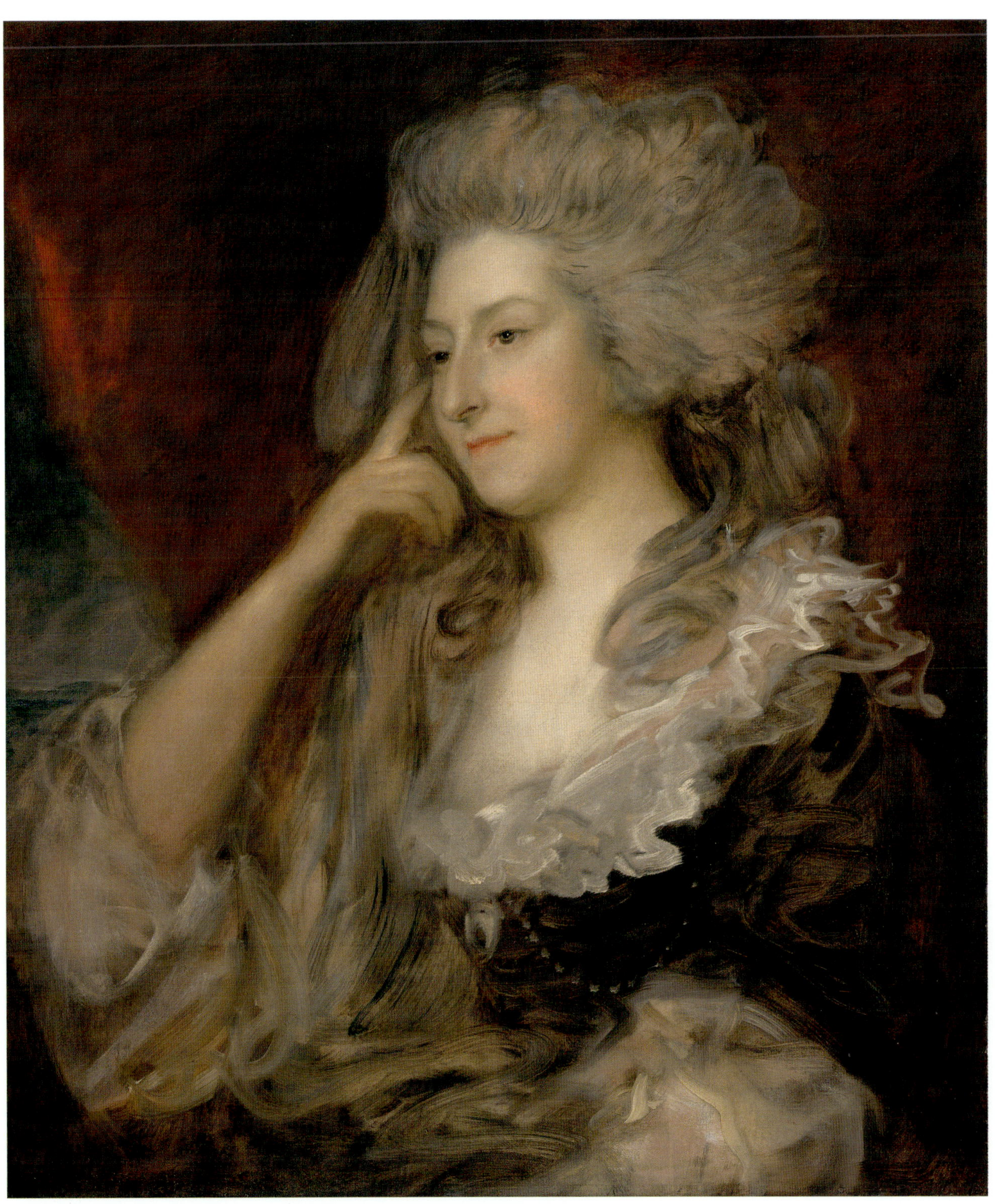

PLATE

9

THOMAS GAINSBOROUGH

Mrs. Siddons

1785

OIL ON CANVAS

49-3/4 X 39-1/4 IN (126.4 X 99.7 CM)

THE NATIONAL GALLERY, LONDON

BOUGHT, 1862

(NG683)

DETAILS APPEAR ON PAGES
63–65

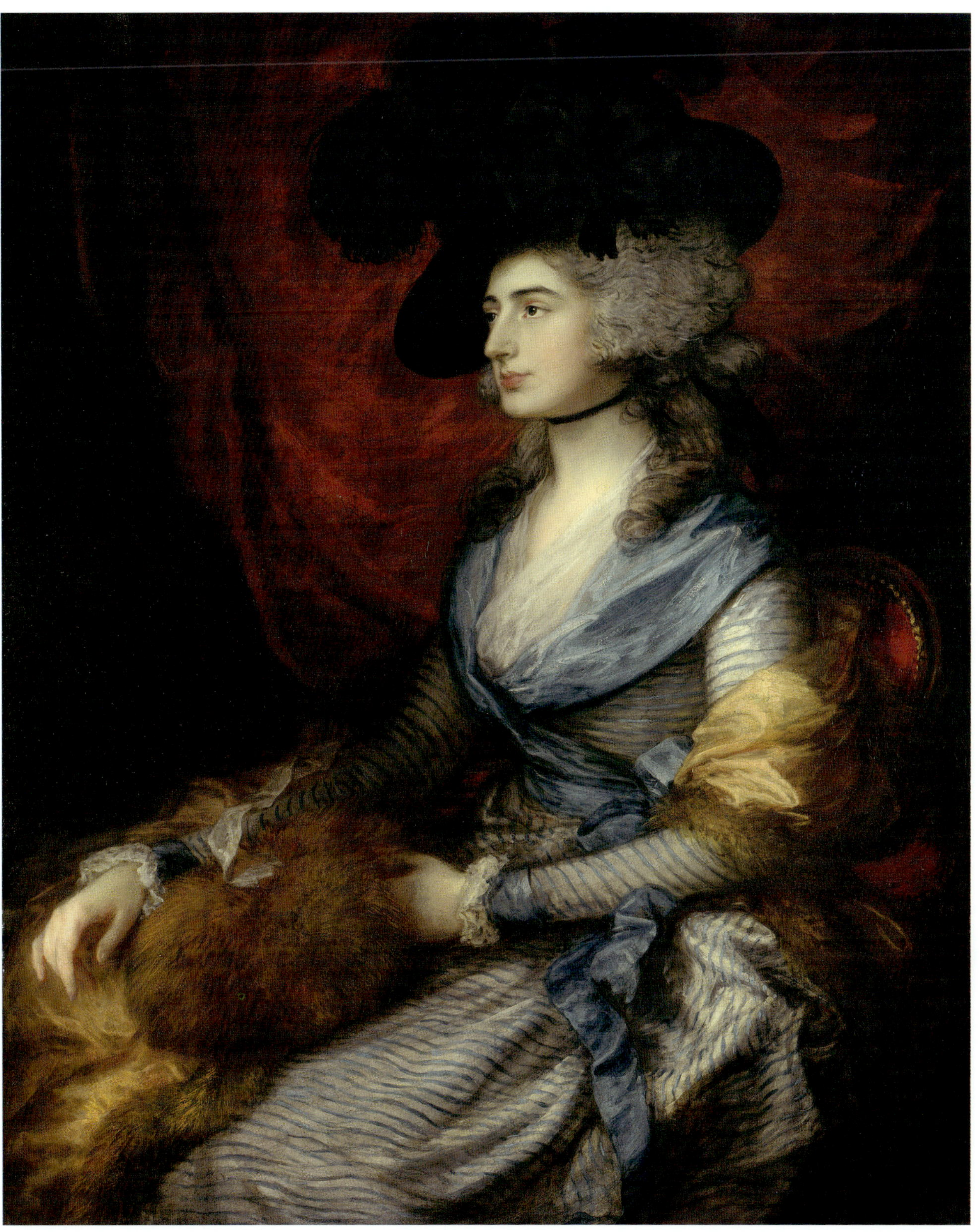

PLATE

IO

THOMAS GAINSBOROUGH
Mrs. Richard Brinsley Sheridan
1785 – 87
OIL ON CANVAS
85-5/8 x 60-5/8 IN (217.5 x 154 CM)
NATIONAL GALLERY OF ART, WASHINGTON
ANDREW W. MELLON COLLECTION
(1937.1.92)

DETAILS APPEAR ON PAGES
1, 2, 4

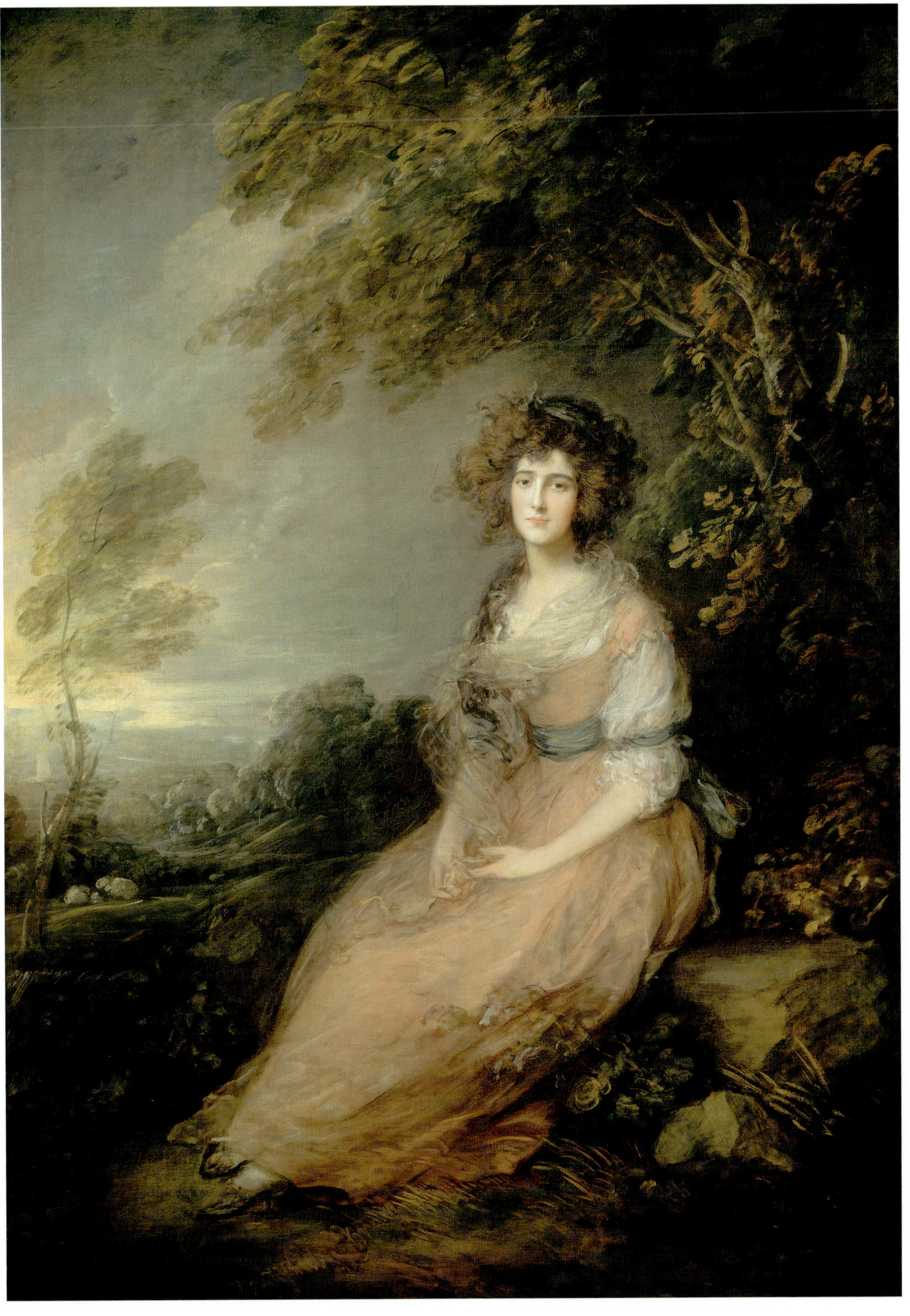

PLATE

II

THOMAS GAINSBOROUGH

The Honorable Anne (Batson) Fane

CA. 1786

OIL ON CANVAS

36 X 27-3/4 IN (91 X 70.5 CM)

KRANNERT ART MUSEUM AND KINKEAD PAVILION

UNIVERSITY OF ILLINOIS, URBANA-CHAMPAIGN

GIFT OF ELLNORA D. KRANNERT

(1973-9-1)

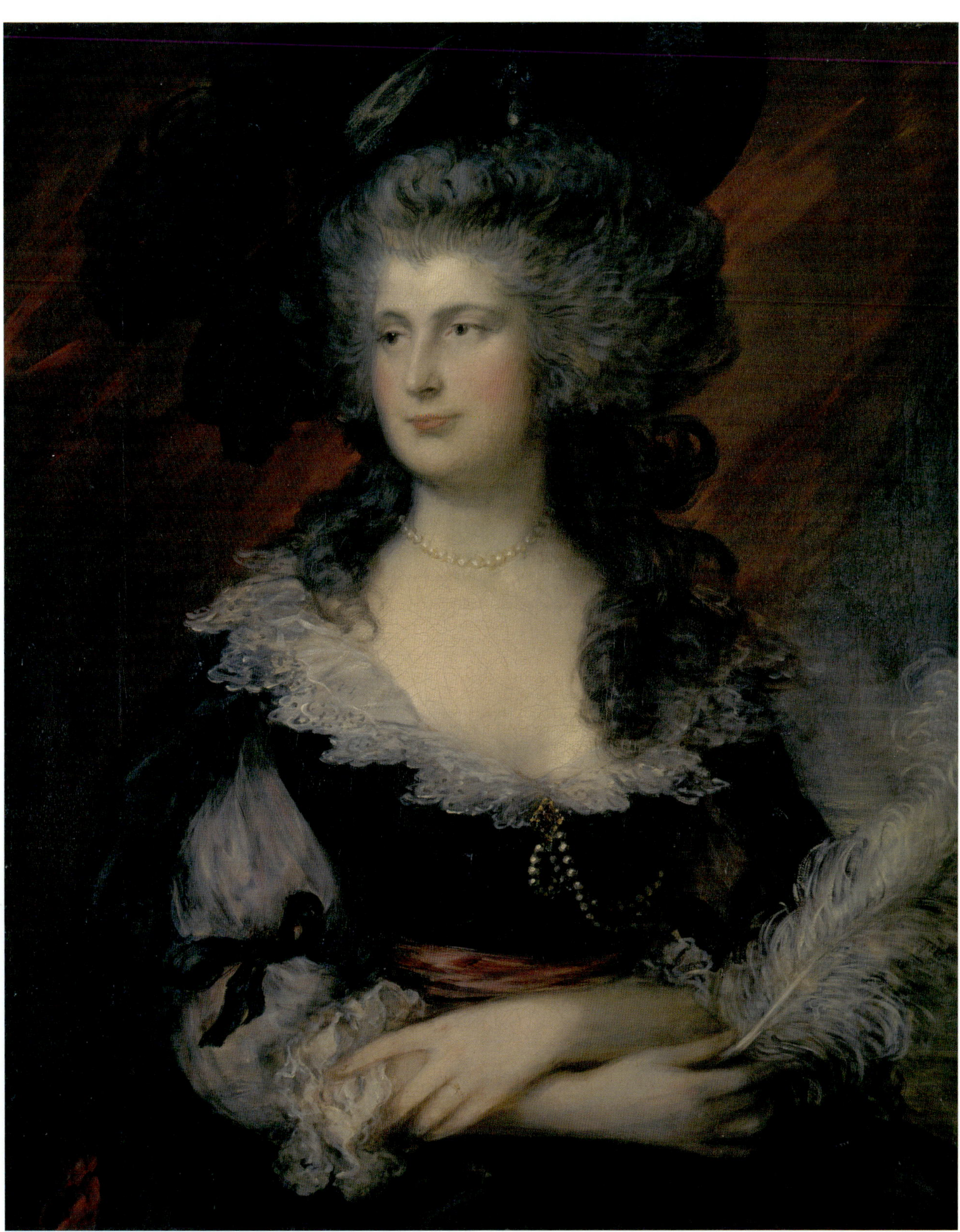

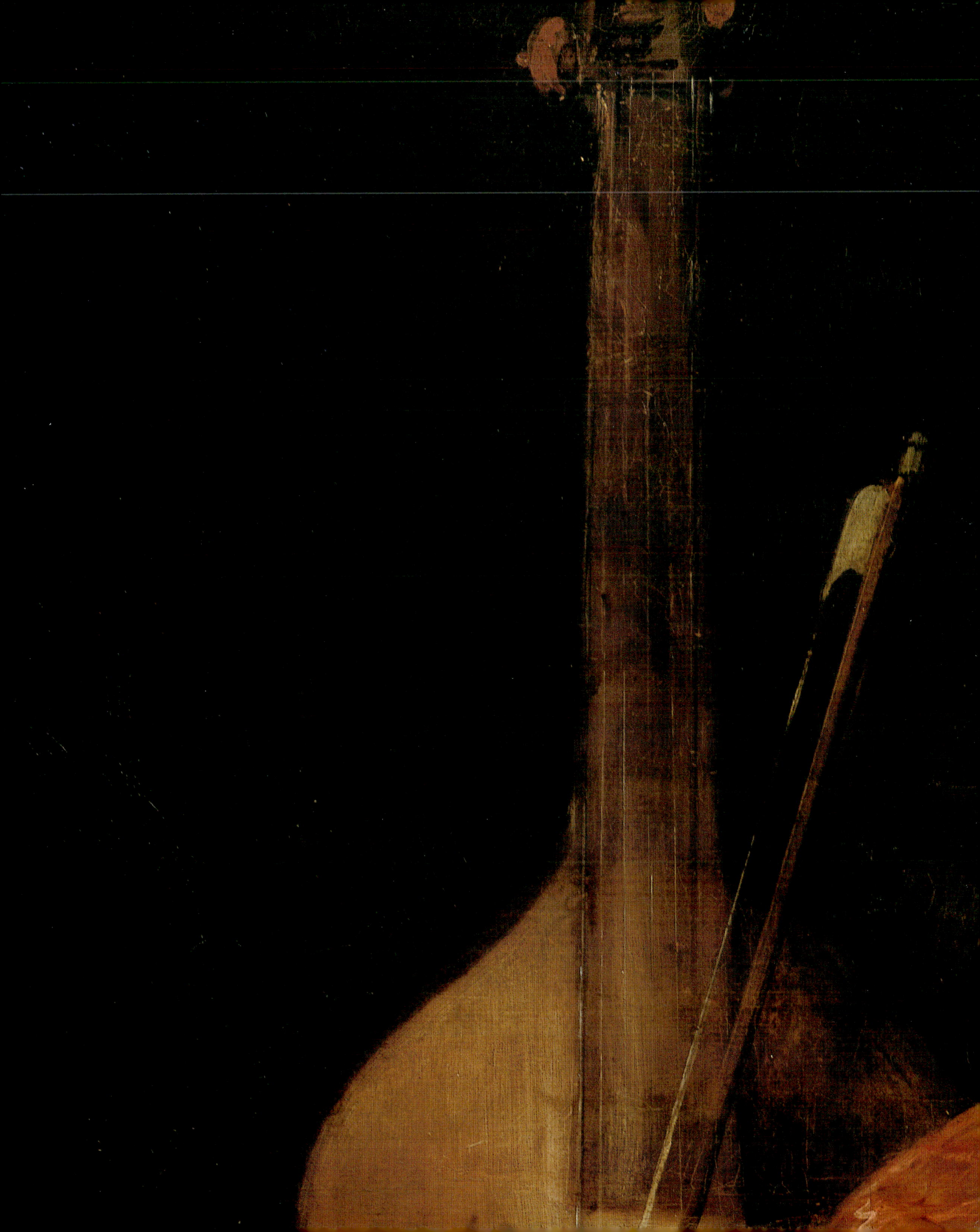

"
A
Favourite
AMONG THE
Demireps " :

Thomas Gainsborough and the Modern Woman

By Benedict Leca

It should seem from this artist's female portraits, that he is a favourite among the demireps. He has, it is plain, been visited by Miss Dalrymple, . . . and other well-known character [*sic*] of the same stamp.

MORNING CHRONICLE AND LONDON ADVERTISER, MAY 25, 1778[1]

W HY WAS THOMAS GAINSBOROUGH, the artist of the quote above, a "favourite" of demireps? The answer is that portraits mattered socially when Gainsborough became the darling of women with a "demi," or half, reputation. Threatening to certain contemporaries because of their power as tastemakers, so-called demireps were the self-possessed, often accomplished eighteenth-century British women featured in the present exhibition whom we think of as modern today for the same reasons they were derided then as "impure": their social and sexual assertiveness combined with their flair for personal style and public exposure ran counter to propriety.[2] Hence women such as the inimitable Ann Ford (PLATE 1), the subject of the Cincinnati Art Museum's Gainsborough masterpiece, who sought to live as a performing musician and defended herself in a pamphlet war, withstood withering scrutiny in the polite society of Georgian England. Such exposure resulted in added attention paid to Gainsborough's touch as a portraitist: for just as they made women "public" (that is, publicly visible), portraits also rendered visible the material presence of the artist, proclaiming his particular manner of painting a female subject. And not just any woman, of course, but often the "It girl" of the moment, whose cultural impact in this case derived from her substance and her style having brushed up against the painter's. For select young women of means, connections, and social ambition the right portrait by the great Gainsborough might cement social standing, even deliver celebrity

---

1

"[Royal Academy Exhibition]," *Morning Chronicle and London Advertiser*, May 25, 1778, 2. I want to acknowledge Michael Rosenthal and Martin Myrone's very useful catalogue *Gainsborough* (London: Tate Publishing, 2002), which alerted me to a number of contemporary periodical sources dealing with Gainsborough's paintings. I would also like to thank all those who kindly read my text, especially Leora Maltz-Leca, Kenneth Brummel, Bill Stott, and Anne Buening.

2

A "higher order of impures," according to one source. Cited in Elizabeth Einberg, *Gainsborough's Giovanna Baccelli* (London: Tate Gallery Publications, 1976), 8.

or notoriety. Gainsborough's portraits also positioned the artist in the context particular to ambitious painting: which woman, painted in what fashion, marked the artist's posture toward both artistic tradition and social etiquette.

Gainsborough owed his success to the fact that he brought heightened visibility and thus cultural relevance — read: power — to women, who, formerly at the margins of society, were now by means of their activities and his portraiture at its center. In this way, he imaged the eighteenth-century woman as empowered and skeptical of traditional gender roles. Gainsborough's portraits were also a new kind of painting. For if the modern woman was a nascent subject in the eighteenth century, so too was the modern, skeptical painter. In Gainsborough's particular case, and in many of the portraits on view in this exhibition, the ambitions of both sitter and painter made for a logical complicity in pushing up against prevailing codes of decorum that governed the painting of women and feminine manners, as well as the social and professional mobility of women and painters. The maverick portraitist, in other words, would have common cause with a sitter who was a woman of renown.

Such an empathetic view of the portrait event (sittings and painting), which I link primarily to contemporary sociability and to the eighteenth-century ethical doctrine of "sensibility," was in fact the basis for creating portraits that redefined the roles that polite society would have prescribed for portraitist and sitter. Gainsborough clearly aimed to edify and empower women, whose progressive allure refracted onto his progressive painting. Contemporaries noted Gainsborough's great skill at capturing a likeness, but often added a caveat about his other defining feature: his spirited brushwork, or touch.[3] For this reason the artist was particular that his paintings be apprehended both for their materiality and their illusionism, mandating that they be viewed at that exact distance from the canvas where impastoed brushwork dissolved into satin fabric. "It was calculated for breast high [hanging] & will never have its effect or likeness otherwise," he specified to the actor David Garrick in instructing him how the latter's portrait should be viewed.[4]

By the eighteenth century, painterly effects had a long history among art theorists and connoisseurs. But the way the forthright execution of Gainsborough's portraits was hitched to his feminine sitters' sex appeal put them among those early modern examples of ambitious portrayals of women that overtly broached desire as constitutive of the engagement among painter, sitter, and viewer presupposed in a painting's textured surface. Gainsborough's modern brand of painting — his individualized touch, his attention to the material and affective properties

[3]
On the point of Gainsborough's incredible skill in capturing a likeness, see William T. Whitley, *Thomas Gainsborough* (London: Smith, Elder, 1915), 91.

[4]
Gainsborough to David Garrick, 1772, in *The Letters of Thomas Gainsborough*, ed. John Hayes (New Haven: Yale University Press, 1996), 108.

of paint, and his skepticism of academic tradition — was specifically predicated on being imaged through fashionable or provocative women. Contemporary critics noted Gainsborough's use of a "very tender and delicate stile of pencilling" to "round [limbs] sweetly and delightfully to the eye," a manner "calculated for tender effect."[5] I want to argue here, however, that the objective of using women as subjects wasn't only to encourage appreciation of painterly painting, but to serve the public display of feminine seductiveness. Indeed, unlike many of the heroes of modernist painting who objectified or otherwise marginalized women — David to Picasso by way of Gauguin and Cézanne — Gainsborough was specifically invested in projecting subversive femininities in complicity with the sitter. What follows, therefore, is an exploration of how Gainsborough conspired with certain notorious women to create portraits that confounded both traditional portraiture and calcified gender roles.

Contemporary popular poems about Gainsborough reveal that beautiful women seductively painted had their effect: "Such charms our *British Nymphs* alone possess, and none but *G—nsb—rough's* pencil can express."[6] If lusciously painted British nymphs could seduce, the appreciation of painterly touch might also edify. The contemporary writer Robert Bromley in an essay on "the cultivation of the fine arts [as] a source of refined polish to the manners" makes it clear that paintings really did matter socially. As Bromley explains, "If the arts in general have this power to humanize and polish the mind, no small share of that polish must be the claim of the pencil [contemporary term for brush], which occupies the first powers of art by which the mind is impressed."[7] Viewing paintings and attending to the painter's mark, which impressed itself on the viewer's mind, thus encouraged good taste and learning, qualities of social benefit. And as per Gainsborough's instructions on assuming the correct place and proper distance from the canvas in order to appreciate both its facture and illusion, it is clear that such directives presupposed active participation from a viewer self-conscious of his or her operative role in perceiving and responding to seductive portraits. Especially when applied to the depiction of women, demonstrative painting meant affective painting, for which Gainsborough expected active, participatory — sensory — looking from the viewer. Peers such as Sir Joshua Reynolds specifically recognized this interactive quality in Gainsborough's painting. Gainsborough's "undetermined manner," according to Reynolds, gave enough of an effect "to remind the spectator of the original; the imagination supplies the rest."[8] In this way the painter's mark initiated a multitude of interconnected dialogues among painter, sitter, and viewer. Indeed, Gainsborough's portraits broached an unprecedented level of engaged appreciation of painting, one that recast the relation of viewer to painting.

5
Anonymous, "A View of Mr. Gainsborough's Gallery," *Morning Herald and Daily Advertiser*, July 26, 1784.

6
Anonymous, "On the Portraits of the Three Princesses, Painted by Thomas Gainsborough," in *An Asylum for Fugitive Pieces* (London: J. Debrett, 1785), 244.

7
Robert Anthony Bromley, "The cultivation of the Fine arts a Source of refined polish to the manners," in *A Philosophical and Critical History of the Fine Arts, Painting, Sculpture, and Architecture* (London: Philanthropic Press, 1793), 1:103.

8
Sir Joshua Reynolds, *Discourses on Art*, ed. Robert R. Wark (New Haven: Yale University Press, 1997), 259.

Gainsborough's modernism was also specifically bound up in the context of the mass market for portraits in eighteenth-century England, which broadened the reach of portraiture as it fed an exploding discourse on its meanings and merits. Portraits were portable, and more adaptable to contemporary visual culture's varied possibilities of display and diffusion than the fixed accessory of the upper-crust interior we tend to imagine. They were copied and distributed as part of a sociable gift economy, and reproduced in prints. Contemporaries collectively engaged painted portraiture in many places besides the exhibition room at the Royal Academy: in civic spaces as well as in private homes, or often, as was customary in the period, in the artist's expanded studio. Gainsborough himself enacted strategies for showing his work, having installed dedicated "shew" rooms as part of his studios in Bath and London to accommodate the stream of visitors. He writes to a friend in 1763 of having sublet the greater part of his house on Abbey Street at Bath "except my painting room and best parlour to show pictures in."[9] For in addition to the parade of scheduled sitters, a multitude of potential clients came to view and assess his portraits. In May 1770, one Dorothy Richardson "calld at Mr. Gainsborough's the Painters, to see his Pictures," while Eliza Orlebar, visiting the studios of Hoare and Gainsborough in April 1774, professed she "greatly preferred the portraits by the latter, as they are such very good likenesses."[10] Sitters could also exploit the artist, just as portraits themselves could repay a visit. The art theorist André Rouquet writes that eighteenth-century British "women especially must have their pictures exposed for some time in the house of that painter who is most in fashion."[11] Philip Thicknesse, for his part, tells us that the portrait of his wife, Ann Ford, "had been carried all over Europe" — that is, besides having been shown for many years in Gainsborough's showroom.[12]

People and images of people thus circulated as part of a new sociability, wherein iconic portraits like Ann Ford's could doubly introduce Gainsborough the artist and his progressive painting, as well as Ann Ford and her brand of empowered femininity, to a multitude of contemporaries in many contexts. In a society that remained largely ambivalent toward the empowerment of women, portraits did not therefore merely mirror relations between the sexes, they actively participated in negotiating the ever-shifting terms between them. In the eighteenth century, the "artist who sought to paint women performers was contributing to an unstable discourse."[13]

9
Gainsborough to James Unwin, Dec. 30, 1763, in *Letters*, 23–24.

10
Hugh Belsey, "A Visit to the Studios of Gainsborough and Hoare," *Burlington Magazine* 129 (Feb. 1987): 107–9. Eliza Orlebar cited in Whitley, *Thomas Gainsborough*, 107.

11
André Rouquet, *The Present State of the Arts in England* (London: Printed for J. Nourse, 1755), 40–41.

12
Philip Thicknesse, *A Sketch of the Life and Paintings of Thomas Gainsborough, Esq.* (London, 1788), 37.

13
Gill Perry, "Ambiguity and Desire: Metaphors of Sexuality in Late Eighteenth-Century Representations of the Actress," in *Notorious Muse: The Actress in British Art and Culture 1776–1812*, ed. Robyn Asleson (New Haven: Yale University Press, 2003), 60.

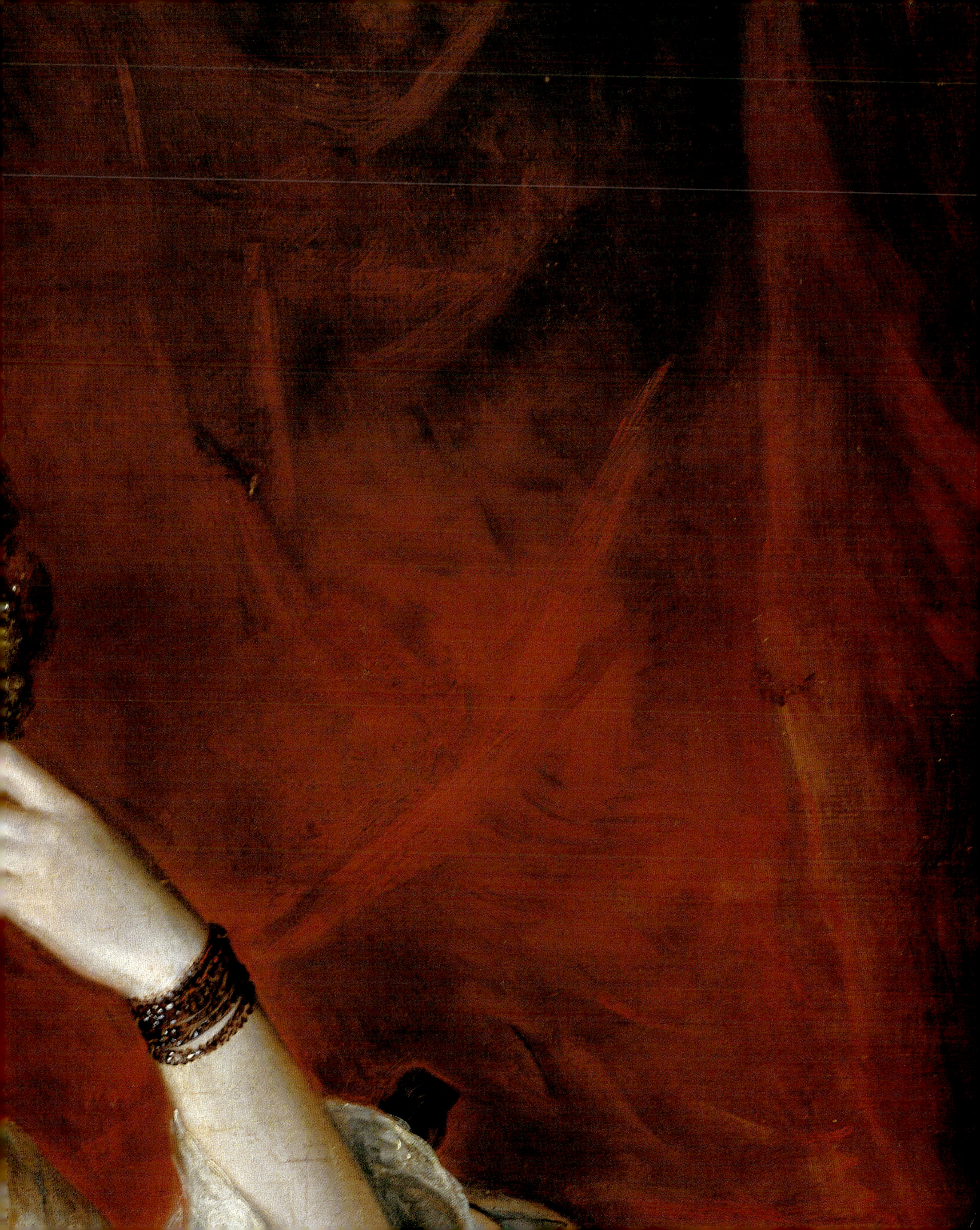

Gainsborough, Reynolds,

AND THE

Gender Dynamics

OF

Portraiture

BEARING IN MIND THIS IDEA of an unstable context in which gender and social identities were being redefined, a comparison of a handful of Gainsborough's portraits of, or including, women with some painted by his great rival, Sir Joshua Reynolds, enables us to differentiate Gainsborough's empathetic, enabling posture toward his feminine subjects from Reynolds's more masculinist portraiture. In such a light, the classic rivalry between Gainsborough and Reynolds was never located just in the realm of technical painting and artistic tradition, but also in the active definition of gender roles. We should always pause before drawing general conclusions about what is a discrete category of sitter for two artists who painted hundreds of women under varying conditions — conditions that might have at times encroached on the painters' own autonomy to make decisions as portraitists. It is nonetheless unsurprising to find a discernible sexism in Reynolds's female portraiture that contrasts with Gainsborough's more permissive depictions. I therefore want to return to Gainsborough by circling back to the idea of portraits as being representations that actively produce certain kinds of subjects and to consider the very different painter Gainsborough was from Reynolds when it came to portraying famous women.

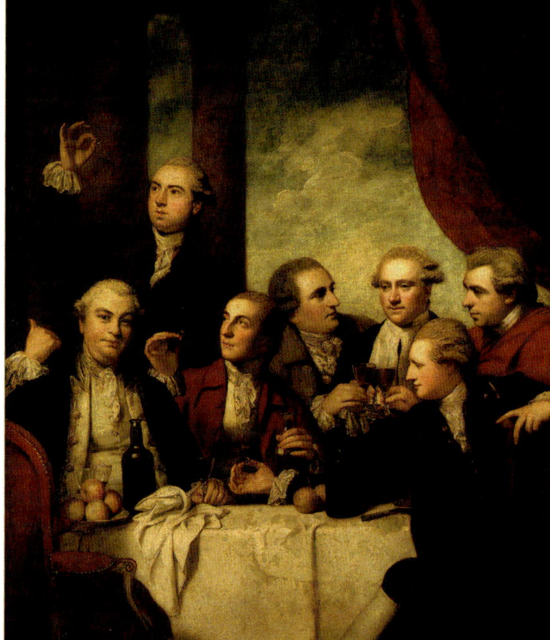

FIGURE 1

SIR JOSHUA REYNOLDS
Group Portrait of Members of the
Society of Dilettanti, 1777
CA. 1777 – 79
OIL ON CANVAS
77-9/16 X 55-7/8 IN (197 X 142 CM)
THE SOCIETY OF DILETTANTI, LONDON

The contrast can first be ascribed to the two men's well-known positions regarding tradition and academicism, with Reynolds, the erudite champion of a learned British grand manner, and the first president of the Royal Academy, predictably positing a more regulated, paternalistic practice than Gainsborough. Two paintings by Reynolds give us a perspective on the often stark gendering of his production, as well as on the entrenched sexism of eighteenth-century British society. Reynolds's example reminds that the enterprising portraitist never lost sight of his bedrock constituency: powerful men. Gainsborough, too, responded to this same clientele, but we can be certain that he could never have produced Reynolds's 1777 *Group Portrait of Members of the Society of Dilettanti* (FIGURE 1). Beneath the upper-class camaraderie, the painting turns on a system of knowing glances and loaded gestures that expressed the sitters' shared interest in female sexuality.[14] Reynolds had in fact joined this dining and literary club for gentlemen in 1766 — something that would have been unthinkable for the maverick Gainsborough — and in 1777, in his capacity as official "limner" to the club, produced this great image of "lewd male merriment."[15] By the same token, *Lady Cockburn and her Three Eldest Sons* at the National Gallery, London (1773, FIGURE 2), surely stands as one of the most charged images of motherhood, exemplifying Reynolds's evident facility with the many related fantasies of such men as our lewd merrymakers: here that of the fertile wife happily mothering sons.

14
See Martin Postle, who cites Shearer West's earlier study devoted to the Society of Dilettanti portraits in " 'Painted Women': Reynolds and the Cult of the Courtesan," in Asleson, ed., *Notorious Muse*, 30–32. See also Shearer West, "Libertinism and the Ideology of Male Friendship in the Portraits of the Society of Dilettanti," *Eighteenth-Century Life* 16 (May 1992): 76–104.

15
Nicholas Penny, ed., *Reynolds* (London: Royal Academy, 1986), 282, cats. 109–10.

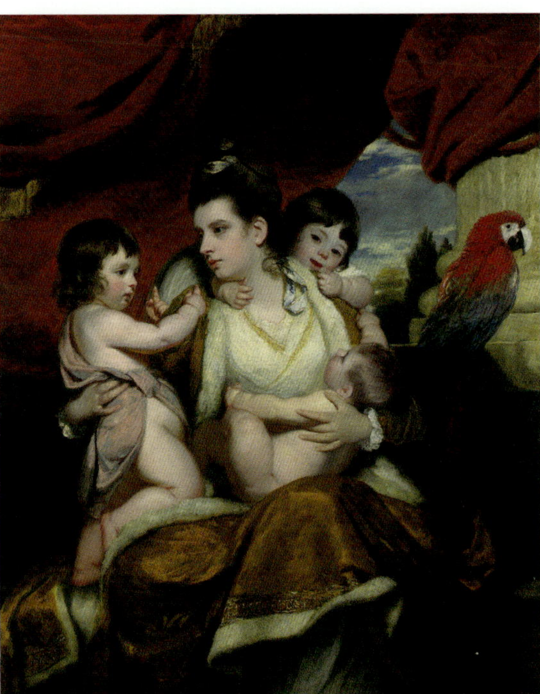

FIGURE 2

SIR JOSHUA REYNOLDS
Lady Cockburn and her Three Eldest Sons
1773
OIL ON CANVAS
55-11/16 X 44-1/2 IN (141-1/2 X 113 CM)
THE NATIONAL GALLERY, LONDON
BEQUEATHED BY ALFRED BEIT, 1906
(NG2077)

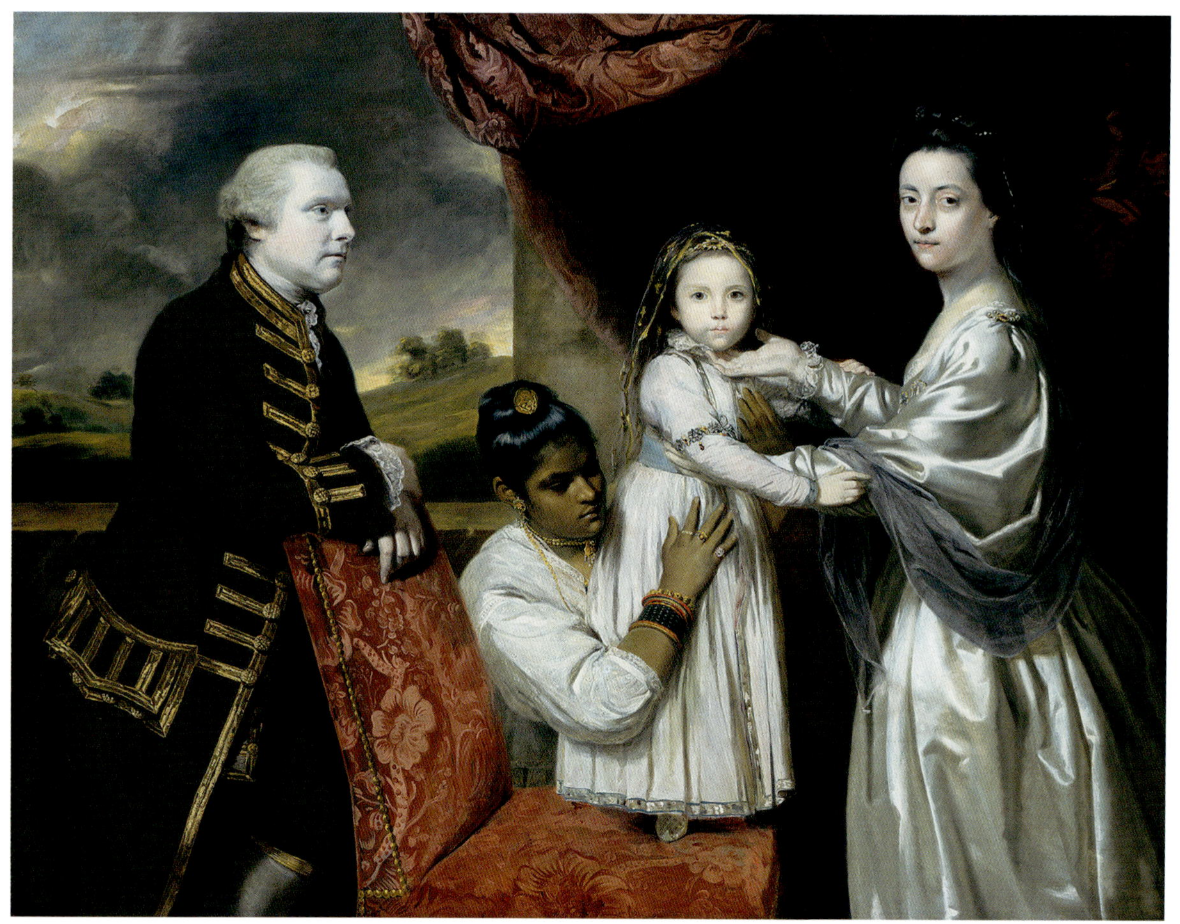

FIGURE 3

SIR JOSHUA REYNOLDS

George Clive and his Family with an Indian Maidservant

CA. 1765 – 66

OIL ON CANVAS

55-1/8 X 67-5/16 IN (140 X 171 CM)

GEMÄLDEGALERIE, STAATLICHE MUSEEN PREUSSISCHER KULTURBESITZ, BERLIN

(78.1)

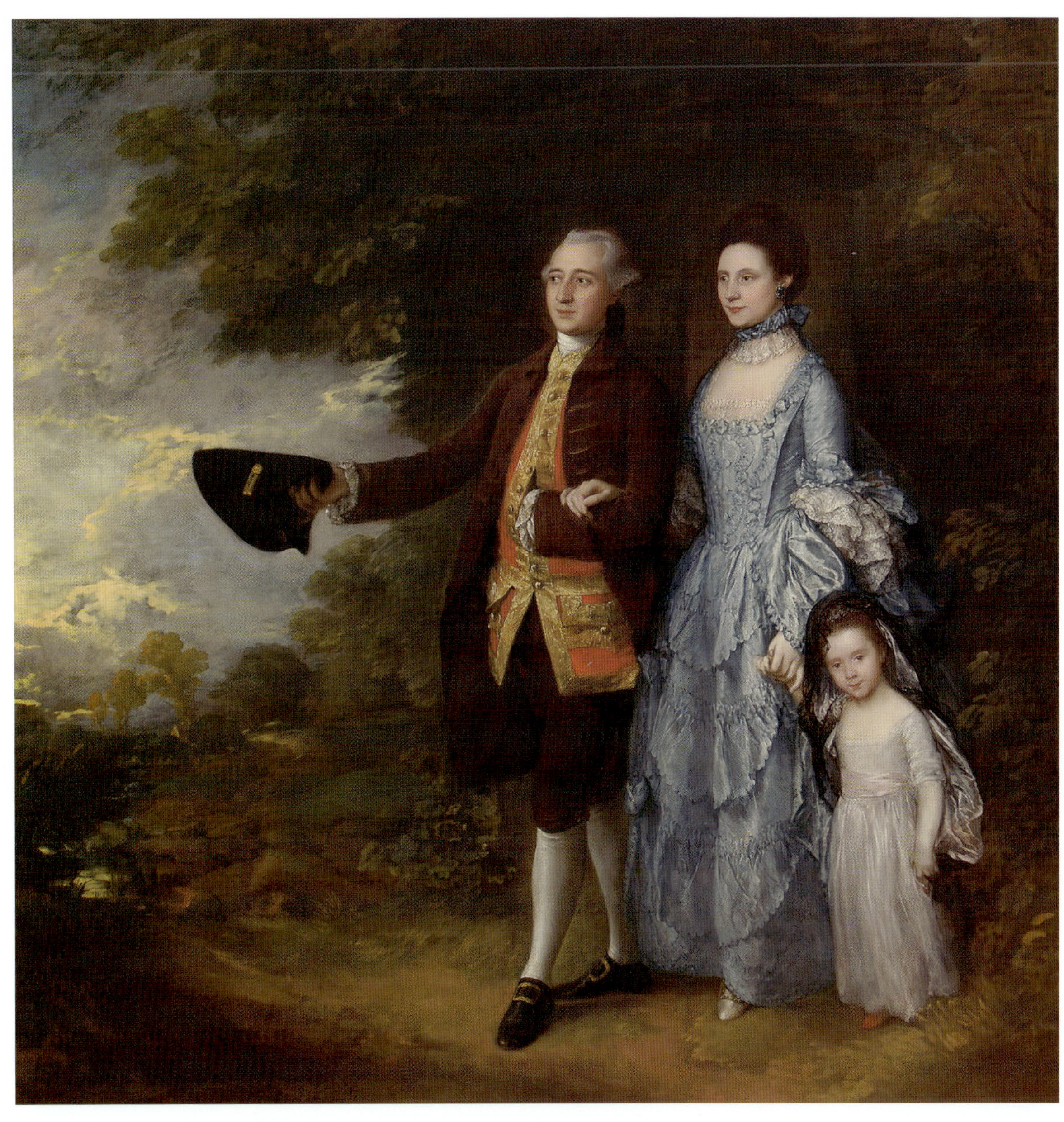

FIGURE 4

THOMAS GAINSBOROUGH
The Byam Family
1762 – 66
OIL ON CANVAS
96-1/4 X 92-1/2 IN (244.5 X 235 CM)
©THE HOLBURNE MUSEUM, BATH
ON LONG-TERM LOAN FROM THE
ANDREW BROWNSWORD ARTS FOUNDATION
(L2001.1)

Also revealing is the contrast formed by a pair of family portraits painted by the two artists around the same time (1762–66): Reynolds's *George Clive and his Family with an Indian Maidservant* and Gainsborough's *Byam Family* (FIGURES 3 AND 4). For much of the century, family portraits such as these aimed primarily to underscore (male) land ownership and familial continuity. While Reynolds's Clive presides over a family vignette in front of a dominating prospect of his lands, Gainsborough's Byam leads his family through his own landscape, gesturing to other holdings. Even though both enforced traditional gender dynamics, the tenor and formal particularities of Gainsborough's conception of a family grouping — and notably the place of the woman in it — suggests an ideological position different from that expressed in Reynolds's painting. Gainsborough's Byam family is shown outdoors, where the couple walk arm in arm in a composite posture adapted from the promenade that doesn't merely convey marital harmony, but also demonstrates Mr. Byam's easy willingness to be outdone by his wife: indeed, Mrs. Byam sports one of the most resplendent dresses ever painted by the artist.[16] Reynolds's Clive family, by contrast, has been disposed according to a more rigid design that cleaves the depicted space between those distinctly available to the family patriarch, George Clive, at left (both public and private), and the darkened, cavernous interior space within which Mrs. Clive and her young daughter evidently belong. What ordinarily might pass as a simple contrast between Reynolds's Baroque pomp and Gainsborough's naturalism reminds us that both of these visual regimes also enabled effects metaphorically suggestive of contemporary models of femininity. For example, the surfeit of greenery in Gainsborough's landscape bespeaks fertility, a conceit adapted most directly from the fecund if not licentious wooded settings of the early-eighteenth-century Frenchman Antoine Watteau. Conversely, for Reynolds, abundant nature has been visibly domesticated to reappear as patterning of interior decoration. And if the public promenade and Gainsborough's dazzling depiction of her dress gave Louisa Byam equal standing alongside her husband, not so at the Clives', where the disparity in clothing between husband and wife is rich in symbolism: as Aileen Ribeiro has noted, George Clive is formally attired while his wife wears one of Reynolds's studio garments.[17]

This view of the portraitist as a purveyor of mediating fictions for a male audience has often been readily applied to Reynolds's portrayals of a number of actresses, courtesans, and demireps. Reynolds's pupil and biographer, James Northcote, emphasized his master's skill in making sitters appear like "ladies."[18] Martin Postle, in a recent essay treating Reynolds's engagement with the cult of the courtesan, affirmed a more pointed objective: Reynolds's fictions of feminine sexuality encouraged a male "fantasy of control and accessibility."[19]

16
John Hayes noted that this was at the time the most elaborate portrait Gainsborough had yet painted. See John Hayes, *Gainsborough: Paintings and Drawings* (London: Phaidon, 1975), no. 57, 212. See also Hugh Belsey, *Love's Prospect: Gainsborough's Byam Family and the Eighteenth Century Marriage Portrait* (Bath: Holburne Museum of Art, 2001).

17
Noted by David Mannings in Penny, ed., *Reynolds*, 217, cat. 49.

18
Nicholas Penny, "An Ambitious Man," in *Reynolds*, 23.

19
Postle, " 'Painted Women,' " 23–55.

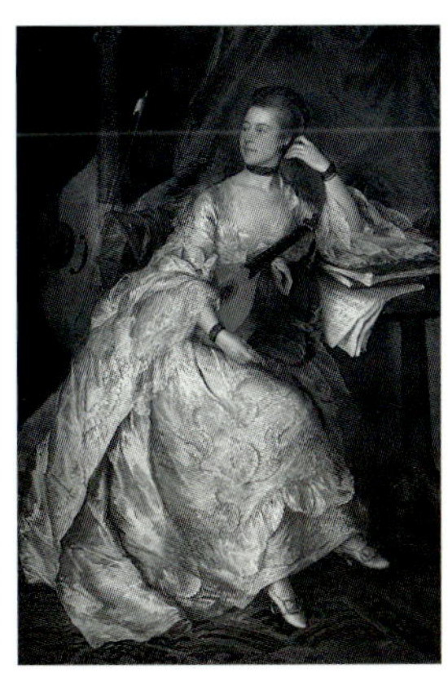

PLATE I
Ann Ford

Both artists of course understood that painting famous women was good for business and their reputation.[20] But as his portraits show, far from conveying fictions of control over his feminine subjects, Gainsborough was complicit in helping them evade it. The two earliest major paintings of a woman of repute by our artists — Gainsborough's *Ann Ford (later Mrs. Philip Thicknesse)* in 1760 (PLATE I) and Reynolds's first portrait of the courtesan Nelly O'Brien in 1762–64 (FIGURE 6) — were almost certainly "showpictures," or among those special works calculated to make a splash in the artists' showrooms or at any exhibition.[21]

We need not dissect the private lives of these young women to understand that they were perceived differently in polite society, thereby making for two divergent portraits. Ann Ford, well-heeled and accomplished, pushed social boundaries by virtue of her career choice as a performing musician and by her relatively combative posture within contemporary society. She authored books and succeeded in earning money as a musician while specifically spurning her family and the overtures of moneyed suitors, notably the Earl of Jersey, to whose advances she responded by producing a pamphlet illustrated with a satirical etching reprising Gainsborough's portrait of her (FIGURE 5).[22] The earl was, of course, exactly the

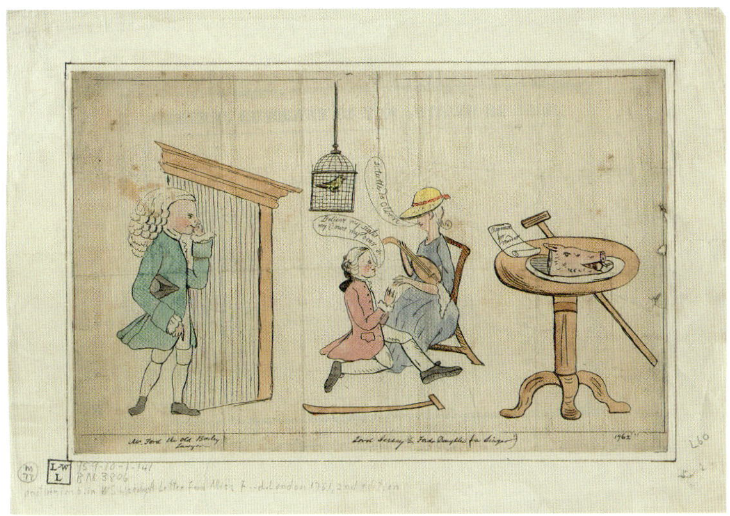

FIGURE 5

The Earl of Jersey and Miss Ford,
frontispiece to *A Letter from Miss F___d to a Person of Distinction*
PUBLISHED LONDON, 1761, ETCHING WITH HAND COLORING, 7-7/8 X 12-3/16 IN (20 X 31 CM)
COURTESY OF THE LEWIS WALPOLE LIBRARY, YALE UNIVERSITY (761.02.00.01)

20
On Reynolds and the cultivation of celebrity through association with famous feminine sitters, see Martin Postle, " 'The Modern Apelles': Joshua Reynolds and the Creation of Celebrity," in *Joshua Reynolds: The Creation of Celebrity*, ed. Martin Postle (London: Tate Publishing, 2005), 24–29.

21
It is Gainsborough's note to Philip Thicknesse, Ann Ford's future husband and the ostensible commissioner of the Art Museum's 1760 portrait, that suggests the latter was in fact *not* a commissioned work, but a showpicture; see Susan Sloman, *Gainsborough in Bath* (New Haven: Yale University Press, 2002), 72. Reynolds's first version of the courtesan Nelly O'Brien (ca. 1762–64) now at the Wallace Collection— a picture the artist apparently kept for over a decade—was surely a calculated showroom piece; see David Mannings, *Sir Joshua Reynolds: A Complete Catalog of His Paintings* (New Haven: Yale University Press, 2000), no. 1353.

22
Michael Rosenthal, *The Art of Thomas Gainsborough* (New Haven: Yale University Press, 1999), 167–71.

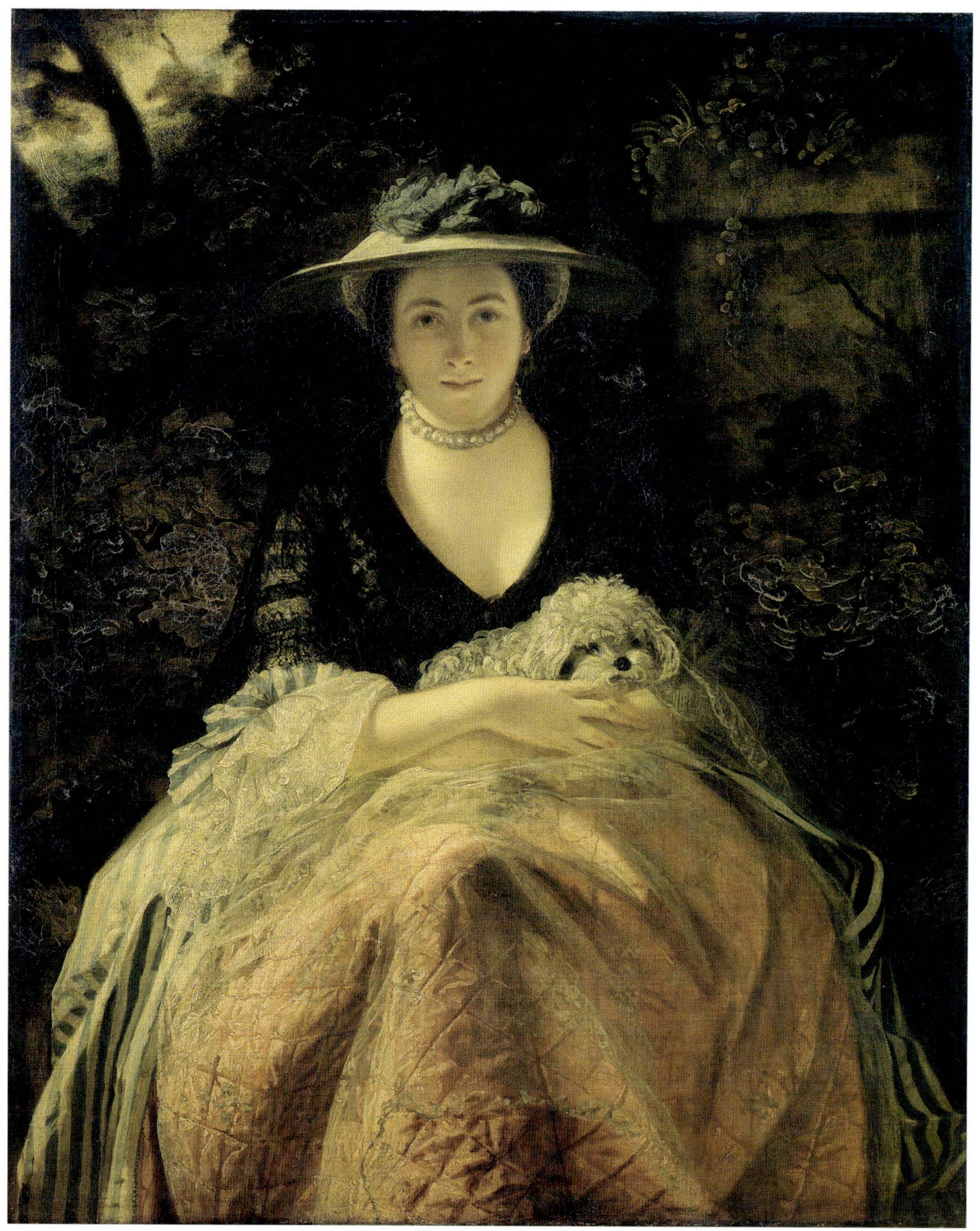

FIGURE 6

SIR JOSHUA REYNOLDS
Miss Nelly O'Brien
CA. 1762 – 64
OIL ON CANVAS
49-3/4 X 39-3/4 IN (126.3 X 101 CM)
THE WALLACE COLLECTION
(P38)

type of man who provided for the livelihood of courtesans such as Nelly O'Brien. Hence the contrasting visual rhetoric, both in terms of the sitter's presentation and address to the viewer, employed by each artist to account for the more subversive character traits of his feminine sitter. The assertive sensuality that Ann Ford and Gainsborough concocted for a *haute bourgeoise* was exactly what Reynolds was attempting to mask when he fashioned a courtesan into one of the "ladies." These contrasting objectives perhaps account for the nearly antithetical poses of the sitters: Gainsborough's is open and Reynolds's is closed. Ann Ford is presented to us arrayed across the canvas in billowing fabric, having adopted a seated posture that allows for a more or less direct address to the viewer.

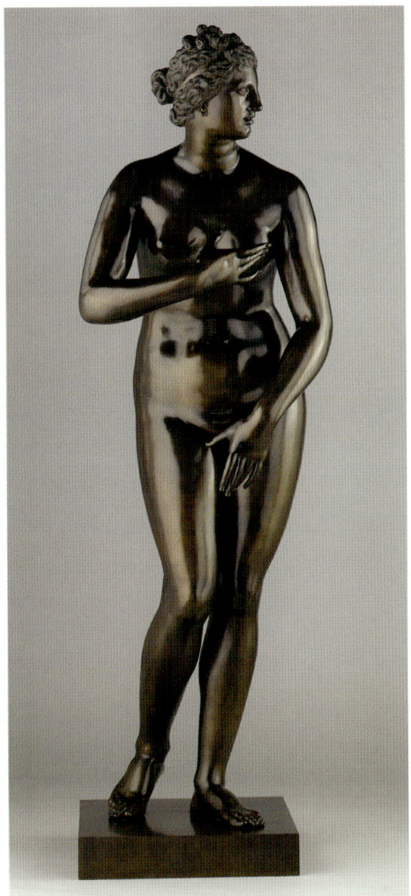

FIGURE 7

PIETRO CIPRIANI
Venus de'Medici
1722 – 24
BRONZE, H 61-1/8 IN (155.3 CM)
THE J. PAUL GETTY MUSEUM, LOS ANGELES
(2008.41.1)

The dramatic sweep of her leg, what we might today read as feminine discretion, was seen by contemporaries as among the portrait's most daring aspects — a forthright intrusion into the masculine realm. Nelly O'Brien, on the other hand, arrives at an entirely different effect owing to her pyramidal form, which gestures back to the Renaissance. Her protruding knee, discernible beneath the pink quilted fabric of her skirt, creates a mountainous bulwark that insists on distance between viewer and sitter.

By one view, these two depictions do indeed represent the contrast between sensual rococo and the more rigid geometry of classicism: Ann Ford is formed of a series of interlocking arabesques, while Nelly O'Brien is enmeshed in a grid of intersecting lines that partitions the canvas. And yet Gainsborough's own possible absorption of antiquity, something scholars have wholly assigned to Reynolds, remind us of his bent for ironic adaptation. The positioning of Ann Ford's right hand, for example, harks back to the class of Greco-Roman Venus Pudica figures, who twist and turn while aiming to cover their mid-body with their hand (FIGURE 7). Such gestures played on the erotic tension between how her hand simultaneously conceals and indicates. In Ann Ford's case, this suggestive iconography was of course qualified by her being clothed. It is in such instances that we need to recall how Hogarth remained Gainsborough's archetype in the use of "ironic and academically inappropriate pictorial cross-references."[23] Fully clothed, Ann Ford had nothing to cover, thus transforming the gesture into a flatly demonstrative one; what was traditionally perceived as modest was now immodesty.

Similarly, instead of creating an image such as Reynolds's *Nelly O'Brien*, which resists alternative narratives, Gainsborough rather seems to have painted himself into Ann Ford's portrait via a sensibility-tinged Hogarthian drama recounted by none other than her husband, Philip Thicknesse. Though the English guitar Ann Ford holds was largely played by women in the domestic sphere (PAGE 59), the painting also depicts a viola da gamba (literally a "leg viol" — positioned between the knees), an instrument that for obvious reasons was more often played by men.[24] Ann Ford was of course known for her skill on this instrument, yet it is Thicknesse who reveals a context to its rather ominous presence as a shadow figure behind the rear curtain. What Thicknesse recounts in his 1788 *Sketch of the Life and Paintings of Thomas Gainsborough* occurred a few years after Gainsborough painted the Cincinnati Art Museum's portrait of Ann Ford, but it suggests a longstanding personal relationship in which portraits served as touchstones of emotional bonds. Thicknesse describes a viola da gamba owned by his wife as the object of an emotionally charged episode between Ann Ford and Gainsborough, who played and collected examples of the instrument. "During the last year of residence at Bath, [Gainsborough] fell in love with Mrs. Thicknesse's viol da gamba," Thicknesse narrates, whereupon she "told him he deserved the instrument for his reward," so as to press her longstanding request for her "husband's picture to hang by the side of [her] own." As Thicknesse tells it, when his wife became aware that Gainsborough had put her husband's portrait aside to complete others, "She instantly burst into tears, retired, and wrote Mr. Gainsborough a note . . ."[25]

The unfinished companion portrait of Mr. Thicknesse was a source of friction between the two men, and while Thicknesse's text is a calculated piece of historical writing, it is nonetheless significant because it not only provides a personal narrative, but also corroborates a view of the ironic artist tweaking social conventions through portraiture.[26] Instead of sanitizing Ann Ford's image, as a portraitist conventionally might, Gainsborough has used his depiction of an

23
Michael Rosenthal, "Gainsborough's *Diana and Actaeon*," in *Painting and the Politics of Culture: New Essays on British Art 1700–1850*, ed. John Barrell (Oxford: Oxford University Press, 1992), 184.

24
Rosenthal, *Art of Thomas Gainsborough*, 167.

25
Philip Thicknesse, *Sketch of the Life*, 20–22, 25.

26
For Philip Thicknesse's own comments regarding this affair, see Robert R. Wark, "Thicknesse and Gainsborough: Some New Documents," *Art Bulletin* 40, no. 4 (1958): 333.

accomplished Ann Ford as the occasion for allusions to alternative narratives. In this way, he establishes a triangulation between himself, Ann Ford's subversive femininity, and the informality — read: suggestiveness — of her posture. Such maneuverings partly explain the contrasting idioms deployed in *Nelly O'Brien* and *Ann Ford*. The pose of Reynolds's Nelly O'Brien descends from the iconic maternal imagery of Christian Madonnas, her folded arms cradling a dog where we might expect an infant. Ann Ford, however, figures at the center of a dynamic composition in which she sits actively surrounded by the attributes of her various accomplishments, crowned as a muse in a modern-day allegory of proficiency in all the fine arts and letters.

As contemporary descriptions as well as her published writings attest, accomplishment was in fact Ann Ford's calling card, in spite of the fact that accomplished eighteenth-century women, particularly when shown as active, continued to be perceived as "a morally subversive and socially disruptive force."[27] The most important period source on Ford, a hagiographic essay published in 1806, strains to emphasize her many talents and codifies what Gainsborough had imaged decades earlier: "At an early period [she] obtained a proficiency in the languages," created "her own [musical] compositions . . ., attained such a degree of perfection in dancing . . . , added to an exquisite voice. [She] draws and paints . . . with great accuracy and elegance."[28] Ann Ford herself articulated this vision of empowered womanhood in her 1800 novel *The School for Fashion*.[29] In a critical dedication to fashion herself, the narrator of Ford's autobiographical work indicts the "erroneous mode of [female] education in which more pains are taken with their external appearance, and frivolous occupations," and peppers her text with passages extolling the superiority of the feminine sex.[30] *The School for Fashion* was in fact only the most sustained articulation of opinions Mrs. Thicknesse had evidently ruminated over for decades. The stated justification of her *Sketches of the Lives and Writings of the Ladies of France*, published in London from 1778 to 1781, for example, was to publicize the idea of an accomplished woman as model. Accordingly, she "claim[ed] no other merit [in authoring the *Sketches*] . . . than that of having the honor of making known to [her] country-women some of their own sex . . . who have rendered themselves, by their superior talents, shining ornaments of the age they lived."[31] Ann Ford was therefore very unlikely to have been a passive sitter when choices were made as to her demeanor and iconography, making Gainsborough's 1760 portrait of her among her earliest attempts at fashioning herself as a woman of substance rather than one of merely stylish amateurism. William Hoare's highly finished drawing of a seated woman (FIGURE 8), created soon after the Cincinnati Art Museum's painted portrait by Gainsborough, conveys the constrained industry that Ford

27
Ann Bermingham, "The Aesthetics of Ignorance: The Accomplished Woman and the Culture of Connoisseurship," *Oxford Art Journal* 16, no. 2 (1993): 10.

28
Anonymous, "Mrs. Thicknesse," in *Public Characters* (London: Debrett, Fores, Hookham and Robinson, 1806), 87–88, 100. I want to acknowledge here Peter Holman, whose 2004 article alerted me to this source. See Peter Holman, "Ann Ford Revisited," *Eighteenth-Century Music* 1, no. 2 (2004): 157–81.

29
See ibid. and also Danielle Grover, " 'Partly Admired & Partly Laugh'd at at Every Tea Table': The Case for Ann Thicknesse (Née Ford) and *The School for Fashion* (1800)," *Female Spectator* 12, no. 3 (Summer 2008): 5–8.

30
Ann (Ford) Thicknesse, *The School for Fashion* (London: H. Reynell, 1800), 1:dedication.

31
Ann (Ford) Thicknesse, *Sketches of the Lives and Writings of the Ladies of France* (London: Dodsley and W. Brown, 1778–81), 1:ix.

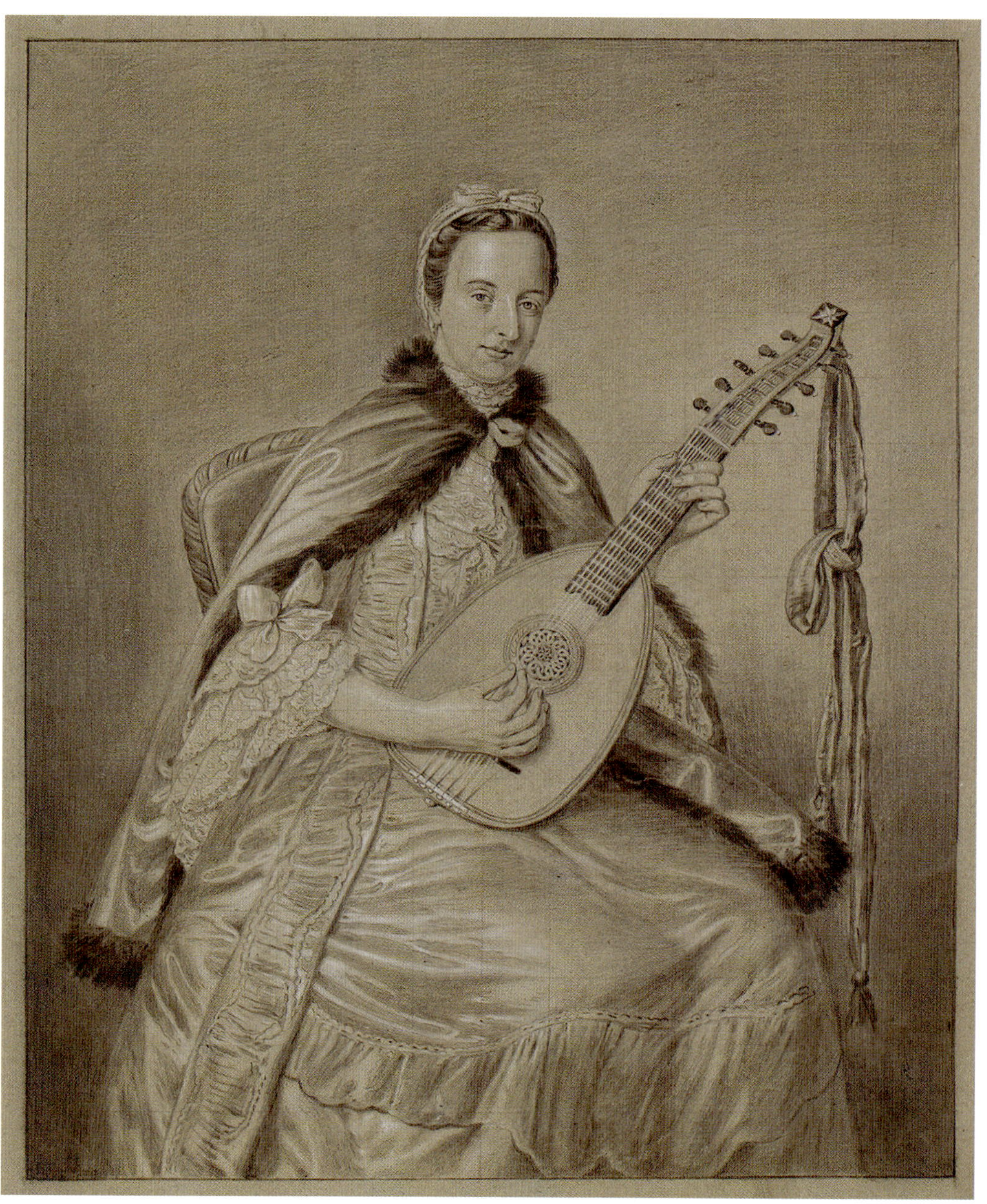

FIGURE 8

WILLIAM HOARE
Seated Woman Playing the Guitar
1707 – 92
CHALK ON PAPER
14-3/8 X 11-3/4 IN (36.5 X 29.8 CM)
METROPOLITAN MUSEUM OF ART
BEQUEST OF WILLIAM K. VANDERBILT, 1920 (20.155.1)

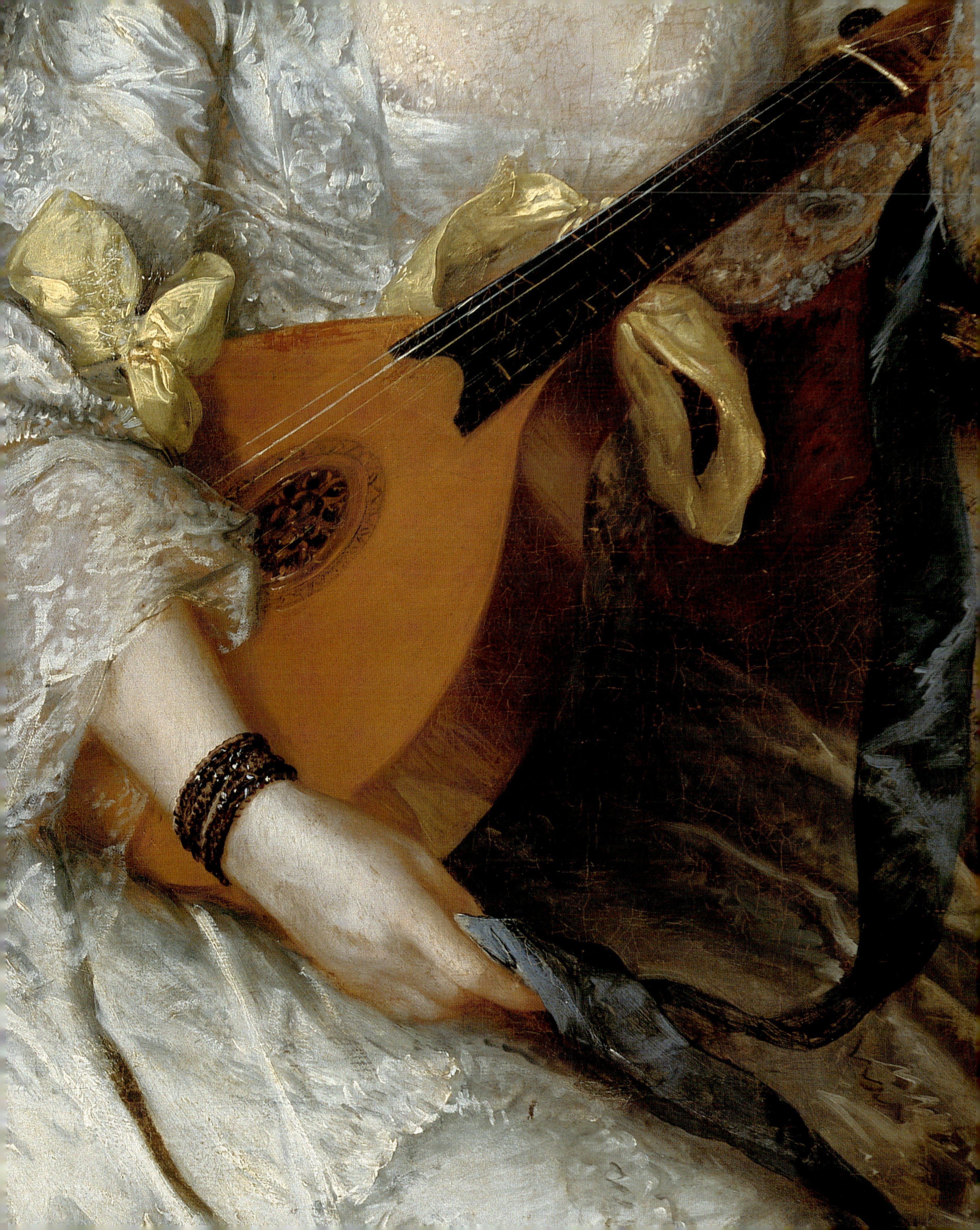

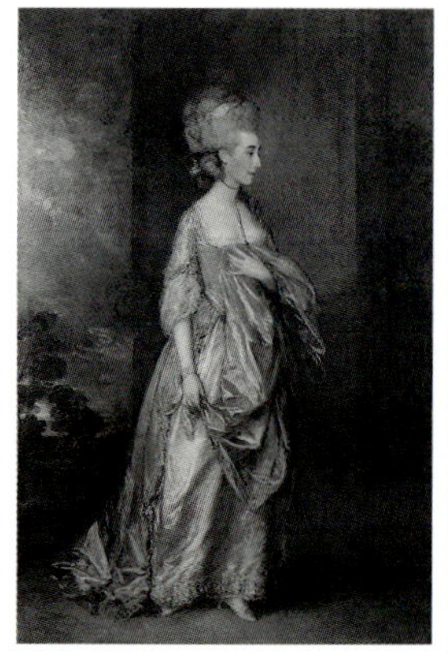

seemingly rejected when she collaborated with Gainsborough. Judy Egerton had it partially right when she glossed this pairing: Hoare does indeed portray "a decorous, demure, and buttoned-up matron." Gainsborough, however, depicts more than a "carelessly decolletée girl," showing us rather a confident woman of substance and refinement.[32]

Beginning in the mid-1770s, with Gainsborough and Reynolds London's two most sought-after portraitists, they repeatedly portrayed some of the same women of renown. We can recall in this light the lost "Demirep Queen, Venus," of George Alexander Stevens's 1772 satirical song, whose wayward path through society included visits to both artists. As the song goes: "Here's the name of each Genius with whom she's a guest: Reynolds, Gainsborough . . ."[33] And so both artists painted the likes of the courtesan Grace Dalrymple Elliott (PLATE 6) and the actress Mary "Perdita" Robinson (FIGURE 9), the latter also commissioning two painted portraits of herself by George Romney.[34] The famed tragic actress Sarah Siddons's outsize reputation means there can hardly be a more charged comparison than the two portraits of her: Gainsborough's *Mrs. Siddons* (PLATE 9), painted in 1785, and Reynolds's *Sarah (Kemble) Siddons as the Tragic Muse*, datable to 1783–84 (FIGURE 10).

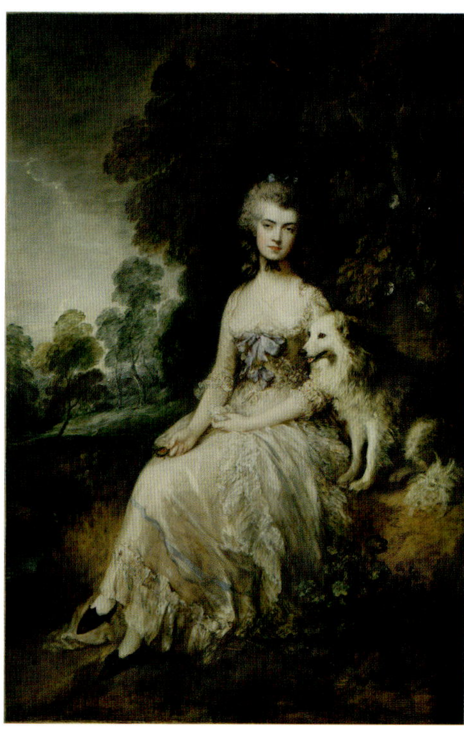

FIGURE 9

THOMAS GAINSBOROUGH
Mrs. Mary Robinson (Perdita)
1781
OIL ON CANVAS
92 X 60-1/4 IN (233.7 X 153 CM)
THE WALLACE COLLECTION
(P42)

32
See Judy Egerton, "William Hoare of Bath," *Burlington Magazine* 133 (January 1991): 47–48.

33
George Alexander Stevens, "The Artists," *Songs, Comic, and Satyrical* (London, 1772), 29.

34
Whitley, *Thomas Gainsborough*, 180.

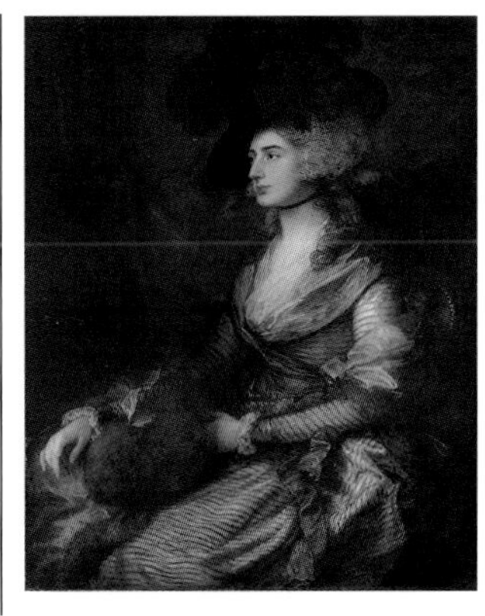

PLATE 9
Sarah Siddons

Born into a family of actors of modest means in 1755, Siddons, in her life and career, followed the ascending social trajectory of the actress as a class of woman, and indeed of the working mother, in eighteenth-century England.[35] Her extraordinary career is well-traveled history, one that began in her own lifetime through the profusion of criticism treating her performances, and the evolving mass of biographical and anecdotal literature that fed a mythology of the private woman far beyond the stage. By the mid-1780s, or the date of the two portraits, Siddons had been appointed Reader in English to the royal children. At this moment her celebrity had also reached its apex: pundits coined the term "Siddonimania" to describe her huge public appeal and affective powers as a dramatic actress; hysterical audiences were said to succumb to "Siddons Fever."[36] Sarah Siddons was thus in every sense a modern tastemaker, especially because she knew how to manipulate the mechanisms of public culture to shape her image: performances and appearances, published commentary, exhibited portraits, prints, and ephemera. As an actress, her professional success depended as much on perceptions of her as a person off the stage as on her skill at playing a part. Inflecting one's personality in a sort of social role playing was also a conventional affectation of learned elite behavior in an age of emergent fashionability, the promenade, masquerades, and public exhibitions. For this reason, Siddons encouraged all the great painters — Romney, William Hamilton, Reynolds, Gainsborough, and Thomas Lawrence — to portray her in many guises, for indeed, painted portraiture was that special medium by which the play between the fictive and actual aspects of her persona could be most directly apprehended.[37]

Few specifics exist as to the actual creation of either Gainsborough's or Reynolds's portrait. Siddons's own bombastic recounting of the sitting for Reynolds is surely apocryphal ("I walked up the steps and seated myself instantly in the attitude").[38] Sitter and painter evidently cooperated, resulting in two portraits of the great actress that were always far more than standard likenesses. Witness the contemporary critic who, having seen Gainsborough's painting at the artist's residence a year after its completion, remarked that "the unpurchased portrait of Mrs. Siddons — with all the graces of private station — still adorns the ante-room, and will adorn it for some time, we fear, so prevalent is the striking form of action and of character over the mild and unimpassioned deportment of private life."[39] Significantly, much the same level of consternation had emerged in response to the portrait of Ann Ford a quarter-century before. Mary Delany, who saw the Ford portrait during a visit to Gainsborough's studio in Bath in

35
Siddons had by 1801 amassed a fortune estimated at £53,000. The literature on Siddons is enormous. I would refer the reader to a recent exhibition catalogue: Robyn Asleson, ed., *A Passion for Performance: Sarah Siddons and Her Portraitists* (Los Angeles: Getty Publications, 1999).

36
See Robyn Asleson's concise and very useful chronology of Siddons's life, "A Sarah Siddons Chronology," in Asleson, ed., *Passion for Performance*, xiv.

37
Shearer West, "The Public and Private Roles of Sarah Siddons," in Asleson, ed., *Passion for Performance*, 30.

38
Mannings, *Sir Joshua Reynolds*, no. 1619.

39
Whitley, *Thomas Gainsborough*, 237. Both were of course "show" pieces. Reynolds's was apparently commissioned by R. B. Sheridan, but clearly conceived with both Gainsborough's earlier portrait and a Royal Academy exhibition in mind (it was shown at the exhibition of 1785). Gainsborough had initially painted his portrait for direct sale, although he never seems to have been intent on selling it.

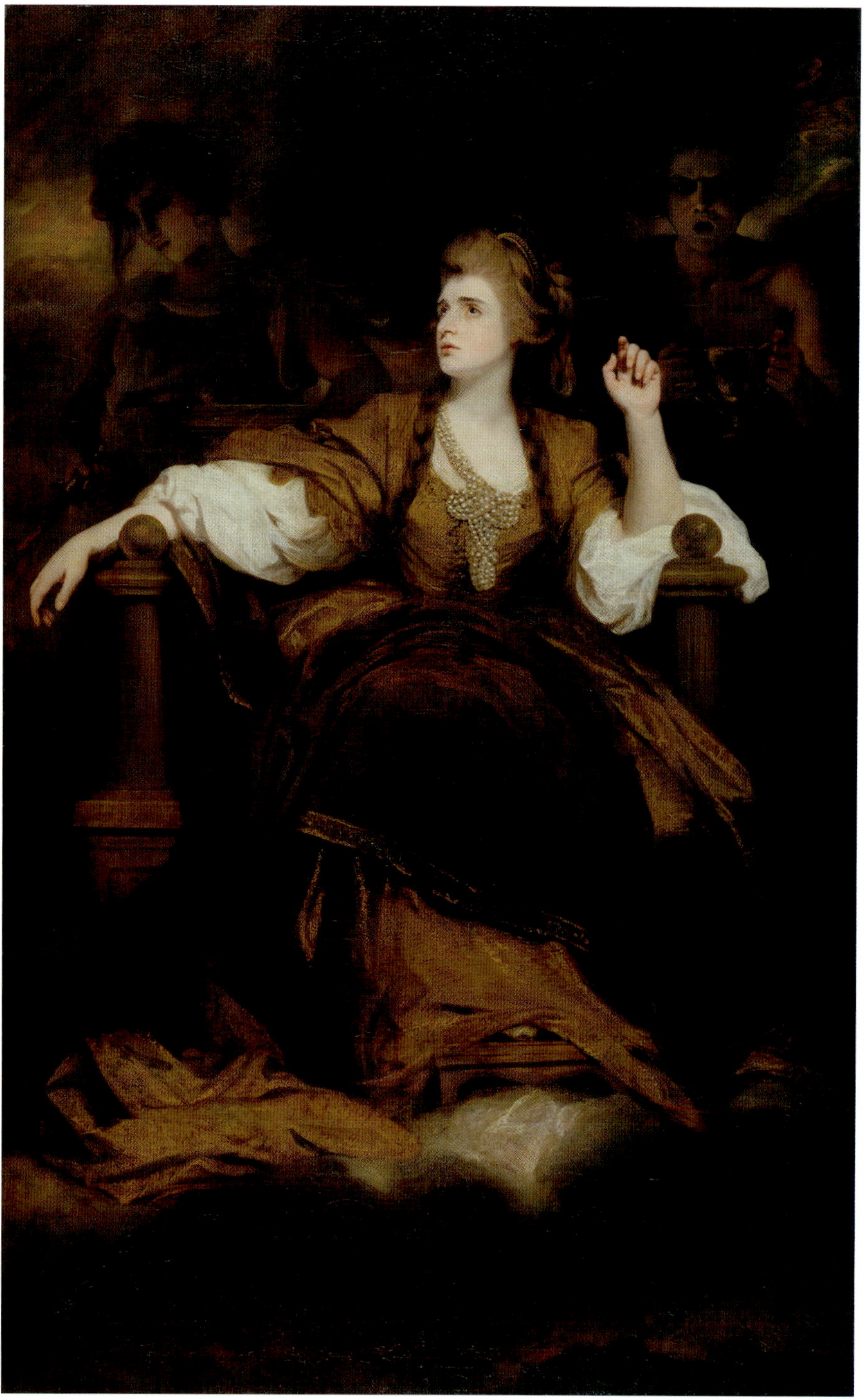

FIGURE 10

SIR JOSHUA REYNOLDS
Sarah (Kemble) Siddons as the Tragic Muse
1783 – 84
OIL ON CANVAS, 94-1/4 X 58-1/8 IN (239.4 X 147.6 CM)
THE HUNTINGTON LIBRARY, ART COLLECTIONS, AND BOTANICAL GARDENS
SAN MARINO, CALIFORNIA (21.2)

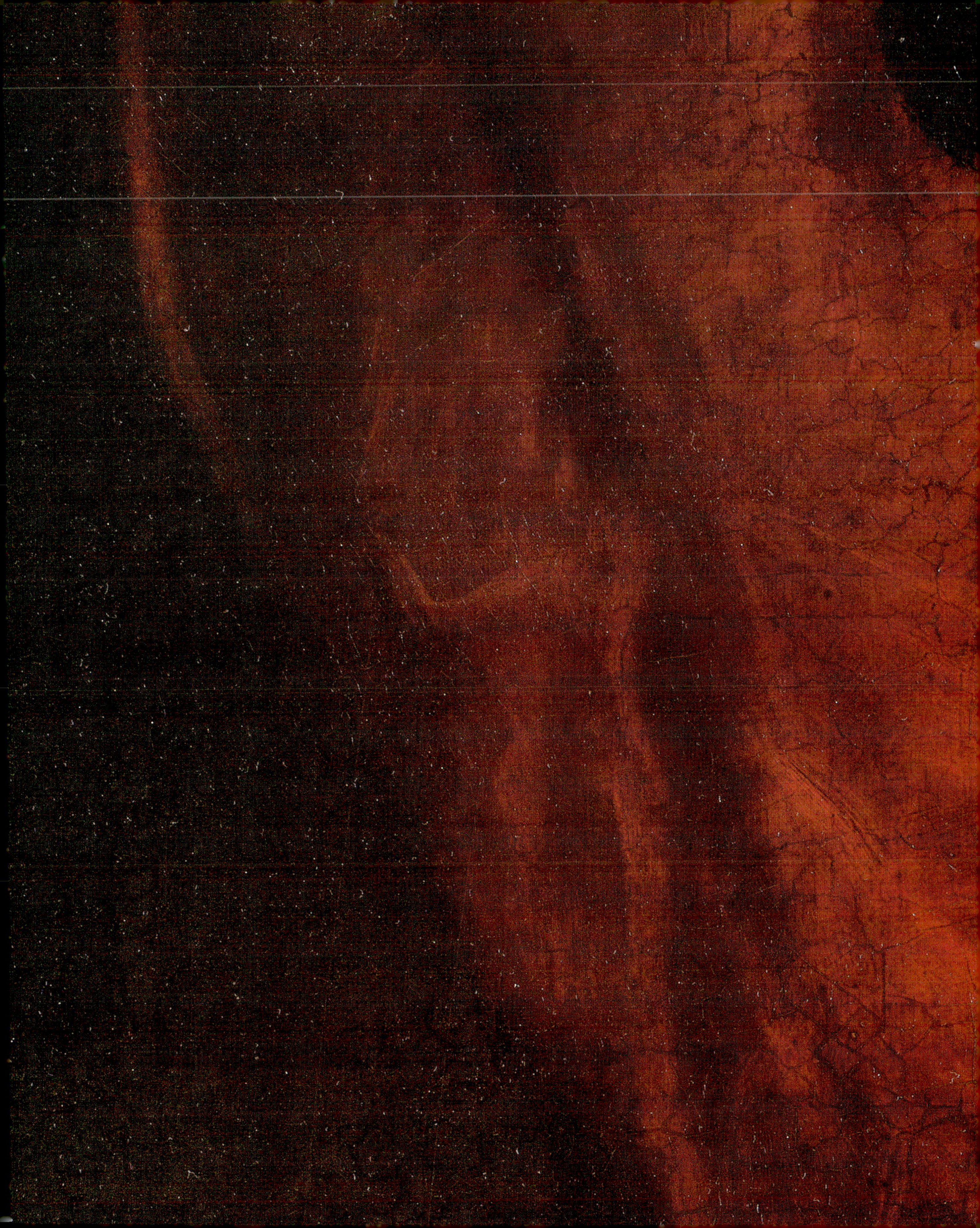

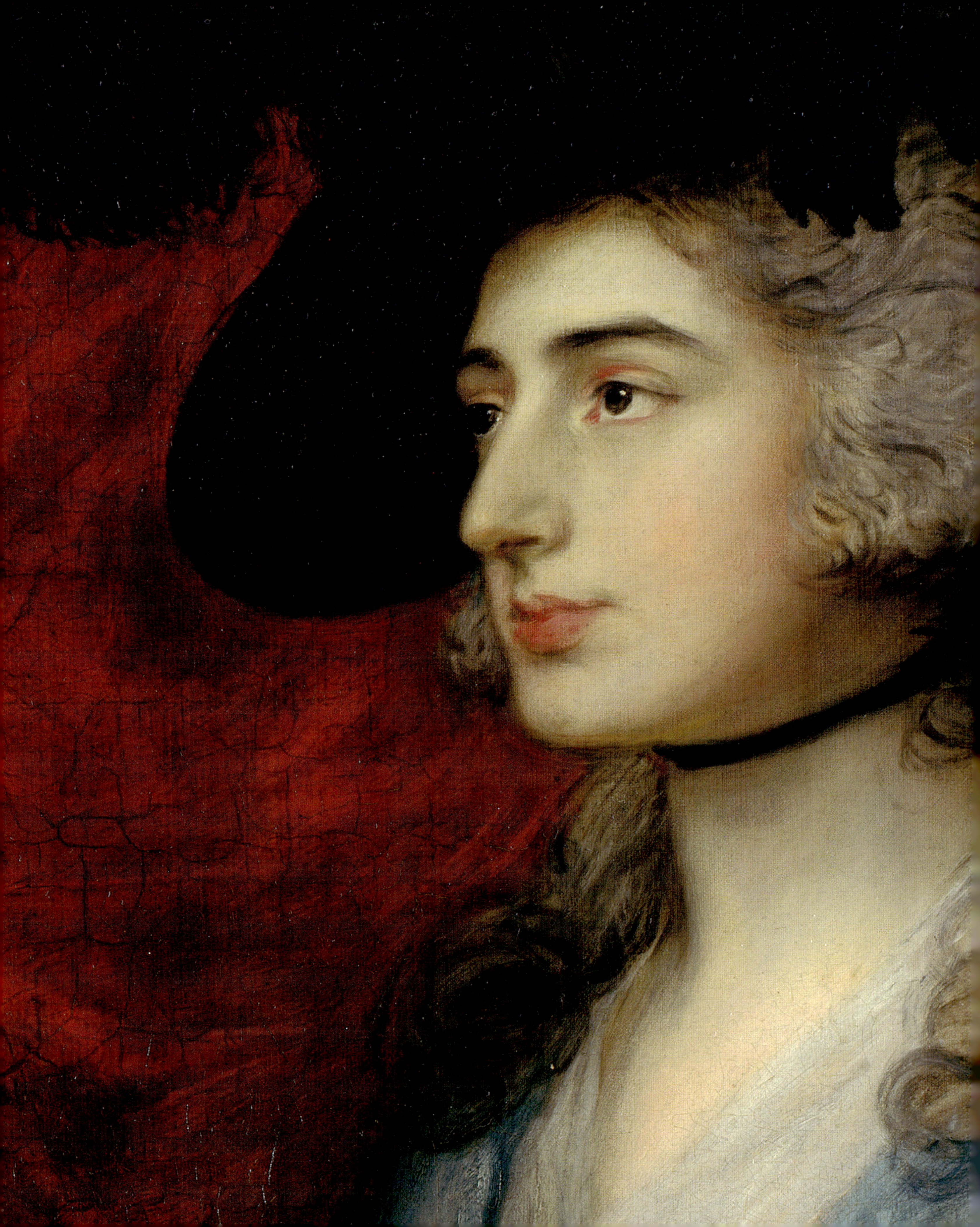

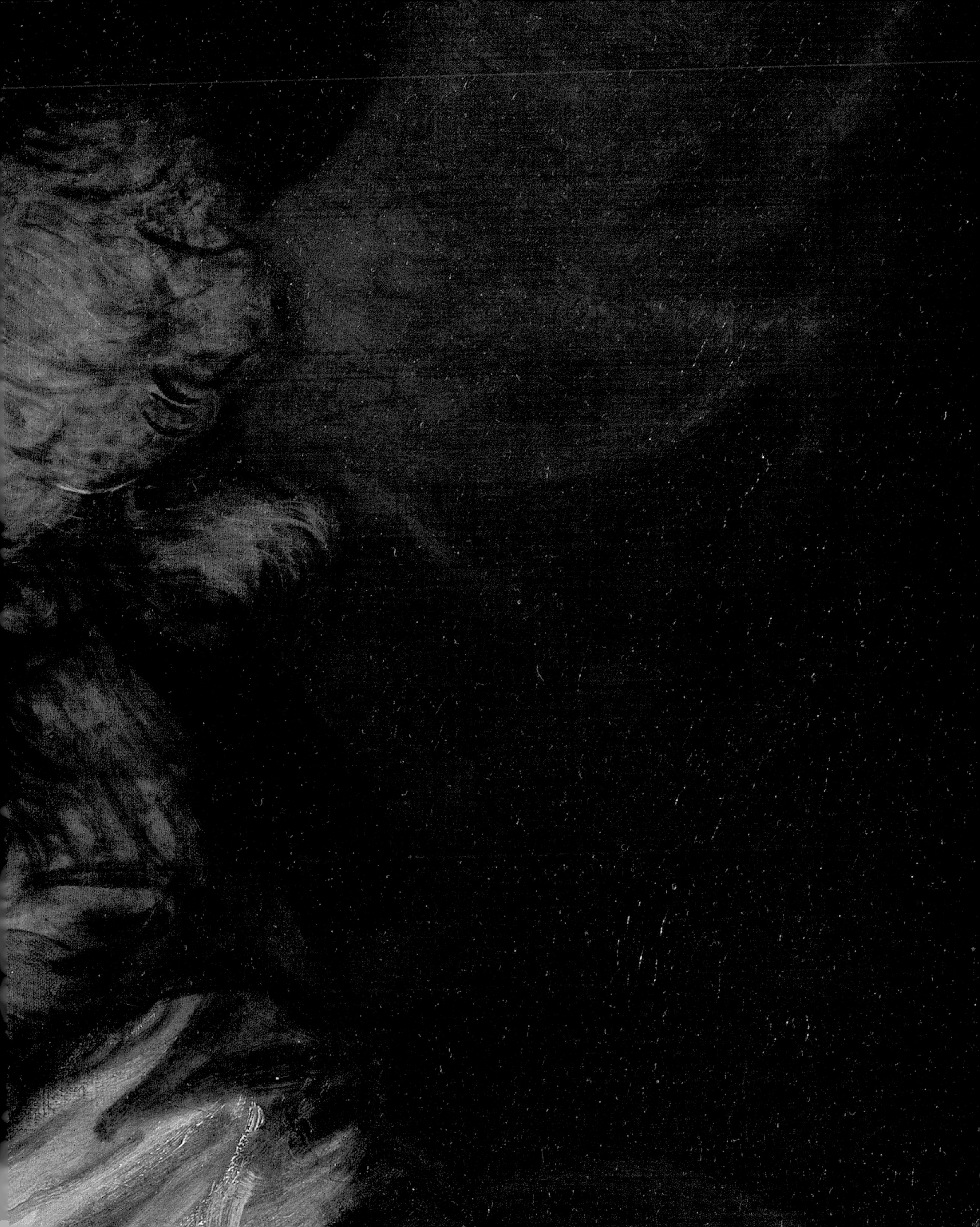

October 1760, deemed it "a most extraordinary figure, handsome and bold," but added that she "should be sorry to have any one I loved set forth in such a manner."[40]

What these breathless reactions across twenty-six years tell us is that Gainsborough was an artist of a calculated and enduring contentiousness, a position largely elaborated in self-conscious contrast to Reynolds, his rival and President of the Academy. We can easily intuit the opposition: Gainsborough's string of distinctively painted masterpieces of exceptional women at odds with Reynolds's idealizing program as expressed in his *Discourses*, the disquisitions on various aspects of academic doctrine that he produced for the benefit of the students at the Royal Academy. The two divergent representations of Siddons therefore resumed the opposition between Reynolds's academic, literary classicism and Gainsborough's emphatic naturalism and demonstrative touch. When Reynolds painted his *Sarah Siddons as the Tragic Muse*, he still believed he could produce modern grand manner portraiture.[41] Here he is in his fourth *Discourse*, in a passage that almost seems to describe his tragic muse:

If a portrait-painter
is desirous to raise and improve his subject,
he has no other means than by approaching it to a general idea.
He leaves out all the minute breaks and peculiarities in the face,
and changes the dress from contemporary fashion to one more permanent,
which has annexed to it no ideas of meanness
from its being familiar to us.[42]

With Reynolds's dramatic picture subtended by this kind of prescriptive rhetoric, we can begin to understand why Gainsborough painted contemporary fashion in the manner that he did. Certainly Gainsborough wasn't shy about expressing "impertinent remarks . . . upon the ridiculous use of fancied dresses in Portraits."[43] For the sake of historical balance, we can recall that Reynolds himself was at this time also painting young women in extravagant fashions — the Frick Collection's *Lady Taylor*, for example (FIGURE 11) — but never with Gainsborough's intention of repudiating academic prescription. Certain sympathetic critics were quick to seize on Gainsborough's singular effect in comparison with Reynolds's theatricality, and one statement by Gainsborough's friend and champion, the critic Rev. Henry Bate, merits attention. "[The] resemblance is admirable," Bate wrote of Gainsborough's Siddons, "and the features are without that theatrical distortion which several painters have been fond of delineating. In addition to the great

40
Cited in Rosenthal, *Art of Thomas Gainsborough*, 167.

41
Reynolds's brand of classicism was a synthetic one, appropriate to painters in training, whereby the artist should extract a composite, perfected ideal from his observations of nature and the Old Masters. In portraiture, Reynolds's goal was always to invest portraiture with gravitas by suppressing particularities, creating grand manner narratives that consciously sought to evoke the mythic and universal.

42
Reynolds, *Discourses on Art*, 469ff.

43
Gainsborough to William, 2nd Earl of Dartmouth, April 8, 1771, *Letters*, 88.

force and likeness . . . the new style of drapery may be mentioned. Mrs. Siddons's dress is particularly *novelle,* and the fur round her cloak and fox-skin muff are most happy imitations of nature."[44]

In setting up a contrast between Gainsborough's naturalism and Reynolds's "theatrical distortion," Bate effectively articulated one of the central constituents of Gainsborough's practice: his naturalistic verve or the physical impact of his virtuosic illusionism in rendering full-length figures.[45] The supplementary dimension was of course gender. As Bate's commentary points out, Gainsborough's "great force and likeness" was equally inscribed in his stunning rendition of feminine fashions — Bate describes Siddons's fox-skin muff as "most happy imitations of nature" — a naturalistic flourish that hardly accorded with the sober decorum of Reynolds's Grand Style.[46] Eighteenth-century viewers registered Gainsborough's characterization of the great actress as surpassing the conventional ("So prevalent is the striking form . . . of character over the mild and unimpassioned deportment of private life," observed one viewer upon seeing the portrait in Gainsborough's studio).[47] For indeed the picture is a play on traditional portraiture, where formal and spatial dissonances or allusions, joined to deliberately provocative fashions and posture, served to increase a subversive shock value.

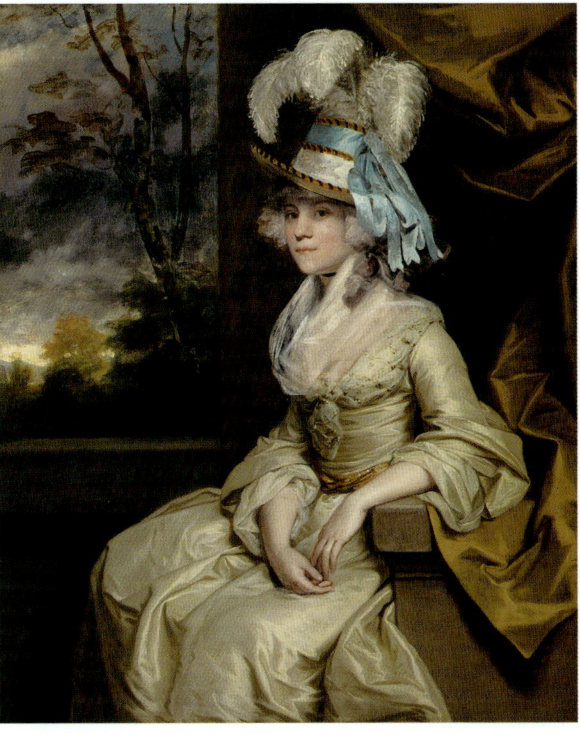

44
Cited in Rosenthal and Myrone, *Gainsborough,* 266.

45
Note how Bate envelops his approbation of Siddons's extravagant fashions and Gainsborough's militant realism in the language of traditionalism—likeness and nature—in a counter-argument to Reynolds.

46
See preceding note.

47
Whitley, *Thomas Gainsborough,* 237.

We can note first how Siddons's physical presence is amplified in Gainsborough's depiction by his choice of the seated figure in the half-length format, a portrait type, as he specified, "calculated for breast high" viewing.[48] This particular pose and scale create a more proximate viewing encounter between subject and viewer, more like the close perusal of a portrait oval, while still retaining the tangible corporeality of the sitter in the viewer's space. Siddons is situated close to the picture plane and therefore proximately to us as viewers before the painting — likely nearer than contemporary manners might have allowed. Reynolds, evoking instead the altarpiece tradition, positions his tragic muse enthroned on a superior register, above human interaction. Although I am suggesting a broad affective appeal for the painting, Gainsborough's Siddons undeniably plays to a male viewer, one who was imagined to be physically near and possibly flirtatious. Visual cues such as the chairback at right indicate how Siddons has moved forward in her seat, and despite her rigid posture, the swirl of fabrics and colors conveys a capacity for movement into our space as a speaking likeness. Gainsborough well knew, of course, that the subtleties of effect of his portrait figures also relied on canvas size, portrait format, and hanging height. When he knew a full-length portrait was to be hung high, he adjusted backgrounds and simplified costumes for a more effective presence from a distance.[49] In the case of Siddons's portrait, a picture kept for years as a trophy display in Gainsborough's showroom, the effect turned on physical proximity. In this constructed setting, propitious for such an embodied encounter, Gainsborough was playing in visual terms on the prevalent popular associations of the ambiguous nature, as one contemporary critic put it, of "an intermediate being known as what is called a Demirep."[50] Certainly, to have known, as Siddons and Gainsborough surely did, that actresses were frequently faulted for their elaborate dress, which was presumed to derive from their illicit liaisons, and to have made her accessories so extravagant and the focus of her portrait, was to affirm an ironic reappropriation of marginal femininity, a maneuver corroborated by the brashness of both sitter and painter.[51] Siddons and Gainsborough were thus in effect collaborators in self-consciously producing seditious art, which in the end led them to create one of the great ambivalent expressions in Western portraiture: inscrutable as the *Mona Lisa*, and yet knowing and present (PAGE 64).

48
Gainsborough to David Garrick, 1772, in *Letters*, 108.

49
See Susan Sloman's discussion of this and related issues in her *Gainsborough in Bath*, 58ff.

50
An Old Rabi, "To Sir John Fielding," *Public Advertiser*, April 27, 1774.

51
On actresses and the perception of their fashions, see Aileen Ribeiro, "Costuming the Part: A Discourse of Fashion and Fiction in the Image of the Actress in England, 1776–1812," in *Notorious Muse*, 109.

The Painter's Pencil

AND THE

Rendering

OF

Femininity

GAINSBOROUGH'S PORTRAITS engendered in this way a complex rhetorical conversation, whereby a viewer's visual appreciation of the painter's mark and of the physical presence of the sitter evolved into "a circular engagement between sitter, viewer and artist."[52] This compound dialogue inhered in the basic function of portraits as (speaking) likenesses of absent sitters, just as it also touched on ideas about the nature of perception itself and indeed on the gendering of painterly effects. A brief reconsideration of the particulars of Gainsborough's demonstrative touch shows how the artist engaged the gendered rhetoric and feminine associations that attached to painterly style in an ironic redirection of the double discourses around women and supposedly "feminine" painting. Indeed, Gainsborough often deliberately located his touch in the very attributes of his feminine sitters, in accessories or rouge, thereby metaphorically investing his unusual paint handling in the progressive feminine identities of his famous sitters.[53]

Just as today, *touch* was a multiplicitous signifier in the economy of eighteenth-century portraiture. Within the aesthetic sphere, touch was the trace of the artist's brush (pencil) and of the painter's gesture, while it also denoted more broadly the artist's manner of painting, that is, his style. In terms of the tactile quality of paint, *touch* also invoked the sensory aspects of touch and thus the larger scientific and philosophical discourses focused on perception and the relative affective power of tactility. Most influentially in the eighteenth century, the Abbé de Condillac, in his *Traité des sensations* (1754), had established the primacy of touch in enabling perception.[54] Likewise, touch's lexical mobility reflected the variety of the term's uses in the social sphere, where physiological reactions, whether from tactile effects or otherwise, had social consequences. A person might be "touched" emotionally by another person or by a portrait, "relationships" that were socially regulated in terms of *tact*, which was literally the sociability of touch. In essence, tact is the capacity to successfully navigate convention, in the world of painting as in the world of manners. To the extent that Gainsborough portrayed certain women who renounced tact, he participated in creating new feminine subjects even as he established a relatively radical artistic persona. The crux of the present exhibition is precisely that Gainsborough's portraits of select women functioned as the sites where both painter and sitter cooperatively affirmed progressive outlooks: the brushstroke, an index of the very point where painter *touched* sitter, functioned in this way as the emblem of their joint self-fashioning.

52
Mark Hallett, "On the Road" (review of Gainsborough exhibition, Tate Britain and National Gallery of Art, Washington, 2002–03), *Eighteenth-Century Studies* 36, no. 4 (Summer 2003): 565.

53
I am indebted here to the following article by Ewa Lajer-Burcharth, which was extremely useful in helping me conceive my discussion of touch as it relates to Gainsborough: "Image Matters: The Case of Boucher," in *Dialogues in Art History, from Mesopotamian to Modern: Readings for a New Century*, ed. Elizabeth Cropper (New Haven: Center for Advanced Study in the Visual Arts / Yale University Press, 2009), 277–303.

54
Etienne Bonnot de Condillac, *Traité des sensations* (Paris, 1754). On Condillac, touch, and perception, see Ewa Lajer-Burcharth, "Pompadour's Touch: Difference in Representation," *Representations* 73 (Winter 2001): 54–88.

Gainsborough was preoccupied with the manner in which he applied paint —
what he called his "touch of the pencil." And this is of course apparent in the
rich and varied surface treatment of his paintings. Accordingly, he was con-
cerned that viewers knew how to appreciate his paintings and apprehend them
from the proper distance. Gainsborough's obituarist in the *Morning Chronicle*,
for example, stated: "His portraits are calculated to give effect at a distance."[55]
Gainsborough himself routinely affirmed the need for a viewer to be properly
positioned: "It was calculated for breast high [viewing]," he instructs one client,
and in the quote below mentions the "force . . . of . . . effect at a proper distance."[56] This very issue regarding the visibility of Gainsborough's touch relative
to his paintings' assigned hanging height at the Royal Academy exhibition was
what prompted the artist in 1784 to retract his submissions early and never to
exhibit there again.[57] We are fortunate that Gainsborough's own pointed statements on the subject of touch and its perception were preserved in a 1758 letter
to a client, the attorney William Mayhew. In remarks worthy of lengthy quoting,
we are witness not only to some of Gainsborough's reasoning, but also to both
the negative reactions his touch elicited and the artist's counterarguments:

> You please me much by saying that no other fault
> is found in your picture than the roughness of the surface,
> for that part being of use in giving force to the effect at a proper distance,
> and what a judge of painting knows an original from a copy by;
> in short being the touch of the pencil, which is harder to preserve
> than smoothness . . .
> I don't think it would be more ridiculous for a person to
> put his nose close to the canvas and say the colours smell offensive,
> than to say how rough the paint lies; for one is just as material as the other
> with regard to hurting the effects and drawing of a picture.
> Sir Godfrey Kneller used to tell them that pictures were not made to smell of;
> and what made his pictures more valuable than others with connoisseurs
> was his pencil or touch. I hope, sir, you'll pardon this dissertation
> upon pencil and touch . . .[58]

Mayhew had in fact complained about Gainsborough's touch being too rough,
a reaction that was prevalent owing to the enduring taste for highly finished
pictures of tight brushwork promulgated by academic notions of "finish."
Gainsborough's touch was, of course, specifically aimed at countering the anonymous smoothened, dutifully prepared finish of the academician. He attempted
to rally the carping Mayhew to his view on the grounds of proper taste: that
is, the connoisseur's taste for distinctly touched surfaces. While we don't know

55
Anonymous, "Thomas
Gainsborough," *Morn-
ing Chronicle*, Aug. 8,
1788, cited in Hayes,
*Gainsborough: Paintings
and Drawings*, 26 and
no. 68.

56
Gainsborough to David
Garrick, 1772, in *Letters*,
108; Gainsborough to
William Mayhew, March
13, 1758, in ibid., 10–11.

57
See Whitley, *Thomas
Gainsborough*, 205–24.

58
Gainsborough to Wil-
liam Mayhew, March 13,
1758, in *Letters*, 10–11.

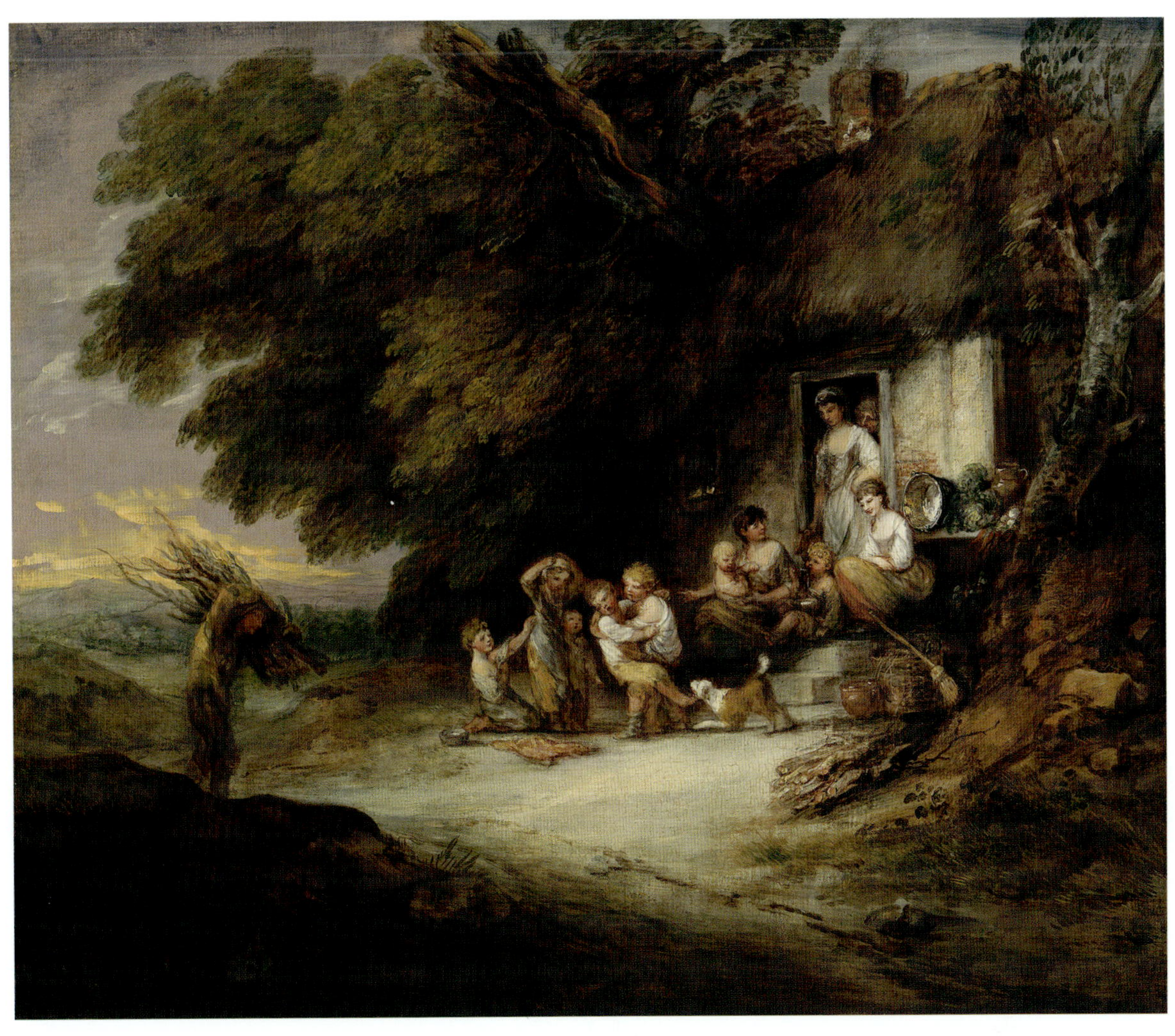

FIGURE 12

THOMAS GAINSBOROUGH
The Cottage Door
CA. 1778
OIL ON CANVAS
48-1/4 X 58-3/4 IN (122.6 X 149.2 CM)
CINCINNATI ART MUSEUM
GIFT IN HONOR OF MR. AND MRS. CHARLES F. WILLIAMS BY THEIR CHILDREN
(1948.173)

DETAIL APPEARS ON PAGE 75

if he won Mayhew over, the exchange does reveal that Gainsborough's touch was self-consciously exercised. Gainsborough specifically aimed to be distinctive, hence the reason his touch — dubbed by contemporaries his "pencilling" — ranked alongside likeness as the distinctive aspect of his portraiture his peers recognized. It is therefore not surprising that in contrast to Mayhew's view, it is a fellow artist, an anonymous eighteenth-century Italian painter, who provides us with a positive review of Gainsborough's rough paint-handling. The Italian's comment is significant for many reasons, not least for what it tells us of the perceived radicality of Gainsborough's manner of applying paint: "What shall I say of the pencilling?" he begins. "I really do not know; it is so new, so original, that I cannot find words to convey any idea of it. I do not know that any artists, living or dead, have managed their pencils in that manner and I am afraid that any attempt to imitate it will be attended with ill success. Were you in London I could only tell you to go and see."[59]

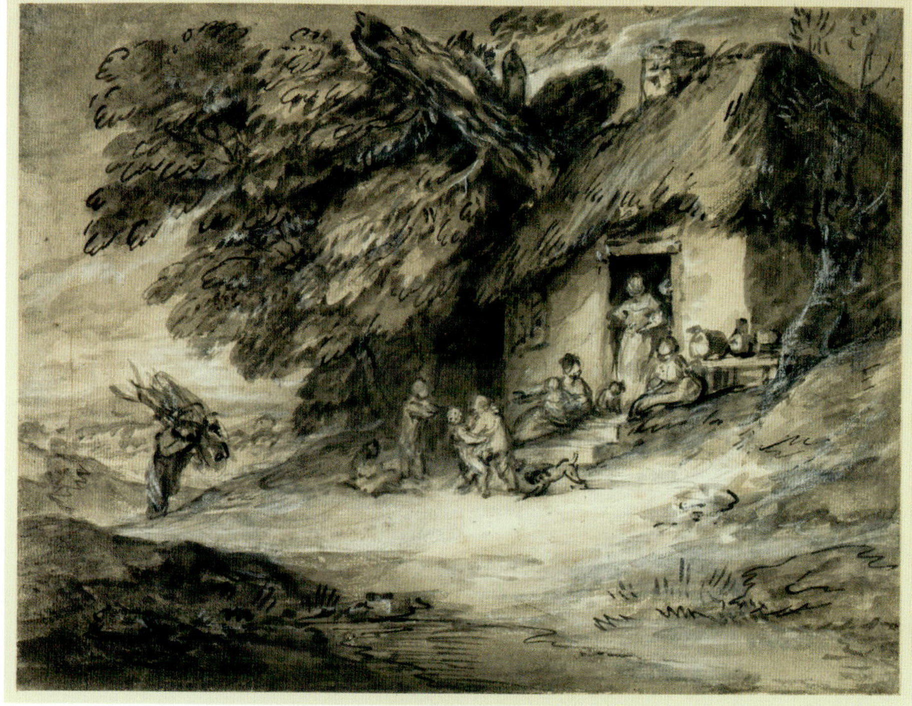

FIGURE 13

THOMAS GAINSBOROUGH
Wooded Landscape with Figures Outside a Cottage
CA. 1778
GRAY AND BLACK WASHES AND WHITE CHALK
10-11/16 X 13-5/8 IN (27.1 X 34.6 CM)
PRIVATE COLLECTION

59
Cited in William T. Whitley, *Artists and Their Friends in England 1700–1799* (London: Medici Society, 1928), 323.

Even if this attention to touch and its affirmation of originality are characteristic tropes of modernist mythology, Gainsborough's touch was, if not wholly unique, at least unusual in its emphasis. To the extent that it identified a distinct artistic personality, the individualized mark also positioned the artist within aesthetic and art historical lineages focused on rough painting dating back to the Renaissance master Titian. I want, however, to address Gainsborough's touch first by returning to the more prosaic reason for self-identification: the marketplace. Gainsborough's "touch of the pencil" was his signature, the means by which, in the artist's view, "a judge of painting knows an original from a copy." As such, it was integral to the very brand that had made him "a favourite among the demireps."[60] To mark a painting was to sign it, and it is with this analogy in mind that we can note one of the great episodes of Gainsborough's marking a canvas with his touch: the streaks of lemon-yellow paint he laid down on the left edge of the Cincinnati Art Museum's 1778 version of *The Cottage Door*, a "landscape" shown at the Royal Academy exhibition of that year (FIGURE 12 AND PAGE 75). Dashed expressively over the canvas with an unevenly loaded brush, the yellow touches affirm themselves as the most pronounced "reliques of [Gainsborough's] hand," reflexive marks of high-keyed color meant to underscore an analogical relation between the artist's creative power and the singular colorism of a distant sky at twilight.[61] We can be sure that the artist meant it as a culminating gesture because, unusually for Gainsborough, he created a preparatory drawing for the painting (FIGURE 13). This drawing shows how he had resolved the composition to near-completion in gray and black wash but without the yellow markings, colored touches of the brush that would have been added as the crowning accent in the finished painting.

Such dramatic painterly notes also featured as part of the artist's broader "pencilling" in many of his portraits, for which a lively touch often took on added resonance when rendering feminine bodies. If one takes the long-view perspective of Gainsborough's career, it is evident that his "pencilling," or painterly style, was hardly constant. But it is in fact from a monographic vantage that we can correctly appreciate the capital importance of the Cincinnati Art Museum's *Ann Ford*. It is the most important of a handful of major full-length portraits dating to ca. 1760 and the painting through which Gainsborough found his voice as a mature painter. As a master statement, the portrait of Ann Ford established the bedrock characteristic of Gainsborough's mature technique, one that he continued to elaborate through to the end of his career: freedom of handling or a general looseness of brushwork. In a letter of the early 1770s, Gainsborough himself communicated the exact terms by which we should assess his style: "freedom [of hand in drawing] is only the manner, in which a Master would do

60
Gainsborough to William Mayhew, March 13, 1758, in *Letters*, 10. "[Royal Academy Exhibition]," *Morning Chronicle and London Advertiser*, May 25, 1778, 2.

61
Anonymous, "Mr. Gainsborough's Pictures," *Diary, or Woodfall's Register*, April 2, 1789, issue 4.

the same thing, different from a stiff handed scholar."[62] Gainsborough of course meant here freedom from academic prescription, intimating also the greater value of expressive handling in relation to the learned rigidity of the history painter.

Gainsborough was thus actively demonstrative and self-affirming in his handling of paint, having developed a signature manner that communicated his individuality and dexterity as well as the traditional ideals of spontaneity, facility, and variety attached to spirited brushwork. For these reasons Gainsborough's "pencilling" is consciously elliptical and suggestive, rather than additive, or "lick'd," the contemporary term still used today to describe more tightly brushed, that is, more finely finished, paintings. Gainsborough describes the value of variety in a statement that reminds us of the omnipresence of the erotic in his integration of painterly materiality with lifelike illusionism: "There must be a variety of Lively touches and surprising Effects to make the Heart dance . . . in Portrait Painting there must be a Lustre and finishing to bring it up to individual Life."[63]

The portrait of Ann Ford is thus generally characteristic of Gainsborough's "pencilling" in the way the paint surface communicates a sense of bristling movement. With a closer look, one is struck by the adaptability of the painter's brush. Gainsborough *demonstrates* an impulsive, liberated hand adept at solving problems of representation through every imaginable effect of the brush: pecks with the tip, loose sinuous strokes, regularized dashes. The square foot of canvas that marks the gravitational center of the composition shows him performing his mastery in depicting the manifold textures of life: stuffs, flesh, the sheen of enameled wood, the hard glint of precious stones (PAGE 76). Note the diaphanous fabric of the sleeve, depicted using the broad application of a translucent whitewash upon which lacework accents are picked out in impastoed touches. Creases in the fabric of the sleeve, meanwhile, resolve themselves at a distance from a mix of serpentine marks topped by dramatic lead-white highlights applied with a dry brush. Again, accents of color — this time the system of yellow knots disposed across the subject's upper body — are among the distinctive marks of the artist, whose penciling with pastelike paint contrasts radically with the adjacent enameled finish of the varnished guitar top. Gainsborough's facility, as he would have it, wasn't therefore only with rough surfaces, but indeed with academic finish itself.

62
Gainsborough to Constantine Phipps, 1771 or 1772, in *Letters*, 92.

63
Gainsborough to William Hoare, 1773, in *Letters*, 113.

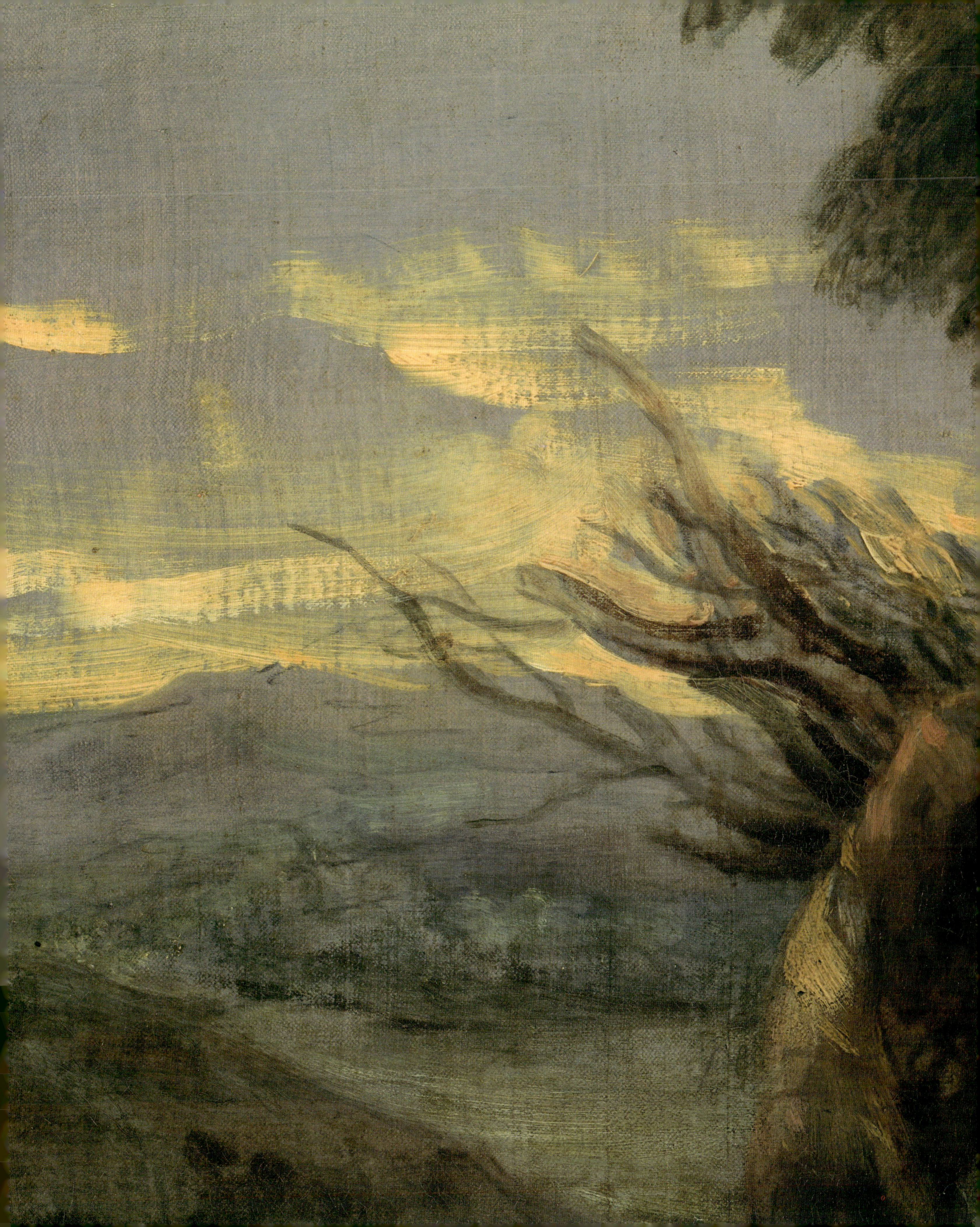

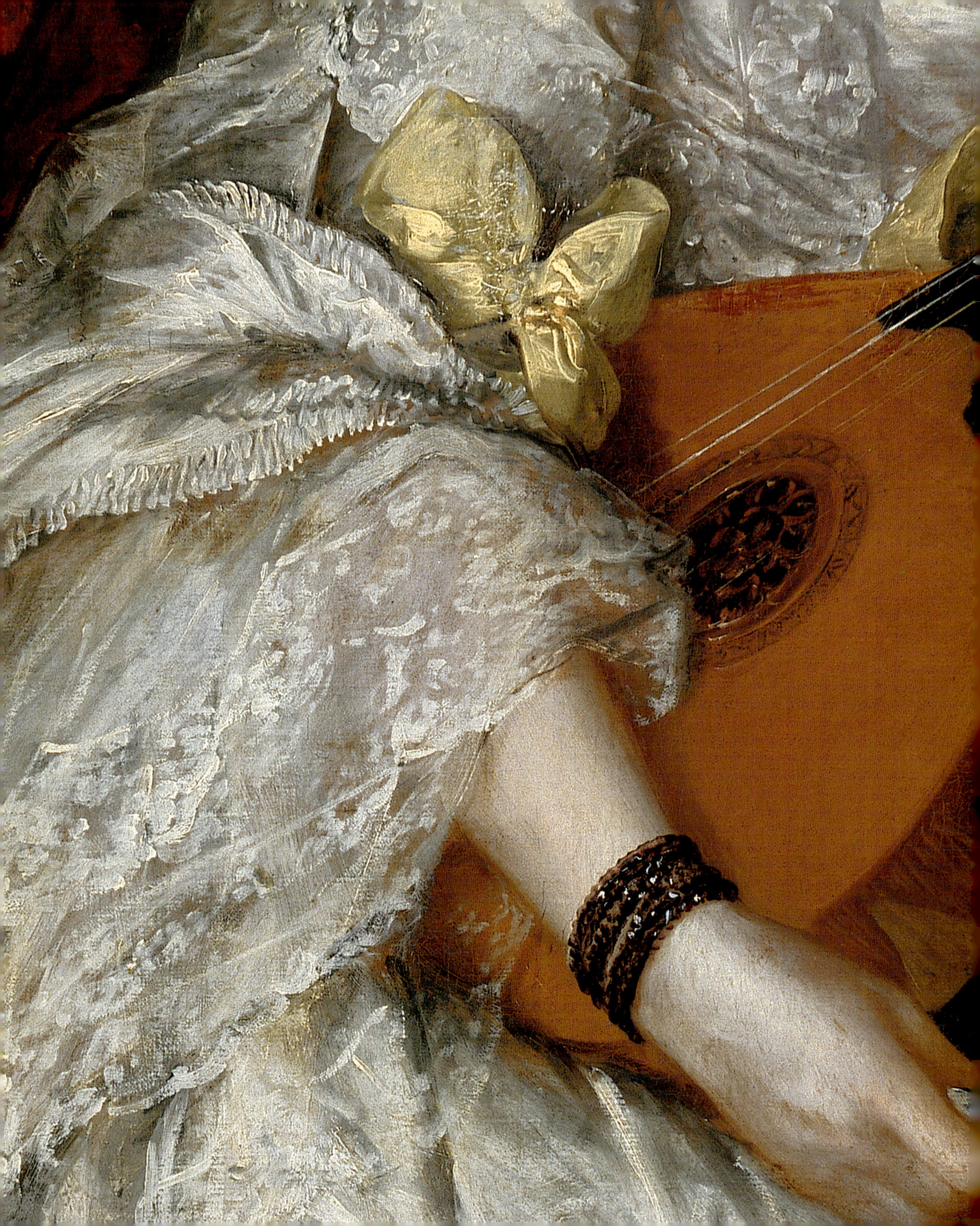

In 1782, nearly a quarter-century after Ann Ford, we find Gainsborough in the midst of his inspired late manner, having painted the portrait of the Italian dancer Giovanna Baccelli using an emphatic penciling that perfectly illustrates his own words about "freedom [of hand in drawing]" being the "only manner" (PLATE 7). His manner here announces itself as a form of willfully tremulous drawing with brush and oil paint. Much of the picture's background is thinly painted with often seemingly quick, smaller strokes that reach from left to right, resulting in a characteristically shifty, shimmering surface that calls attention to itself, even if at the time not always favorably. Gainsborough's friend William Jackson of Exeter, for example, recounting the painter's manner in general terms, judged that the painter had in fact "failed by affecting a thin washy colouring, and a hatching style of penciling."[64] Similarly, Reynolds, in his famous fourteenth *Discourse* assessing Gainsborough's touch, first praised his "hatching manner [which] did very much to contribute to the lightness of effect . . . in his pictures" only to then fault it as an "unfinished" or "undetermined manner."[65] Contemporaries in any case recognized Gainsborough's painterly touch as being in tension with the more contained handling prescribed by academic decorum. The reviewer for the *London Chronicle*, for instance, having seen Gainsborough's eleven submissions to the 1782 Royal Academy exhibition, which included the portrait of Giovanna Baccelli, observed "as usual, a proud rivalship exists between the pencil of the President and that of Mr. Gainsborough."[66]

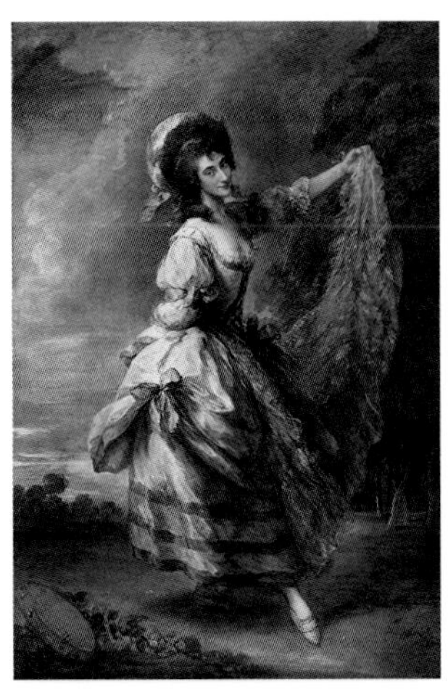

PLATE 7
Giovanna Baccelli

This antagonism was predictably gendered, with Gainsborough's faulty feminine effects contrasted to Reynolds's ideal masculine grand manner, an aesthetic opposition which appeared even in some of the earliest art historical treatments of Gainsborough's own career. Gainsborough's sketchy manner, seen by some as less noble because of its resonance with the painterly atmospheres of Antoine Watteau, is either criticized or omitted, while his self-avowed debt to the Flemish Baroque master Anthony Van Dyck is highlighted as the determinant influence. Reynolds, along with many other contemporary art writers, referred to French "flutter" and other such terms to criticize excessive painterliness. Here is Reynolds in a much earlier 1752 critique of French Rococo art in which he enumerates his objections to "ornamental" painting in language that seems to anticipate the Cincinnati Art Museum's *Ann Ford*: "affected turns of the head, fluttering draperies, contrasts of attitude and distortions of passions . . ."[67] Reynolds's astonishment at his rival's "magick" never diminished, as it no doubt forever evoked Watteau's gossamer forms. In his tribute to Gainsborough some four decades later, Reynolds

64
William Jackson, "Character of Gainsborough," in *New Annual Register, or General Repository of History, Politics, and Literature for the Year 1798* (London: S. Hamilton, 1799), 34.

65
Reynolds, *Discourses on Art*, 258–59.

66
Cited in Rosenthal and Myrone, *Gainsborough*, 136.

67
Joshua Reynolds, cited in Edward Morris, *French Art in Nineteenth-Century Britain* (New Haven: Yale University Press, 2005), 5.

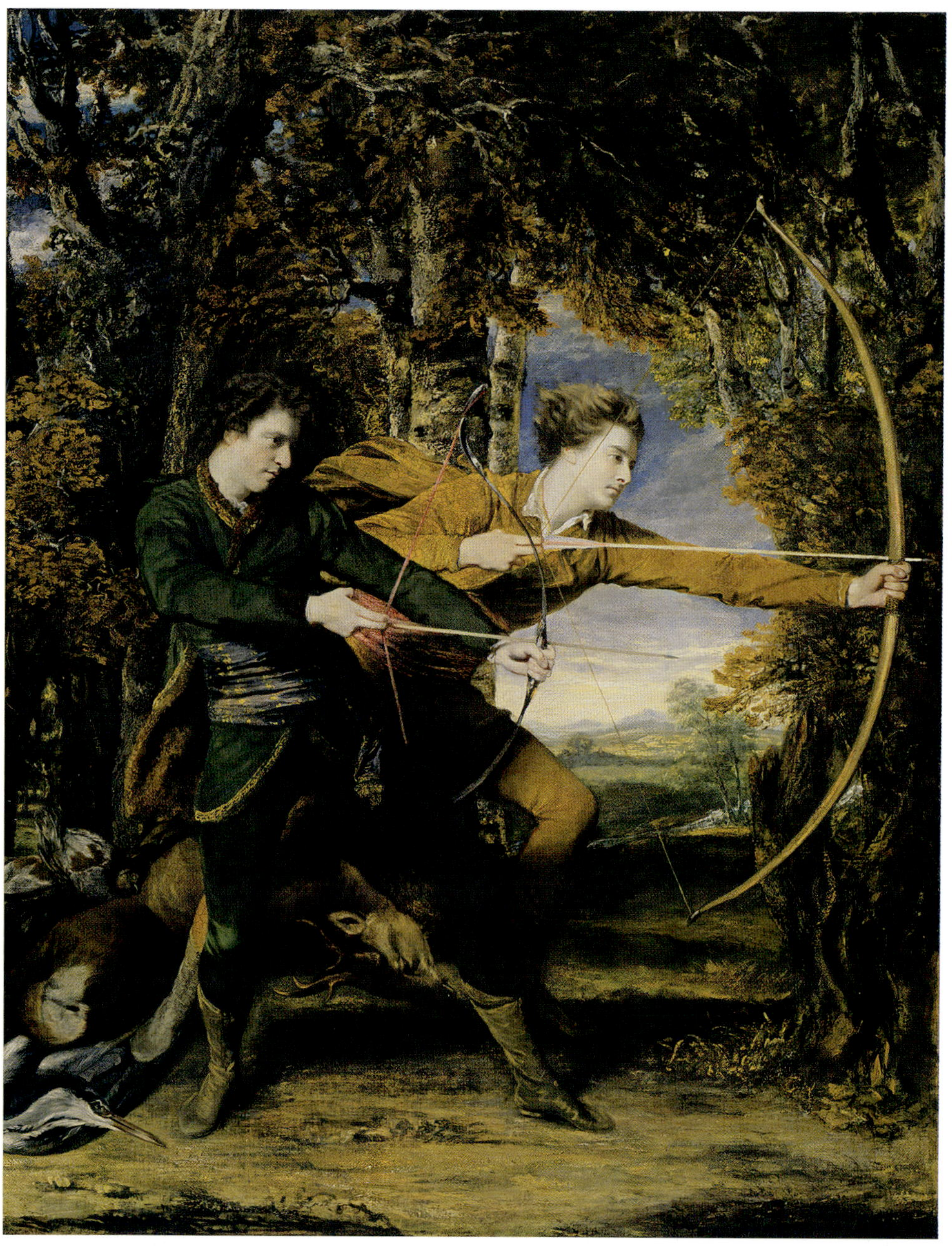

FIGURE 14

SIR JOSHUA REYNOLDS
Colonel Acland and Lord Sydney: The Archers
1769
OIL ON CANVAS
92-15/16 X 70-7/8 IN (236 X 180 CM)
TATE
PURCHASED (BUILDING THE TATE COLLECTION FUND) WITH ASSISTANCE
FROM THE NATIONAL HERITAGE MEMORIAL FUND, TATE MEMBERS,
THE ART FUND (WITH A CONTRIBUTION FROM THE WOLFSON FOUNDATION)
AND OTHER DONORS, 2005 (T12033)

DETAIL APPEARS ON PAGES 80–81

speaks of "all those odd scratches and marks, which, on close examination, are so observable in Gainsborough's pictures . . . this chaos, this uncouth and shapeless appearance, by a kind of magick, at a certain distance assumes form." For William Jackson, Gainsborough had "failed" when he took up "thin colouring . . . But when . . . he painted in the *manly* substantial style of Vandyke, he was very little, if at all, his inferior."[68] In other words, Gainsborough was better when he painted like a man, or calculatedly deployed a looser touch within the parameters of established traditions of grand manner (masculine) impasto.[69] Reynolds provides us with two ready examples of "broad" painting in the grand manner. *Lady Cockburn* wears an embroidered gown trimmed with impastoed highlights that learnedly ape Rembrandt (FIGURE 2). In the stunning *Colonel Acland and Lord Sydney: The Archers* (FIGURE 14), which is manly in scale and theme (the hunt), Reynolds employs a thick, mottled surface to render imitatively the actual roughness of the tree bark and the brush that surrounds the two figures (PAGE 80).

It is further on in his fourteenth *Discourse*, however, where Reynolds distills Gainsborough's art down to mere "effects . . . of colour," that he implicitly fixes his rival in the realm of the feminine. For in the art theoretical dyad between color and line, color was conventionally configured in terms of the fleeting, the insubstantial, and the feminine: "Gainsborough . . . cultivated those effects of the art which proceed from colours; and sometimes appears to be indifferent to or neglect other excellencies."[70] It is important to note here that Reynolds was not just talking about color per se but also about its textured application in a manner recalling how the great Venetians applied their exotic coloring as "*colorito.*" Accordingly, the term *colorito* encompasses both color and the resultant effects of the brush in applying it.

This understanding of color as being inextricably fused to touch in the eighteenth century is corroborated by the painter and theorist Jonathan Richardson, who in his *Essay on the Art of Painting* defines the term "Handling" as follows: "By this Term is understood the manner in which the Colours are left by the Pencil upon the Picture." Richardson goes on to establish what was to become a convention of any discussion on touch: deviant or ham-handed touch, commenting that handling (touch) might be "well, or Ill as 'tis perform'd with a curious, expert; or heavy, clumsey hand."[71] Reynolds was thus reprising an established adage when he addressed the pitfalls of touch in his eleventh *Discourse*, delivered to the Academy and its students in December 1782, a mere six months after Gainsborough's portrait of Baccelli and his other submissions had caused

68
My emphasis. William Jackson, "Character of Gainsborough," 34.

69
Likewise, contemporary critics such as George Vertue established "broad and great" compared to finished portraits; see Carol Gibson-Wood, *Jonathan Richardson: Art Theorist of the English Enlightenment* (New Haven: Yale University Press, 2000), 60–65.

70
Reynolds, *Discourses*, 259–60.

71
Jonathan Richardson, *An Essay on the Theory of Painting* (London, 1725), 164.

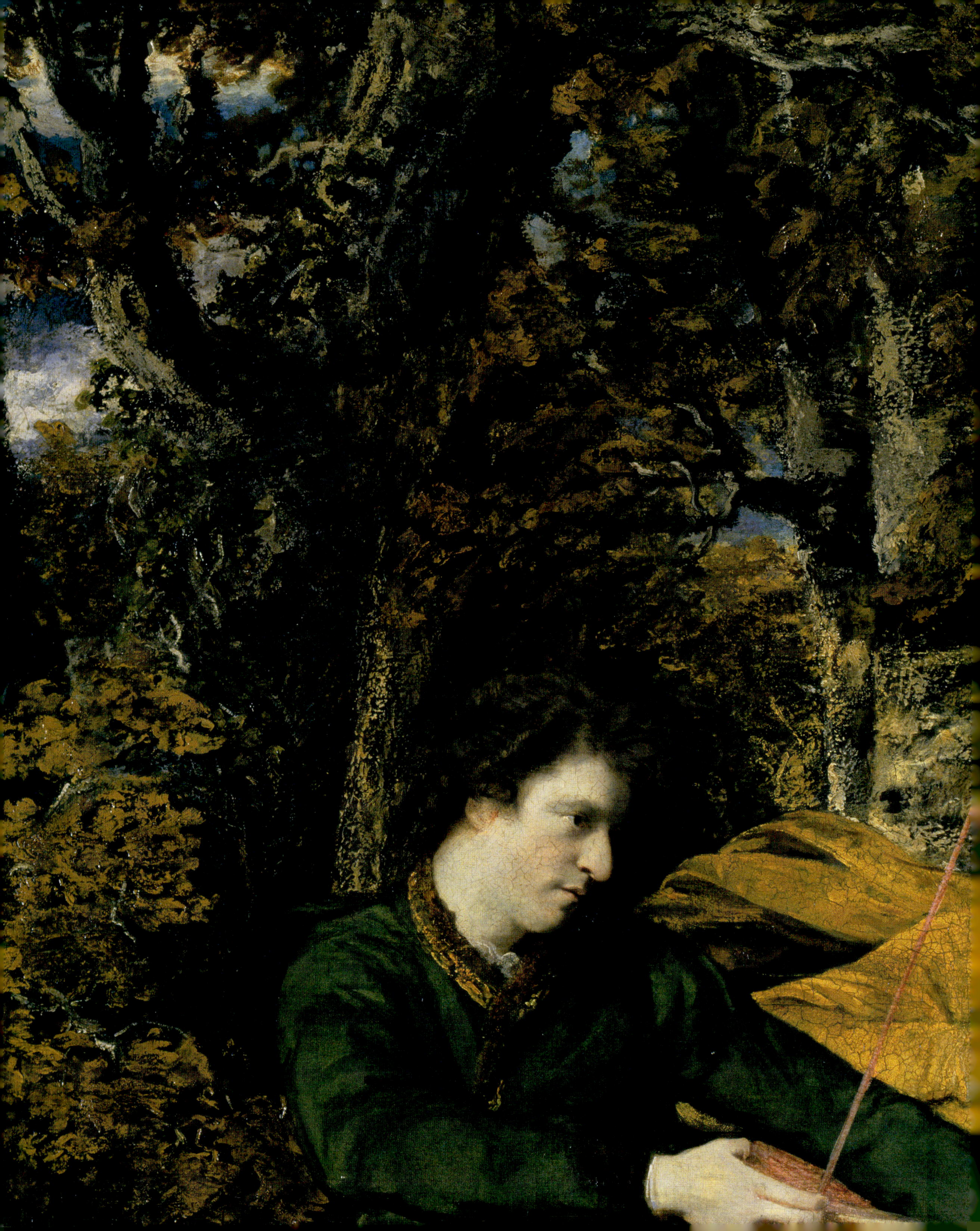

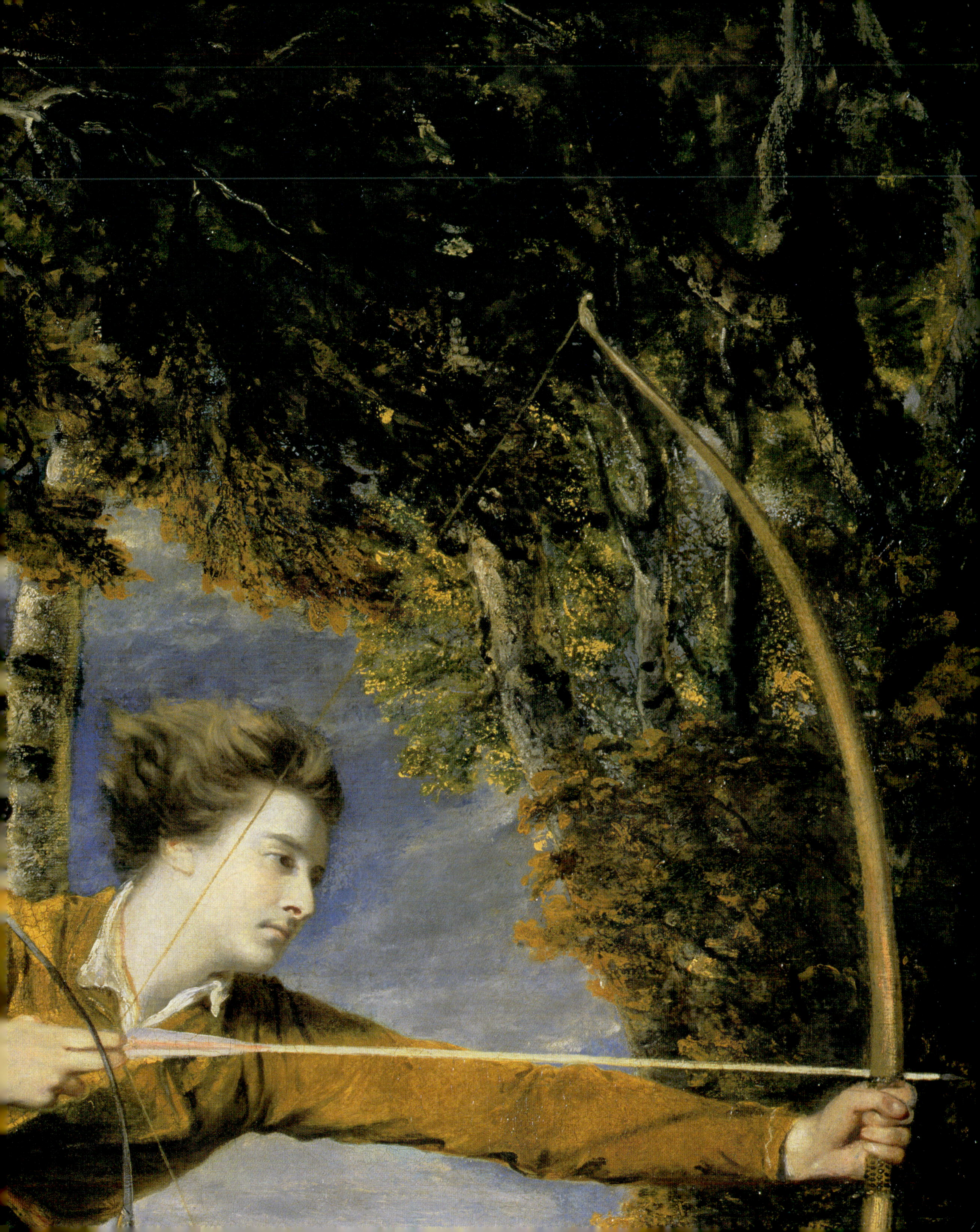

a sensation on account of their "pencilling." Gainsborough, of course, espoused Rubens and Van Dyck as his models; nonetheless, the substance of Reynolds's lesson still applied: painters should be wary of the seductiveness of impastoed colors from Italy: "Many artists . . . have ignorantly imagined they are imitating the manner of the Titian, when they leave their colours rough, and neglect the detail; but, not possessing the principles on which he wrought, they have produced . . . absurd, foolish pictures; for such will always be the consequence of affecting dexterity without science."[72] Reynolds's probity as Royal Academy president precluded more accusing language toward women, but his enumeration of the shortcomings of so-called ornamental painting — "affected turns of the head, fluttering draperies, contrasts of attitude and distortions of passions" — leaves little doubt as to how he gendered indecorous painting.[73]

Other critics were less hesitant about locating the root of supposedly deviant practices squarely in the world of women. For all times, it seems, not only the bodies of women but also their virtue were implicated in the critique of paintings, with formal and technical deficiencies in pictures fused to the imputed moral shortcomings of female sitters or to "unsavory" women more generally. Witness an anonymous 1795 review railing against the ill effects of "ornamental" painting. The author conflates pictorial "excess" with the "ornaments of a courtesan," linking it, in turn, to French vice and finally to the unnatural:

> There is a taste spreading abroad for gaudy hues, glittering effects and
> mechanical fopperies dazzling to weak-sighted connoisseurs and
> unfledged students — with the meretricious ornaments of a courtesan,
> they lure the idle and inexperienced . . .
> If this extravagant perversion of all taste is not checked and exposed . . .
> we shall . . . degenerate into all the vices of French frippery and affectation,
> to the utter exclusion of Nature.[74]

In contrast, Gainsborough deliberately continued his brand of "feminized" rough painting not only to counter masculinist practice, but also to validate his painting on the very terms by which it might be negatively classified as "feminine." Painterly and colorful, Gainsborough's work could easily be seen as related to French "flutter" (Reynolds). But here again, as we saw previously with Mrs. Siddons's extravagant fashions, Gainsborough upends established biases through a sort of reappropriation and reversal. That Gainsborough's touch was most visibly located in the luxury accessories of a foreign demirep such as Baccelli overtly announced it as constitutive of an alternative, sensory kind of painting.

72
Reynolds, *Discourses*, 195–96.

73
Cited in Morris, *French Art in Nineteenth-Century Britain*, 5.

74
Cited in Kay Dian Kriz, *The Idea of the English Landscape Painter: Genius as Alibi in the Early Nineteenth Century* (New Haven: Yale University Press, 1997), 45.

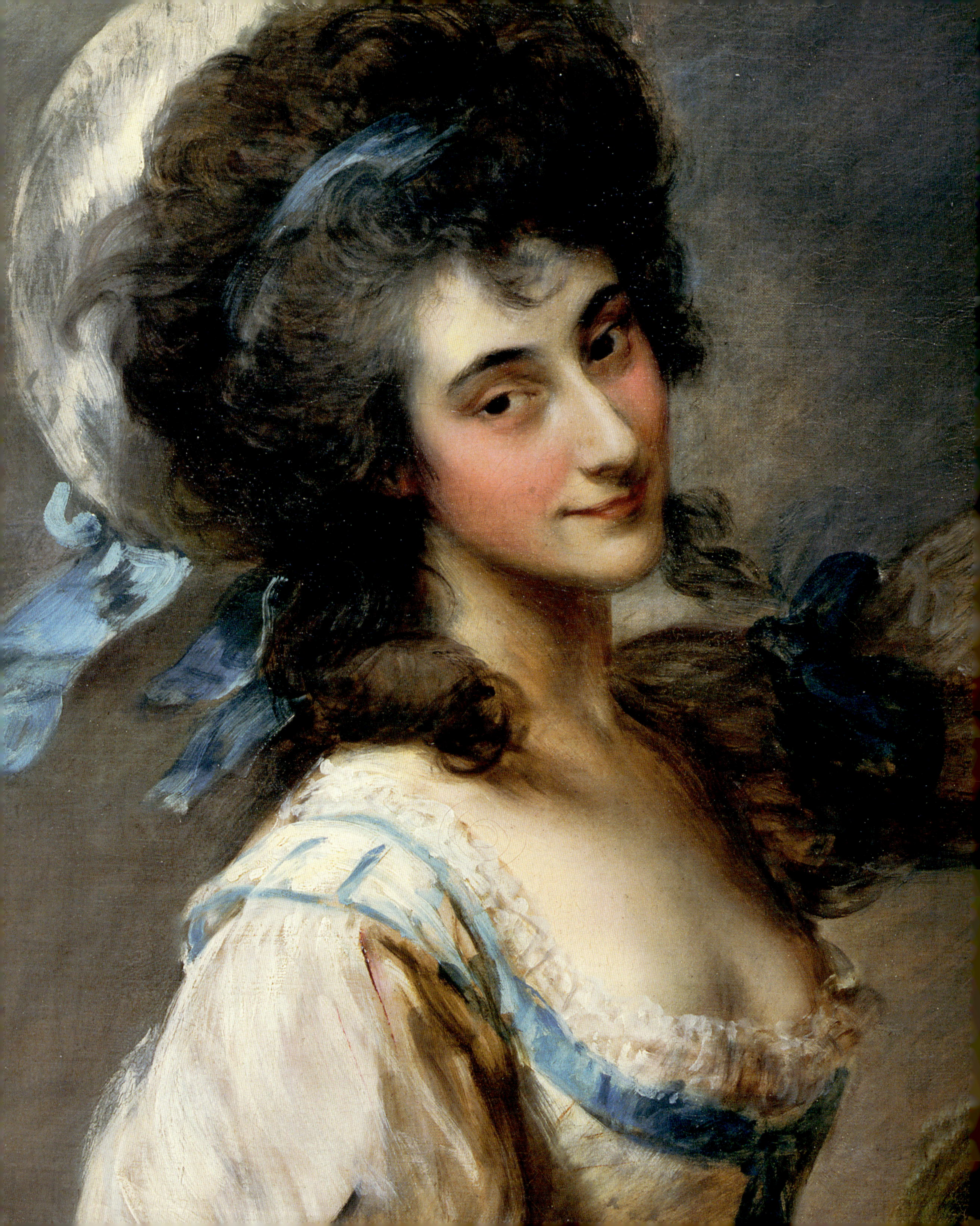

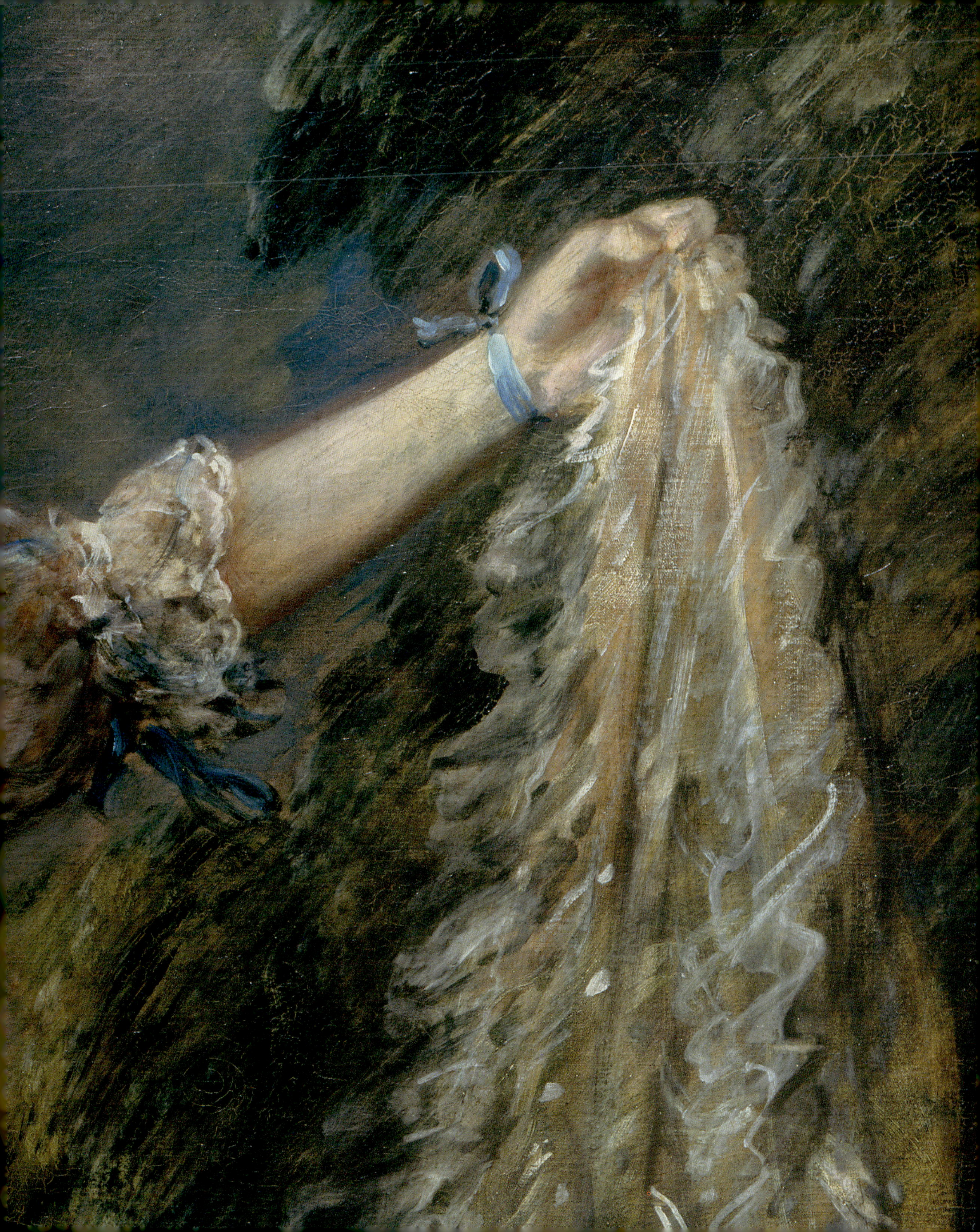

Certainly he wanted to hold our attention with the profusion of paint strokes that forms Baccelli's apron, a diaphanous fabric evasive to the gaze and silken to the touch (PAGE 85). The point is that the very demonstrative strokes that complete the illusion refer back to the artifice of the painter, who has impolitically marked his picture with one especially visible mark: the single, continuous stroke of gray emanating from the center of the canvas that forms the front of the dancer's dress and the edge of her apron (PAGES 88–89). Through this bombastic stroke, Gainsborough was appropriating femininity precisely to counter the dominant art theoretical discourse that denigrated "feminine" effects.

Some contemporary critics duly zeroed in on the artist's inspired painting of the dancer's makeup. This was exactly as intended, for we know that Gainsborough had for years been criticized for his coloring of faces, notably of courtesans'.[75] His coloring was thus at one level applied ironically, something that seems only occasionally to have been recognized. A comparative assessment in the contemporary *Gazetteer and New Daily Advertizer* of Baccelli's portrait and that of Lord Camden addresses the shifts in Gainsborough's coloring, noting that the artist now knew to use "all that soberness of colouring, which corresponds with the gravity of the object" — that is, Lord Camden. Baccelli, on the other hand, was a "contrast rather than a companion," first because she was a public woman (a dancer); second, on account of her emphatic coloring appropriate to a demirep. According to the *Gazetteer* critic, to portray "an Italian Opera Dancer, the artist was not only obliged to vivify and embellish, but if he would be thought to copy the original, to lay on his colouring thickly: in this he has succeeded, for the face of this admirable dancer is evidently *paint painted*"[76] (PAGE 84).

75
See, for example, Anonymous, "(Royal Academy Exhibition): Mr. Gainsborough [. . .]," *Morning Chronicle and London Advertiser*, April 25, 1778.

76
Anonymous, "Royal Academy Exhibition" (review), *Gazette and New Daily Advertiser*, May 1, 1782.

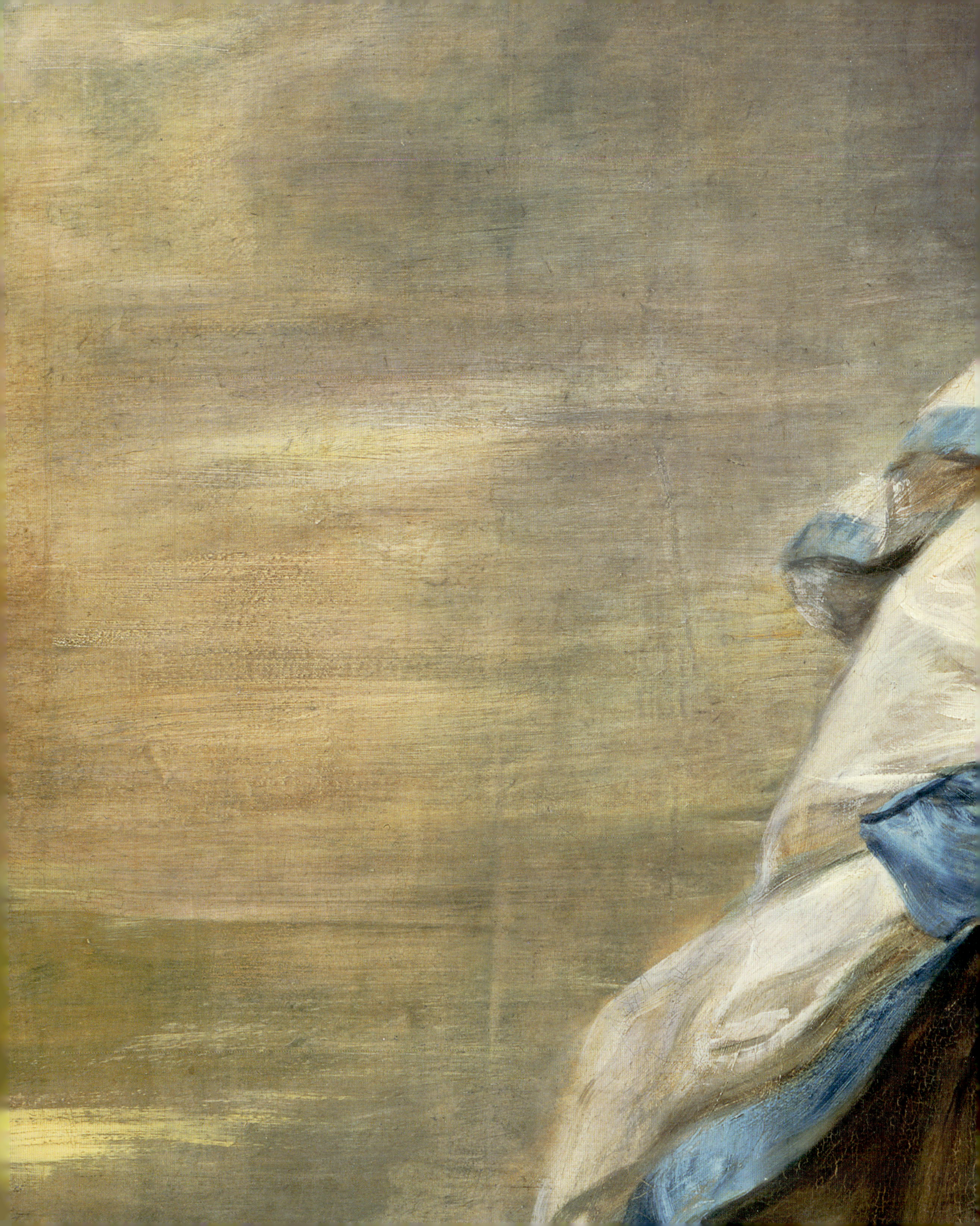

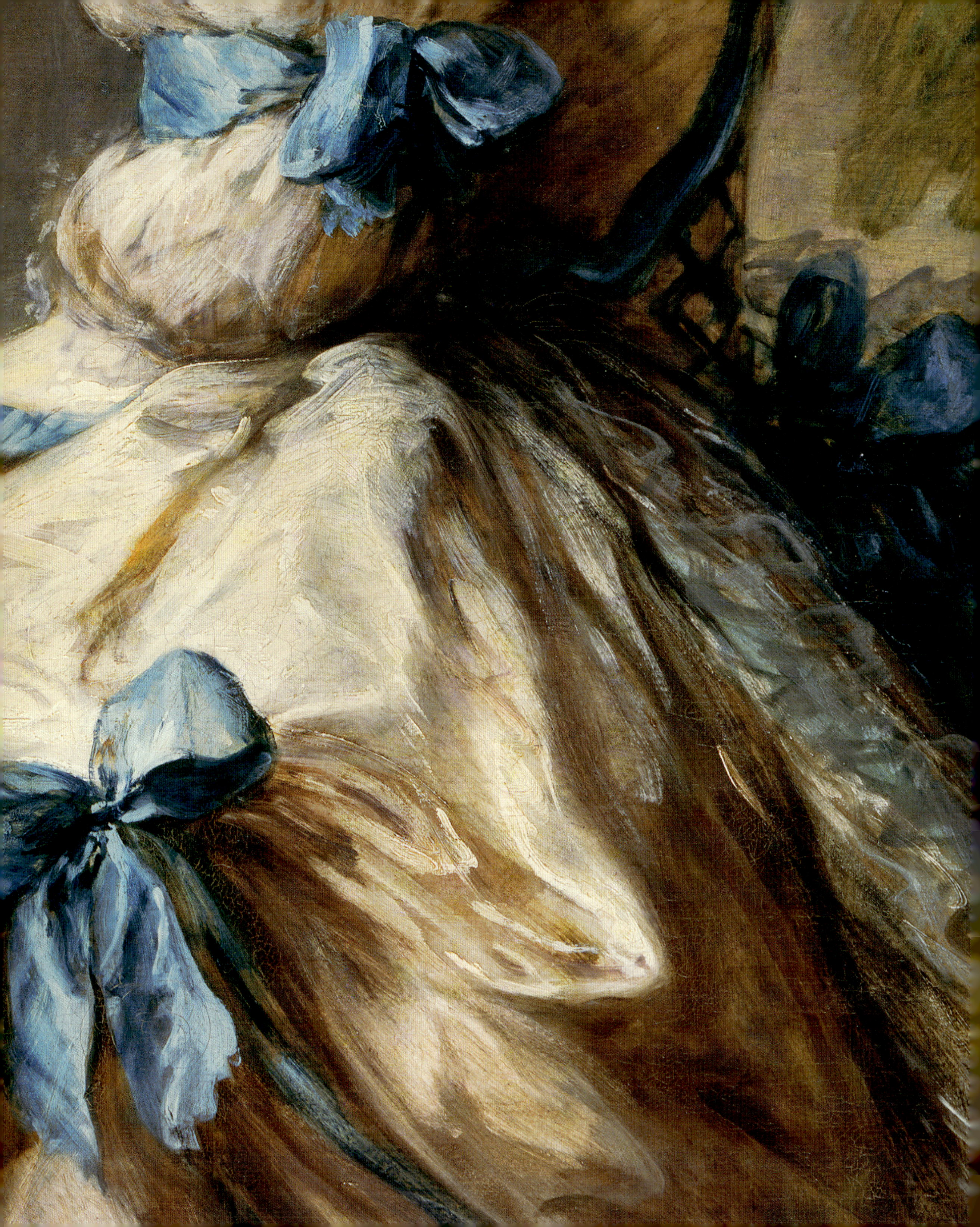

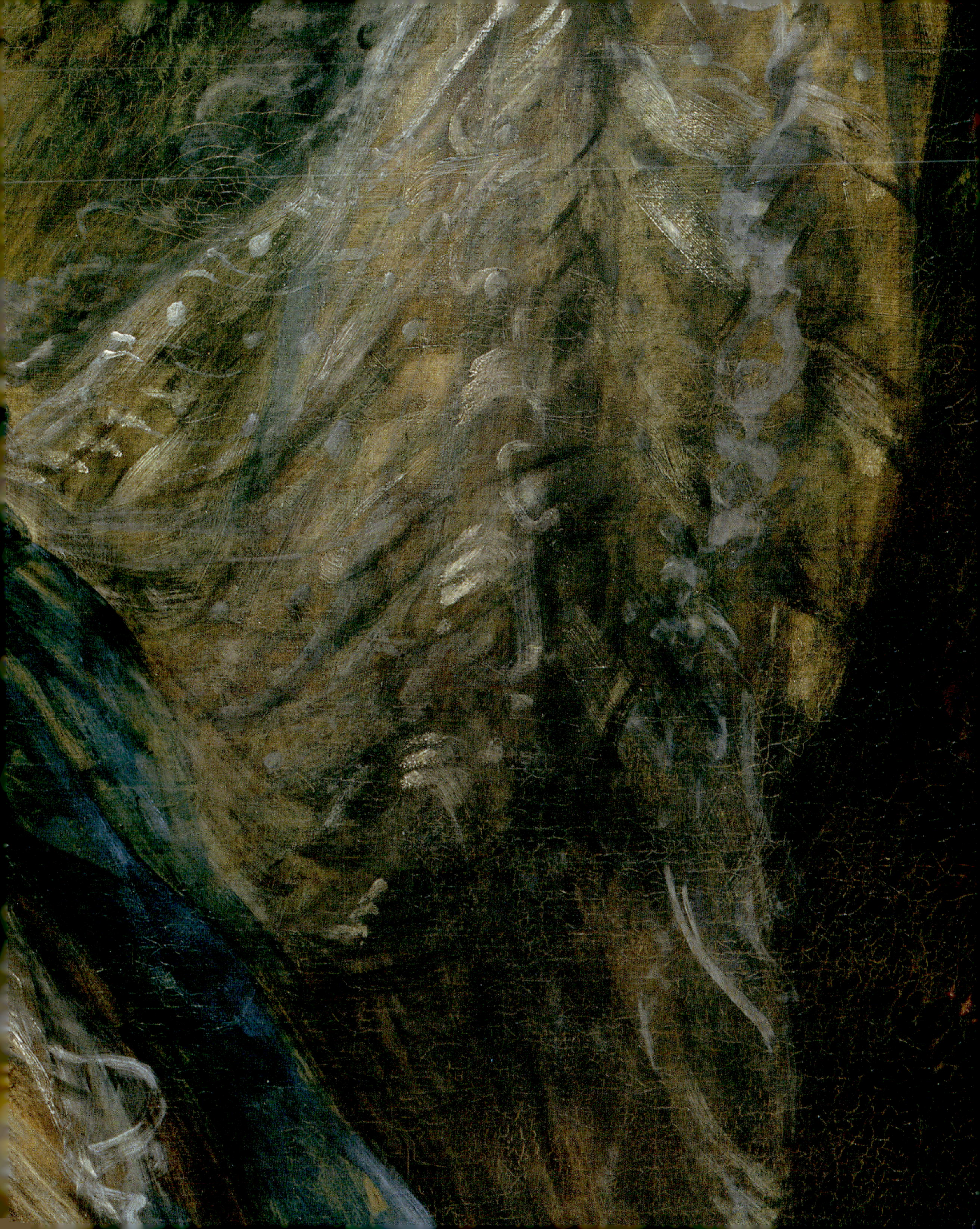

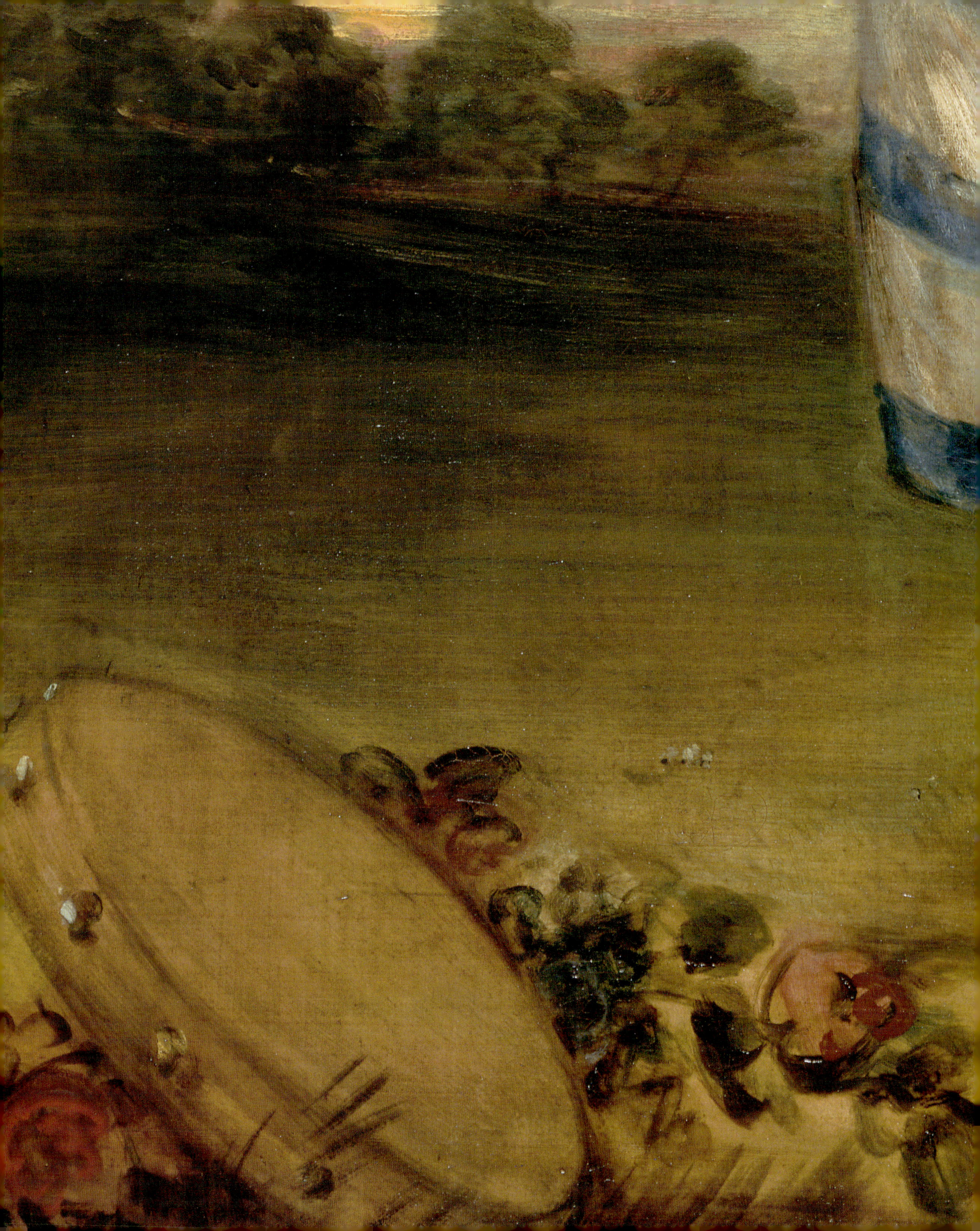

MODERNITY IN PAINTING was thus tied up in the depiction of women: here the painter's touching of the dancer's rouged cheek elicited musings on the relationship between the materiality of paint and its illusionistic potential. We can also be sure that when Gainsborough conflated his touch with her rouge, he was hardly looking to vivify on moral terms, as the anonymous critic above would imply, but rather to flout this very type of chauvinism. Typically the art press negotiated feminine sex appeal in portraits from the conventional positions of the moralizing or the mildly complimentary. In painting, as we saw in the case of Mrs. Siddons, Reynolds packaged actresses and courtesans in theatricalized, grand manner set pieces that provided for a male "fantasy of control and accessibility."[77] In literature the same fantasies were often articulated through archetypal caricatures, such as the scheming woman, with disguise and deception being the staple traits of the demirep. As per the novelist Fielding's formulation, demireps were women "who intrigue with every man [they] like under the appearance of virtue."[78] Thomas Horde, in a play of the mid-1780s, defines a demirep as "a female made up of spirits and motion, that bids defiance to space and extent, and traverses the globe in a whirlwind."[79] Such a woman could become particularly discomfiting in a suspicious collaboration with a shifty portraitist, a producer of the masquerades that might obscure discernible signs of class and morality. Hence, in the portraiture chapter of his book-length assessment of British art at midcentury, the contemporary critic André Rouquet warns of foreign-born women and "the[ir] barbarous art of daubing [their] cheeks with a glaring red."[80] Portraitists were to avoid abetting this false feminine fashion for heavily rouged cheeks by not painting them — in other words, they were admonished to refrain from doing what Gainsborough had deliberately done in painting Giovanna Baccelli.

Gainsborough was obviously invested in the exact obverse of conventional prudishness, that is, in the seductive potential of painting and of women, an objective made doubly visible by his touch as well as by the forthright allure of the women his touch described. We can safely speculate at this juncture that allure was a cooperative endeavor between Gainsborough and sitters such as Ann Ford, Giovanna Baccelli, Sarah Siddons, or Grace Dalrymple. As Rouquet had noted, eighteenth-century British women liked to "have their pictures exposed for some time in the house of that painter who is most in fashion."[81] Fashionability and sex appeal would seem even to have been a competition between sitters. In June 1785 the *Morning Herald* mentioned that "[Grace Dalrymple] is at this

77
Postle, " 'Painted Women,' " 30–32.

78
Henry Fielding, *Tom Jones* (London, 1749), 264.

79
Thomas Horde, *The Empirick; an Entertainment in two acts* (Oxford: W. Jackson, ca. 1785), 21.

80
Rouquet, *Present State of the Arts*, 48.

81
Ibid., 40–41.

time sitting to Mr. Gainsborough and surveys, with triumphant air, the portrait of the toe-poised Baccelli, which is placed in the Gallery of that distinguished painter."[82] In any case, the portraits in this exhibition need not presuppose only a male viewer. For "in a world prior to visual animation," Marcia Pointon tells us, "paint on canvas . . . provoked strong feelings of empathy."[83] That is, in the eighteenth century both men and women reacted physically to painted portraiture of women.

Our own visual appreciation of Gainsborough's "paint painted" touches thus mirrors that of eighteenth-century viewers of both sexes. It equally corresponds to some of the bedrock concerns of eighteenth-century "sensibility": the widely adopted existential doctrine founded on emotional and empathetic sociability that offered much to the sociable portraitist. Richardson codified portraiture's adaptation of the sociable aspects of sensibility when he described the ideal of a sensible gentleman-portraitist in his *Essay on Painting*: "A portrait painter must understand mankind and enter into their characters, and express their minds as well as their faces: and as his business is chiefly with people of condition, he must think as a Gentleman, and a man of sense."[84] Samuel Johnson affirmed the deeper emotional bonds of "sensible" portraiture when he noted that a portrait's primary purpose was to "diffus[e] friendship, and renew tenderness."[85] And Gainsborough's own "sensibility" could hardly be questioned if one takes stock of the many contemporary remarks that attest to his being a man of feeling. He was, for example, skilled at the viola da gamba and "always play'd to the feelings."[86] For Philip Thicknesse, the artist's story required a pen "equal to [Gainsborough's] own inimitable pencil, to hold forth the powers it possessed, or the tender feeling of his heart."[87]

"Sensible" interchanges were in any case more than subjective feelings in the realm of ethical philosophy, since they were enacted in Gainsborough's immediate and intimate relations with the demireps he painted. For this reason it is helpful to concretize such portrait encounters (usually a series of sittings) in the surviving details of Gainsborough's studio and painting practice as the site and activity that produced sensitive painterly touches. It is first meaningful to consider Gainsborough's Abbey Street studio in Bath, where he painted the Cincinnati Art Museum's *Ann Ford*, in geographic terms: that is, enmeshed in the commercial fabric of the city above a "purveyor of lace and ribbons," which also sold fashionable accessories, perfumes, powder, flowers, and haberdashery.[88] In other words, as he painted Ann Ford, Gainsborough was part of the luxury goods industry that catered to fashionable women. A handful of

82
Cited in Einberg, *Gainsborough's Giovanna Baccelli*, 31.

83
Marcia Pointon, " 'Portrait! Portrait!! Portrait!!!,' " in *Art on the Line: The Royal Academy Exhibitions at Somerset House 1780– 1836*, ed. David Solkin (New Haven: Yale University Press, 2001), 103.

84
Richardson, *Theory of Painting*, 22.

85
Samuel Johnson, "The Idler," *Universal Chronicle*, Feb. 24, 1758. I want to thank those members of the C18-Listserv who provided me with the exact bibliographic citation for this quote.

86
Anonymous, "Anecdotes of the late Mr. Gainsborough, the Portrait-Painter," in *The Beauties of Magazines, Reviews, and other Periodical Publications* (Edinburgh: George Mudie, 1788), 2:67.

87
Thicknesse, *Sketch of the Life*, 3.

88
See Sloman, *Gainsborough in Bath*, 51–52.

contemporary descriptions also set the exact scene and tenor. In one of his letters, Gainsborough himself describes his partitioned workspace and showroom, mentioning how he had rented out his house "except my painting room and best parlour to show pictures in."[89] Philip Thicknesse speaks of being received "in [Gainsborough's] painting room, in which stood several portraits," and of helping the artist search for "a good painting room as to light, a proper access."[90] The painter Ozias Humphry specifies the studio and showroom as a more shadowy space of gauzy visions: "[His portraits], as well as his landscape, were frequently wrought by candle-light, and generally with great force and likeness. But his painting room — even by day a kind of darkened twilight — had scarcely any light, and I have seen him, whilst his subjects have been sitting to him, when neither they nor the pictures were scarcely discernable."[91] Humphry remarks elsewhere that "in the latter part of his life he painted chiefly by candlelight, which became his inclination."[92] Gainsborough thus used a combination of controlled natural light and artificial light, laying down the basic strokes of a composition — what he felt to be "of the last [i.e., the greatest] importance" — in a dim twilight as he progressively introduced more light to finish his picture.[93]

Gainsborough's London lodgings and studio at Schomberg House from 1774 to 1788 would have afforded the artist a generous space of some thirty-five feet long and twenty-five feet wide — an area expansive enough to have served as a "saloon" for the purpose of showing his pictures beginning in 1784.[94] Thicknesse communicates the basic but critical detail about the painter in action. Gainsborough painted standing up: "Those who have sat to Mr. Gainsborough know, that he stood, not *sat* at his palate."[95] Gainsborough ranks among the great alla prima painters of the Western canon, meaning he worked from the living model and directly onto canvas, a procedure that self-consciously underscored the artist's sensibility and the reactive aspect of painting. Visible evidence of facility and spontaneity were in this way the byproducts of sensations felt before the sitter, a conception of artistic process that prefigured later romantic and modernist articulations of it.

Here the artist's touch and ideas of the tactile reappear time and again as the cognitive basis of a portrait's creation, apprehension, and effect in an eighteenth-century society of senses and politeness. Gainsborough, as a rule, would not work on a portrait without the sitter being present, as he affirmed to a patron in a 1771 letter: "to make any alteration . . . require[s] . . . Her Ladyship comes to Bath for that purpose, as I cannot (without taking away

89
Gainsborough to James Unwin, Dec. 30, 1763, in *Letters*, 23–24.

90
Thicknesse, *Sketch of the Life*, 11 and 15.

91
Ozias Humphry, R.A., in Whitley, *Thomas Gainsborough*, 391.

92
Ozias Humphry, R.A., in Hayes, *Gainsborough: Paintings and Drawings*, 25.

93
See Susan Sloman's excellent discussion of Gainsborough's studio practice and his command of lighting and surface effects in *Gainsborough in Bath*, 58ff and 62.

94
Whitley, *Thomas Gainsborough*, 109–12.

95
Thicknesse, *Sketch of the Life*, 35.

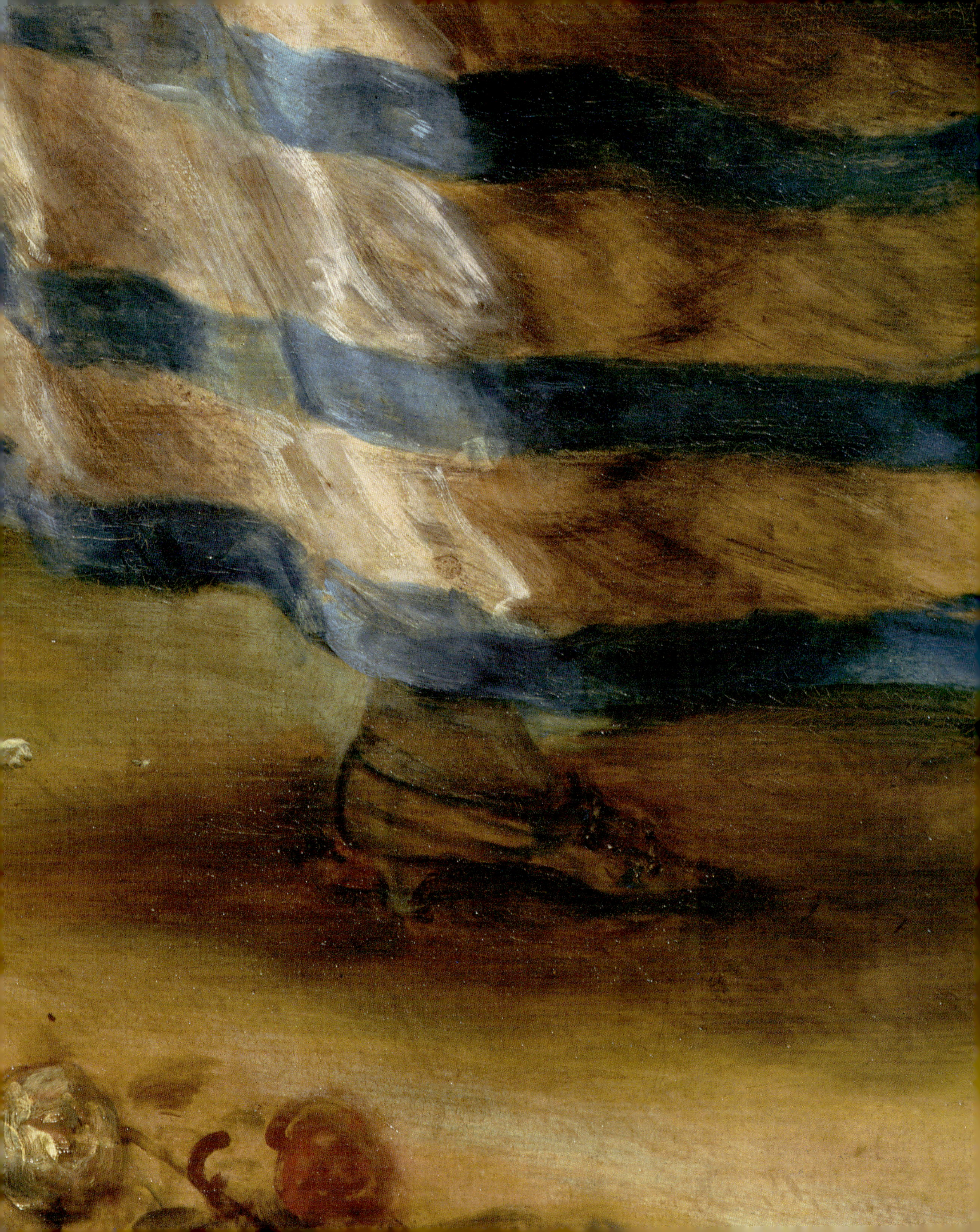

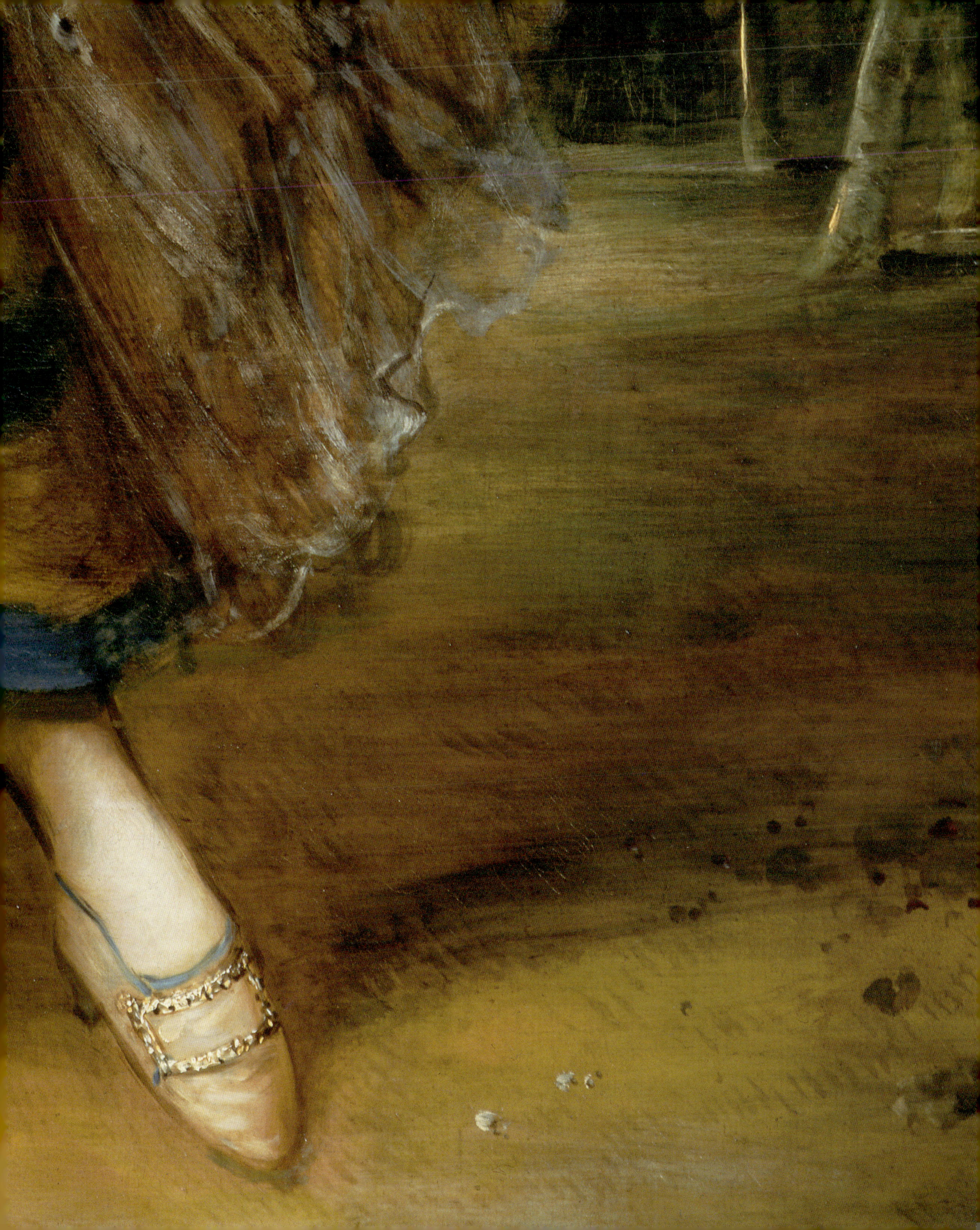

the likeness) *touch* it unless from the life."[96] From the life also needed to be a productive physical interaction between painter and subject, and Gainsborough was evidently handy at using words to make his sitters comfortable. According to his friend William Jackson, Gainsborough's conversation was "gay, lively — fluttering round subjects, which he just *touched*."[97] Likewise the painter's touch could move like the orator's words, especially when depicting sitters who were speakers. Gainsborough himself described this melding of sight, touch, and hearing in his discussion with his patron Rev. Dr. William Dodd of the effects of the latter's portrait on his parishioners. Gainsborough here recounts to his patron how he had hidden and positioned himself to see and hear the reactions of Dodd's intimates, having "peep[ed] & listen[ed] through the keyhole of the door of the painting room on purpose to see how much you *touch* them out of the pulpit as well as in it."[98]

It is nonetheless Gainsborough's manner of applying paint that offers perhaps the most ready example of this kind of multi-sensory engagement between painter, sitter, and portrait. Gainsborough's contemporary John Thomas Smith relates the way the artist "paint[ed] portraits with pencils on sticks full six feet in length and his method of using them was this: he placed himself and his canvases at a right angle with the sitter, so that he stood still, and touched the features of his picture exactly at the same distance at which he viewed his sitter."[99] In this last description, we are called to imagine the rather charged scene of Gainsborough wielding his celebrated pencil at the tip of six-foot prosthetic limbs, standing before his subject, herself standing immediately next to her portrait being touched by the artist. We can imagine the appeal for the painter, who, in Gainsborough's case, was especially keen to explore issues of pictorial invention, effect, and engagement — that is, to convey to the viewer the physical experience of such an encounter. According to the contemporary art theorist Francesco Algarotti, a painter should "so manage his pencil, as, by the magic of it, make enraptured spectators fancy themselves there along with him."[100]

Little wonder that by the eighteenth century the studio was already long mythologized as an erotic space. The easy analogy of touching paint on canvas and touching bodies allows us to safely speculate on more risqué interactions than those conventionally required of a portrait sitting, especially when artistic lore — think of the ancient painter Apelles and his nymphs — established a "tradition," while the inequitable power dynamics between the artist and his model made sexual exploitation a reality of studio life. It was on account of such situations that the portrait sitting had long held a tinge of the illicit, so-called gallant

96
Gainsborough to William, 2nd Earl of Dartmouth, April 8, 1771, *Letters*, 87.

97
William Jackson, *The Four Ages; together with Essays on Various Subjects* (London, 1798), 183.

98
Gainsborough to William Dodd, Nov. 24, 1773, in *Letters*, 121.

99
John Thomas Smith, *Nollekens and his Times* (London, 1828), 1:186, cited in Hayes, *Gainsborough: Paintings and Drawings*, 24.

100
Francesco Algarotti, *Essay on Painting Written in Italian by Count Algarotti* (Dublin: T. and J. Whitehouse, 1765), 60.

encounter. The Elizabethan miniaturist Nicholas Hilliard bemusedly describes the "drawer" (artist) and his presumed traffic in "lovely glances, wittye smilings, and those stolne glances."[101] Analogously, the eighteenth-century art theorist Gérard de Lairesse suggests that a generic portraitist should be a confidant enabling an intimate discussion, while ever aware of the appropriate boundaries. Accordingly, the painter "should . . . discover . . . in what circumstance lies . . . the favorite pleasure [of the person sitting]. [And] if the sitter himself do, by his talk, discover his own bent, the painter ought to humor it to the last, whether it be jocose or moderate." Lairesse is sure to use the masculine pronoun to detail such an engagement — the informality of which would have been problematic for any woman to entertain — while embarking on a sequence of admonitions regarding appropriate studio imagery that confirms the reality of the perceived sexual economy of the portraitist's world: "Painting-rooms are often hung with such smutty pictures as frequently put virgins to the blush, or alter their countenance . . .; in a painting-room there ought not to hang the wanton picture of *Mars and Venus catch'd by Vulcan*."[102]

The graphic satirist Thomas Rowlandson's genial caricature of the portraitist in his milieu offers us a glimpse, even if comically, into the foibles and intrigue surrounding the studio visit (FIGURE 15). In a satire on grotesque people's blind mania for likenesses, we witness the partitioning of the portraitist's worksite, with the studio or painting room walled off — as we know Gainsborough's was — from the more ample space of the showroom. According to the critic Rouquet, "Every portrait painter in England has a room to shew his pictures, separate from that in which he works," a fact that could only have further fetishized the actual workplace of the master.[103] Accordingly, we see the portraitist's valet on the left of Rowlandson's scene having performed his function of ushering the stylish young woman toward the entrance of the sectioned-off painting room, where the artist welcomes her, his "pencil" at the ready. Gainsborough himself alluded to this issue when he joked to his friend William Jackson that if his servant were to inappropriately turn away a "hansom [*sic*] Lady . . . 'tis as much as his life is worth."[104]

With portraitists known for their "smutty pictures" and assiduous courtship of "wom[e]n of quality," who themselves "intrigue[d] with every man," satirists played on the many possibilities.[105] Recall, for example, G. A. Stevens's satirical song in which "Demirep Queen, Venus" was "a guest [to] Reynolds, Gainsborough."[106] As we know, Gainsborough adored women. Philip Thicknesse recounts that Gainsborough had ruined "a lady's picture on purpose to have her chatt while she set for another to be better done."[107] Reynolds, for his part,

101
Nicholas Hilliard,
"A Treatise Concerning
the Arte of Limning"
(c. 1600), cited in John
Gage, "Saving Faces,"
Art History (December
1993), 666.

102
Gérard de Lairesse, *The
Art of Painting* (London,
1738), 2:349.

103
Rouquet, *Present State
of the Arts*, 42–43.

104
Gainsborough to William Jackson, Sept. 2,
1767, in *Letters*, 42.

105
Fielding, *Tom Jones*, 264.
Rouquet, *Present State
of the Arts*, 38–39.

106
Stevens, "The Artists,"
29.

107
Philip Thicknesse, cited
in Rosenthal, *Art of
Thomas Gainsborough*,
160.

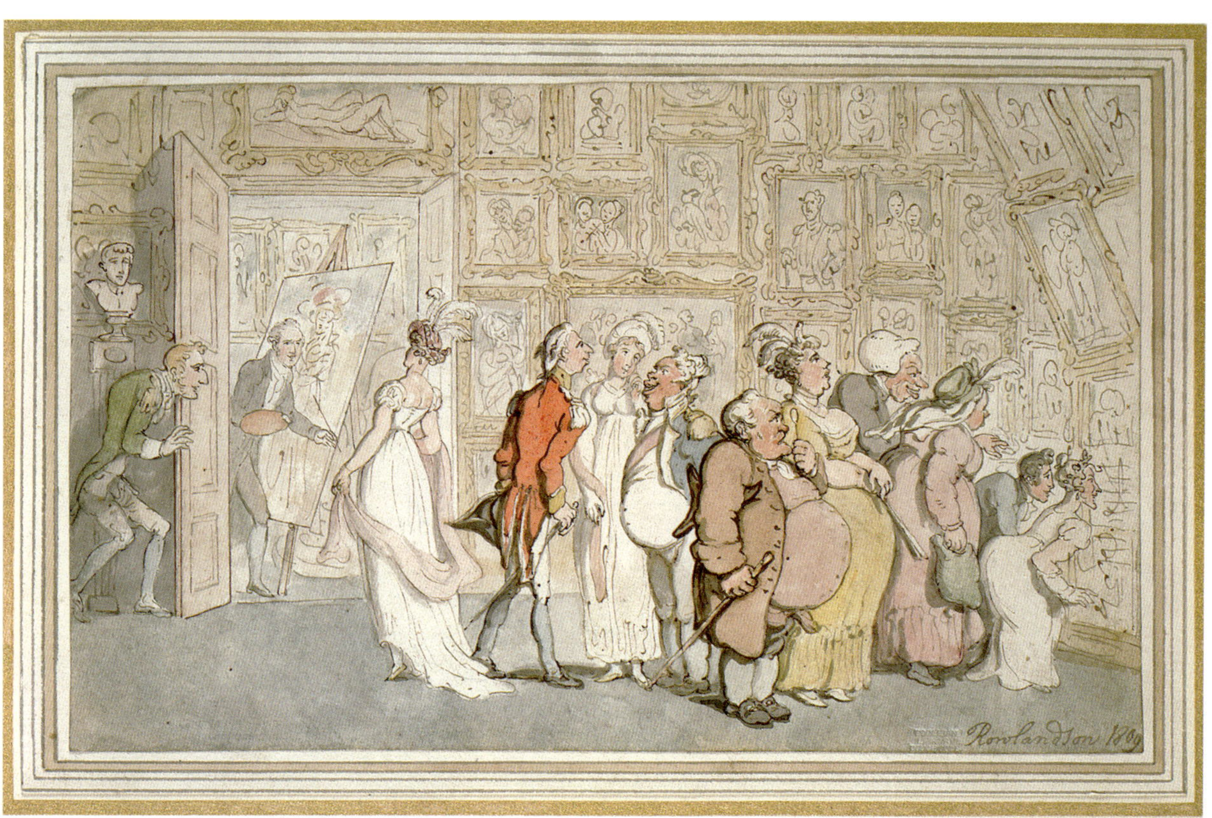

FIGURE 15

THOMAS ROWLANDSON
The Portrait Painter's Anteroom
1809
PEN AND BROWN INK AND WATERCOLOR OVER INDICATIONS OF GRAPHITE
4-7/8 X 7-15/16 IN (12.4 X 20.1 CM)
ASHMOLEAN MUSEUM, UNIVERSITY OF OXFORD
(WA1863.1179)

was rumored to have possibly bedded many of the great beauties who sat for him, such "as 'Lady L—r', who was said to habitually view the artist's picture collection after hours."[108] The sensible painter was in fact known to be susceptible to feminine charms, which might be recognized, for good or for ill, in his painting. Writing of Reynolds's turn with Mrs. Robinson, one critic spoke of a collaboration that had produced an as yet unimaginable painting: "We have not been told of some of the astonishing Effects which her charms produced in the Artist employed."[109] According to a 1779 *Town and Country Magazine* column, "Lady L—r" sat for Reynolds mornings and evenings so that "the knight [Reynolds] should give a resemblance of her in the most natural way."[110] As for Gainsborough — self-described as "deeply read in petticoats" — we can recall my opening epigraph, which indicates it was "plain [he had] been visited by Miss Dalrymple . . . and other [demireps]."[111]

Prurient details aside, the point here is the need to reframe the intimacy of the portrait encounter as one that is ultimately unknowable as well as often beyond the dichotomized gendering usually assigned to the interchange between male portraitist and feminine sitter. As in the case of many of the paintings in the present exhibition, Gainsborough's feminine sitters were often of greater prominence — and certainly wealth — than the artist himself. Yet to the extent that demireps were essentially as marginal as any portrait painter, we can again presume a complicity between painter and sitter that fell within the broader realm of "sensibility." On one hand, sensibility was another form of what we think of as sympathy or even sociability, both of which encouraged the physical, emotional, and social bonds that impelled the meetings, sittings, and viewings required of portraits, just as they governed what effects were sought and achieved through portraiture. If painterly effects might be understood to reflect the artist's feelings, the painter's mark functioned then, as now, as the central signifier integrating multiple registers of meaning in an expansive view of sensibility. How painter and sitter reacted emotionally to one another during the "portrait event" influenced the way the painter applied his paint, which in turn elicited particular reactions from viewers. Additionally, one of the hallmark characteristics of eighteenth-century sensibility was its attention to the sensory, affective powers of people and things, again making both the creation and consumption of portraits a matter of emotional reactions to both people and portraits. "Sensible" portraiture intensified both an "awareness of another's feelings and an ability to enter into them."[112] And significantly, sensible physical awareness, whereby strokes of paint impressed themselves on the eye or mind of the viewer, meant that sensibility, broadly understood, was predicated "on a mode of vision that in turn depended on touch."[113]

108
On this topic see Postle, " 'Modern Apelles,' " 24.

109
Saint James Chronicle, April 27, 1782, cited in Gill Perry, "The Spectacle of the Muse: Exhibiting the Actress at the Royal Academy," in Solkin, ed., *Art on the Line*, 111–25.

110
Postle, " 'Modern Apelles,' " 24.

111
Gainsborough to John Henderson, June 27, 1773, in *Letters*, 116.

112
Ann Bermingham, "Gainsborough's *Cottage Door*: Sensation and Sensibility," in *Sensation & Sensibility: Viewing Gainsborough's "Cottage Door*," ed. Ann Bermingham (New Haven: Yale University Press, 2005), 8.

113
Ibid., 13.

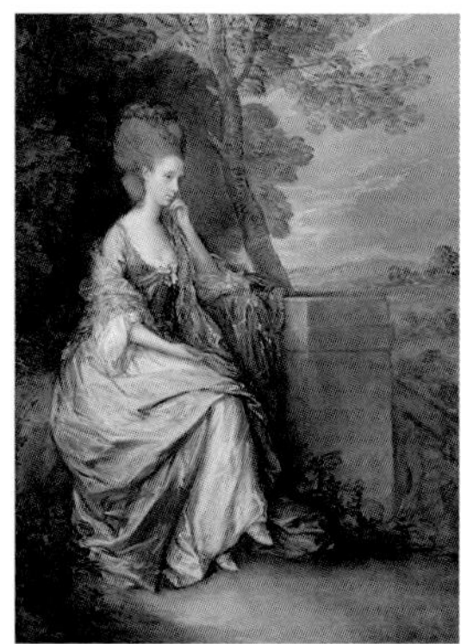

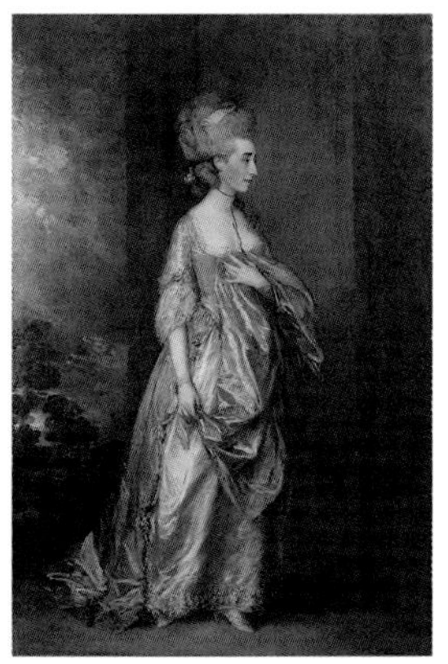

I therefore want to conclude with a brief look at two of the portraits that elicited such a spate of pointed critical reactions in 1778: *Anne, Countess of Chesterfield* (PLATE 5) and *Mrs. Grace Dalrymple Elliott* (PLATE 6). In these two portraits we can discern our "favourite" painter having both entered into his sitters' feelings through paint and successfully positioned his painting and sitter within the continuum of tradition. In the words of Ann Bermingham, "femininity is constructed by being set within the social order in a certain way, and within a particular relationship to high art."[114] Gainsborough was certainly aware of his relationship to high art when he painted the two portraits in 1778, just as he was well aware that his inflections of femininity were going to have their impact on the hidebound world of Georgian London. Indeed, Gainsborough submitted thirteen paintings to the scrutiny of the Royal Academy exhibition in the spring of 1778 — the most ever up to that point. And the critical reaction to the portraits certify that Gainsborough's grand statement was effective in generating discussion not only of women and his paintings of them, but also, as he would have it, of perception itself as it is figured through these special women.

Gainsborough succeeded in producing a new type of modern, grand manner portraiture that was technically and formally forward-looking, as well as inclusive of more progressive feminine identities. For indeed both portraits play on the dynamics of feminine sexual and social affirmation as made visible in Gainsborough's touch. We might presume thus that Countess Chesterfield's dress was the result of a special portrait sitting in which, with the help of the willing portraitist, this daughter of a reverend might have wanted to project a bit more spice. In what is a metaphoric undressing of the sitter, a large swath of Chesterfield's dress is unresolved, being essentially composed of radical slashings of the artist's brush. In a showpiece at the Royal Academy exhibition this was of course no inattention to finish on the part of the artist, but rather a calculated engagement of the viewer into a tactile/visual — sensual — dialogue. It is tempting here to rejoin this sensible painting to one of the seminal and yet somewhat underreported sources of Gainsborough's demonstrative painting: the earlier French art theorist Roger de Piles, whose *Principles of Painting* had a longstanding influence in eighteenth-century England and on Gainsborough specifically.[115] Indeed, if we imagine Gainsborough's rather risqué gambit as an invitation to something more, de Piles's is perhaps the most apt commentary. In a critical train of thought focused on taste in drawing, he arrives

114
Bermingham, "Aesthetics of Ignorance," 6.

115
De Piles had already been substantially translated into English in the first decade of the eighteenth century: *An Abridgement of the Lives of the Painters, The Idea of the Perfect Painter* (both trans. London, 1706), and the *Dialogue upon Colouring* (trans. London, 1711). And his *Cours de peinture par principes* was widely available in English by the 1740s (see, for example, the J. Osborn edition of 1743).

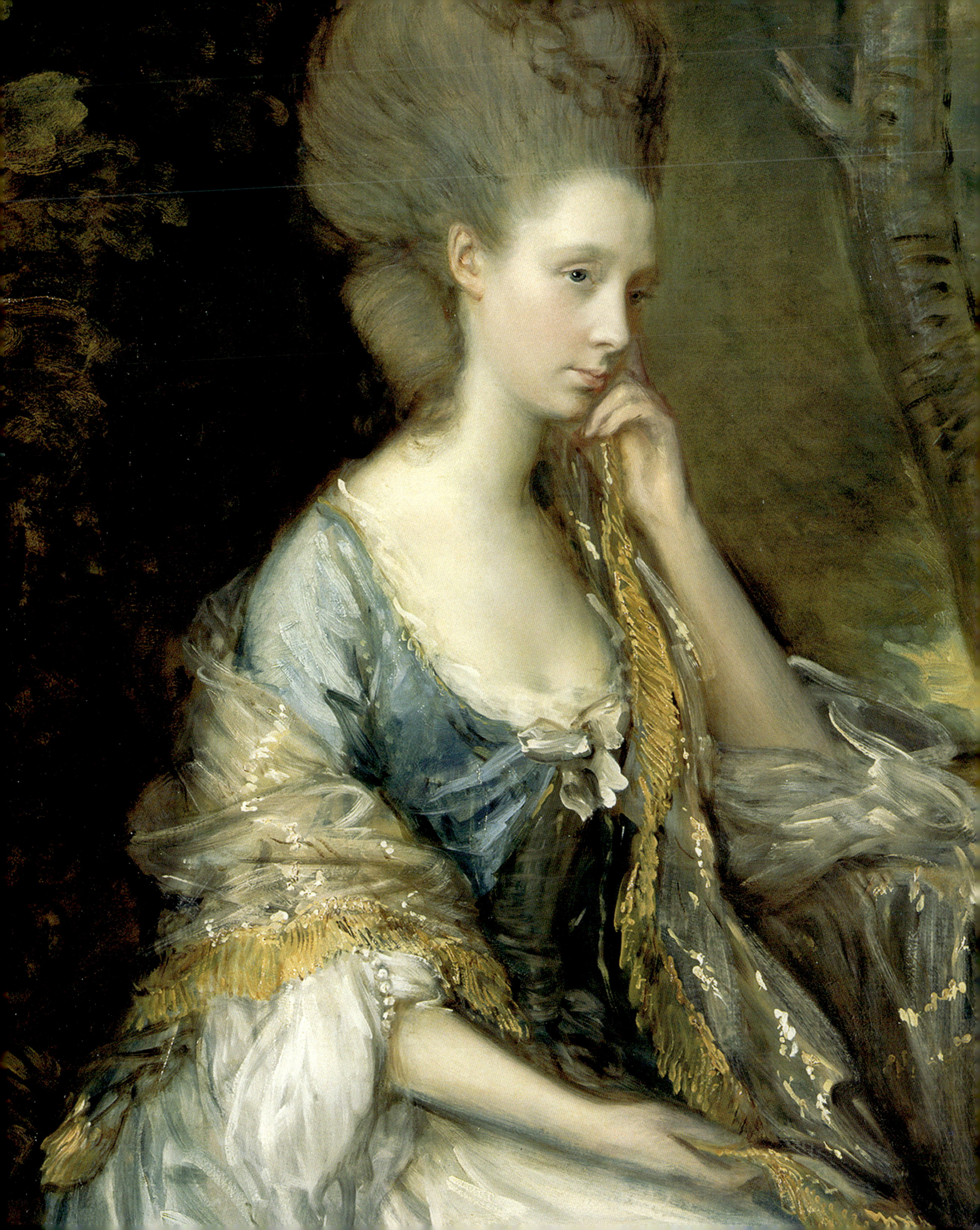

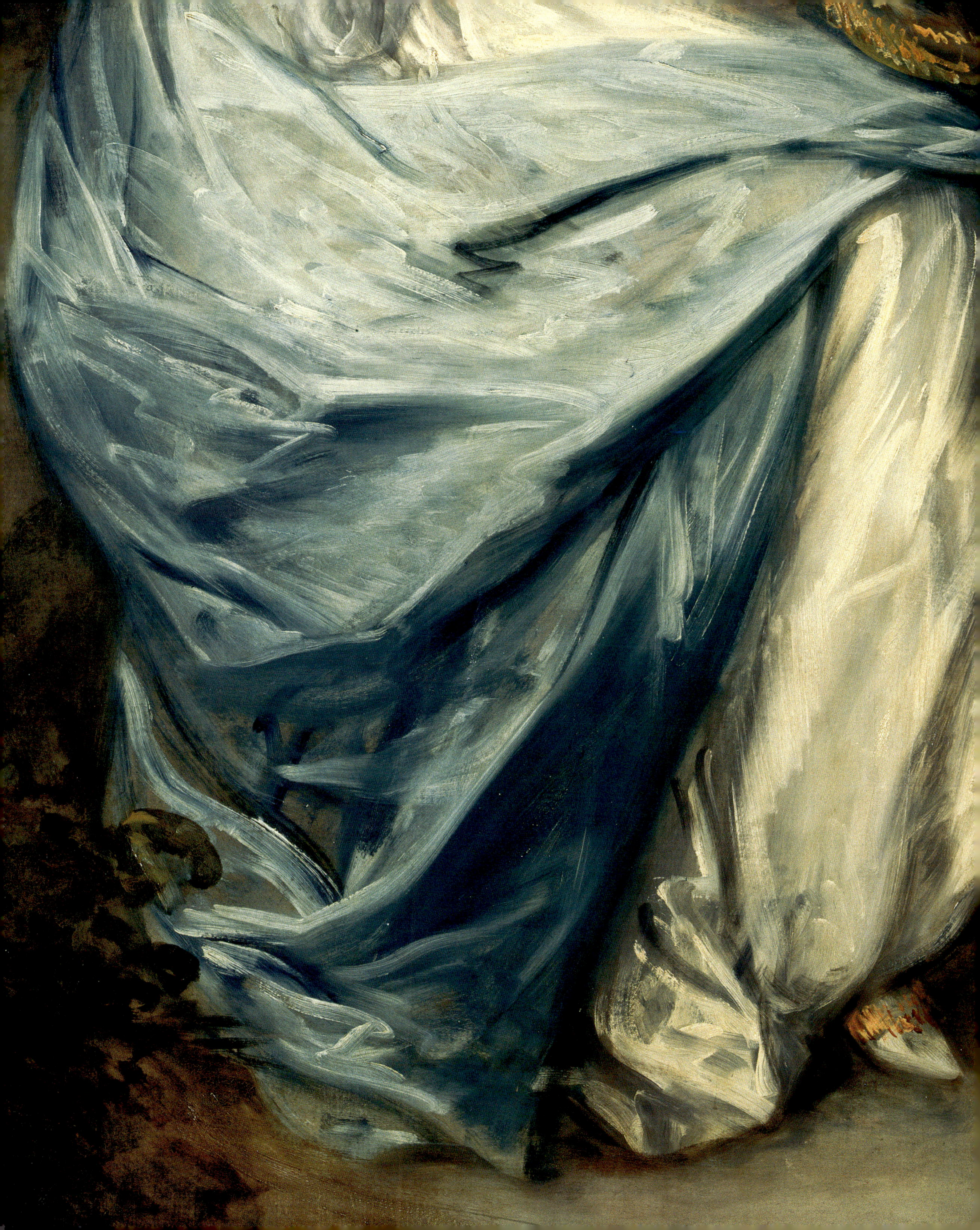

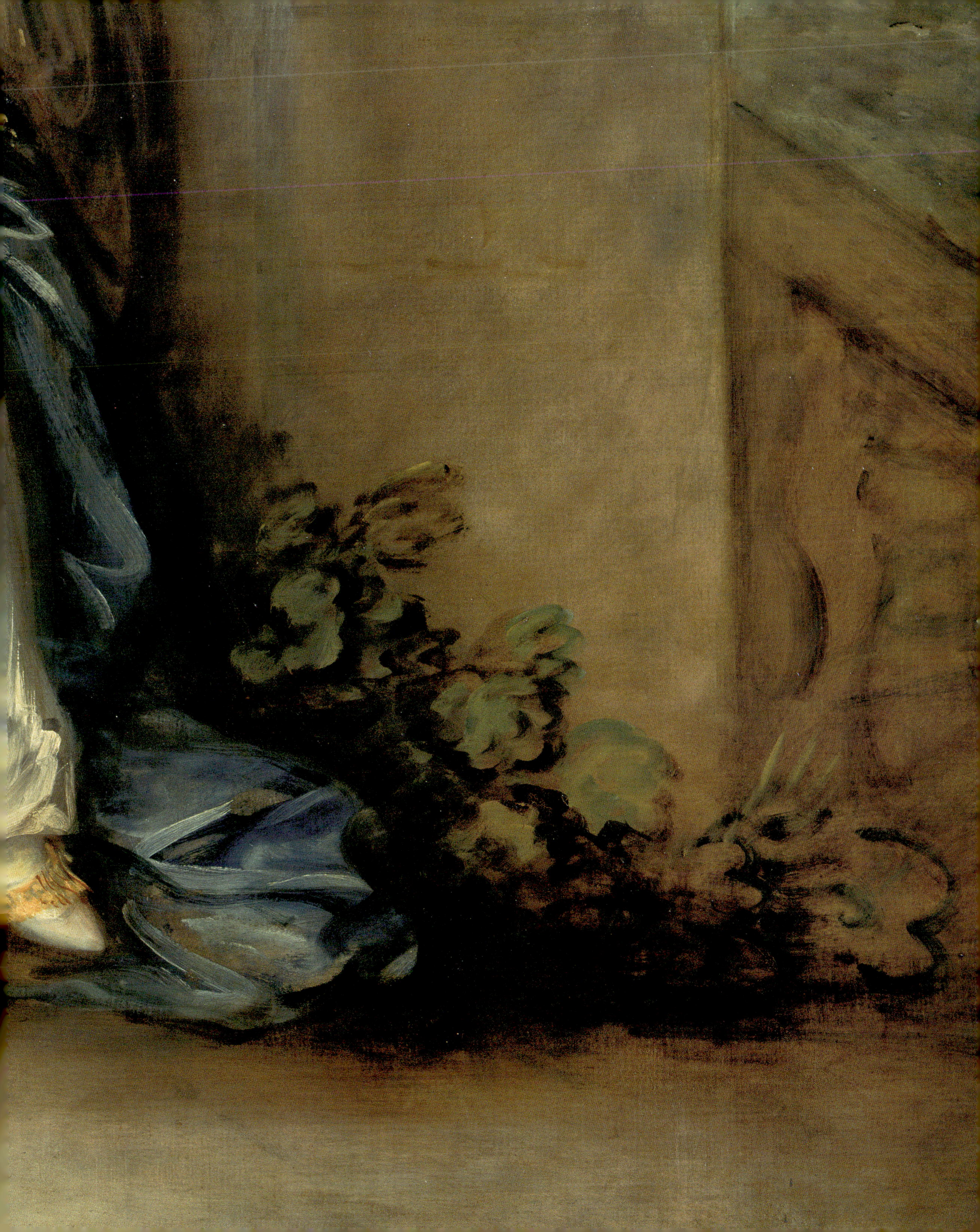

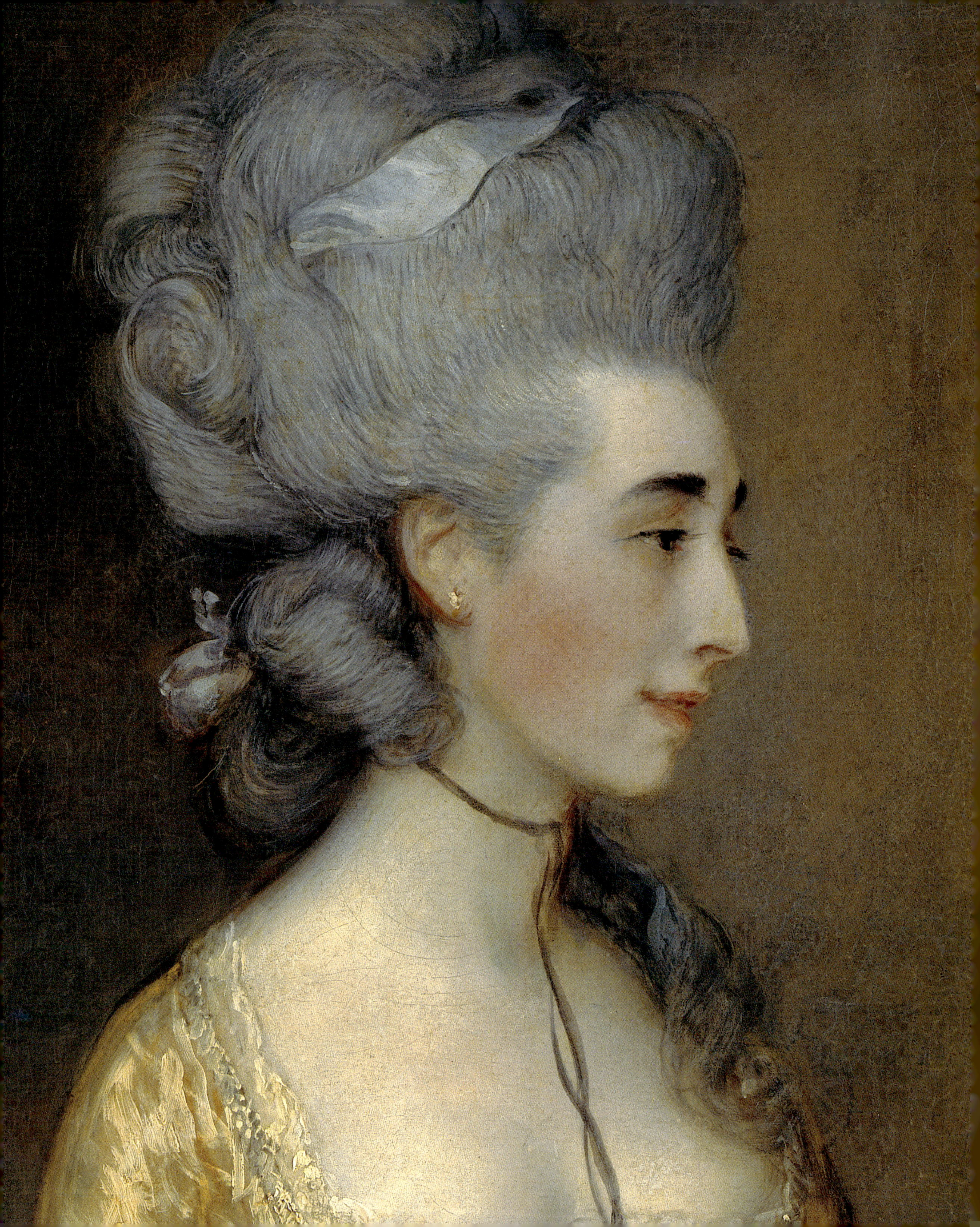

at "passion in Painting" by way of elegance and character: "passion in Painting," according to de Piles, "is a movement of the body accompanied by certain lines on the face, which mark an agitation of the soul."[116] The newspaper critic and Gainsborough's friend, Sir Henry Bate-Dudley (formerly Rev. Henry Bate), seems here to have been at the ready to underline the "merit" of Gainsborough's shifty technique while implicitly linking it to an ascribed assertive sexuality of the sitters, as if perhaps to invite the viewer to move closer:

> [Gainsborough] has been reproached with negligence in finishing,
> but if his pieces be viewed at a proper distance, which,
> as it is manifestly his design . . . this imputation will appear
> totally without foundation.
> The portraits which he has exhibited on this occasion
> consist chiefly of *filles de joye*, and all are admirable likenesses,
> No. 114, particularly being that of the beautiful
> Mrs. [Grace Dalrymple] E[lliott].[117]

Conversely, if Bate-Dudley looked to color his commentary with aspects of the libidinous, Gainsborough knew to invest his depiction of the notorious courtesan Grace Dalrymple Elliott with the visible attributes, not of sex, but of sensibility: her hand, here conjoined to that of the artist's sensible touch, gathers folds of painterly fabric to her bosom (her heart), indicating in no uncertain terms the emotive, animating potential of this new modern mode of expressive feminine portraiture (PAGE 106). "A portrait is animated when a spectator might almost mistake it for real life," explains *The Artist's Repository and Drawing Magazine* in the late 1780s.[118] Those contemporary critics who entered into dialogue with Gainsborough's portrait of Dalrymple described it in just these mutually reinforcing terms of apt touch and animating sensibility: "[The portrait of Dalrymple] appear[s] with inexpressible delicacy, united with the utmost force and truth; and the touch of the artist is uncommonly exquisite . . . [and an] inexpressible sensibility that animates the whole figure."[119] Through Gainsborough's modern portraiture, new progressive — essentially modern — femininities could now be fully realized. To be portrayed provocatively by the painterly painter, especially for the politically disenfranchised women of the eighteenth century, meant the ability to enter into various dialogues, or, crucially, to gain greater or more favorable representation in the public sphere of eighteenth-century society.

116
Roger de Piles, *Cours de peinture par principes* (Paris, 1709), 145.

117
Sir Henry Bate-Dudley, "Thomas Gainsborough, R.A.," *Morning Post and Daily Advertizer*, April 27, 1778.

118
Anonymous, "A Dictionary of Principles, and Terms of Art," in *The Artist's Repository and Drawing Magazine* (London: C. Taylor, 1784–94) 3: 12.

119
Cited in Whitley, *Thomas Gainsborough*, 155.

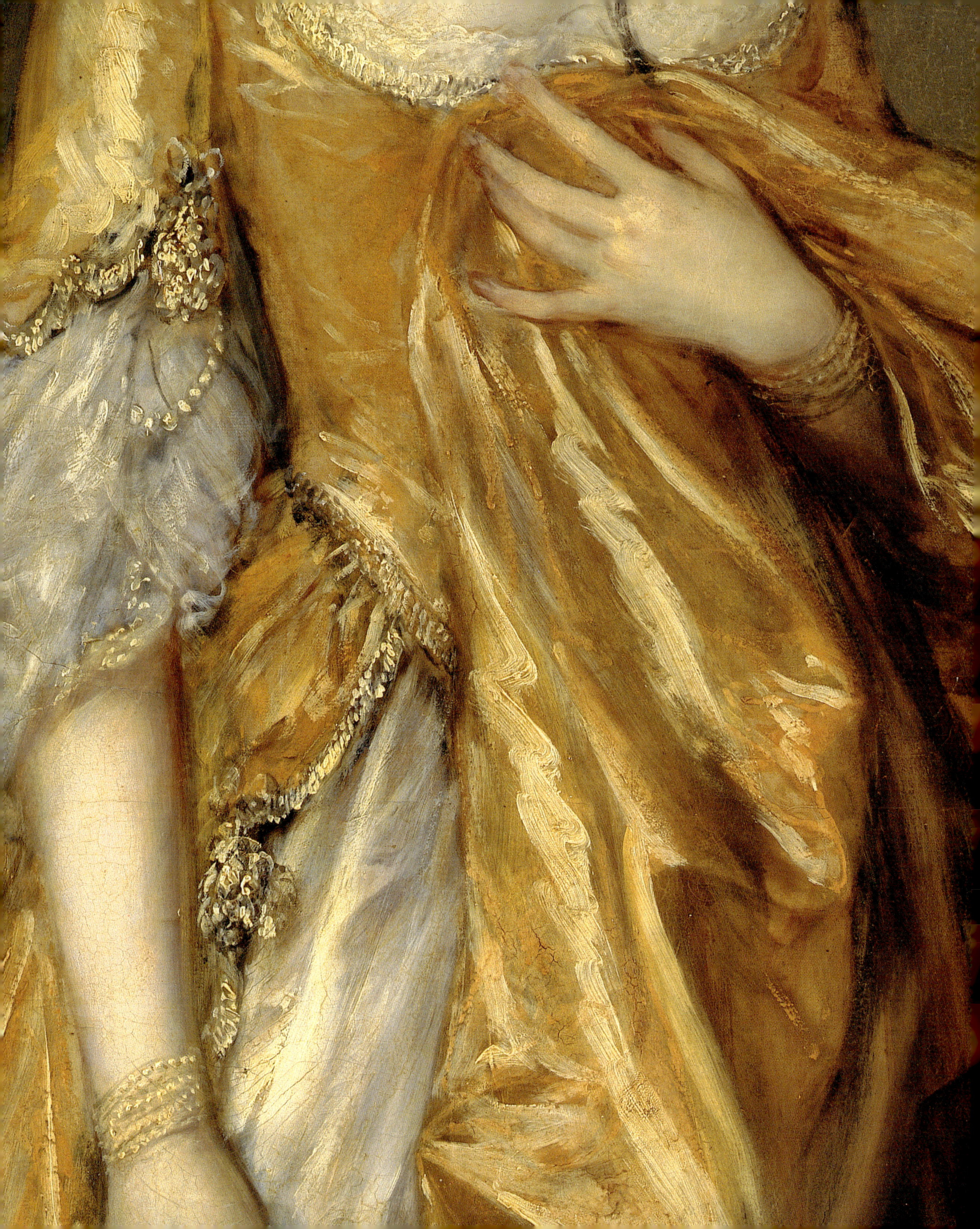

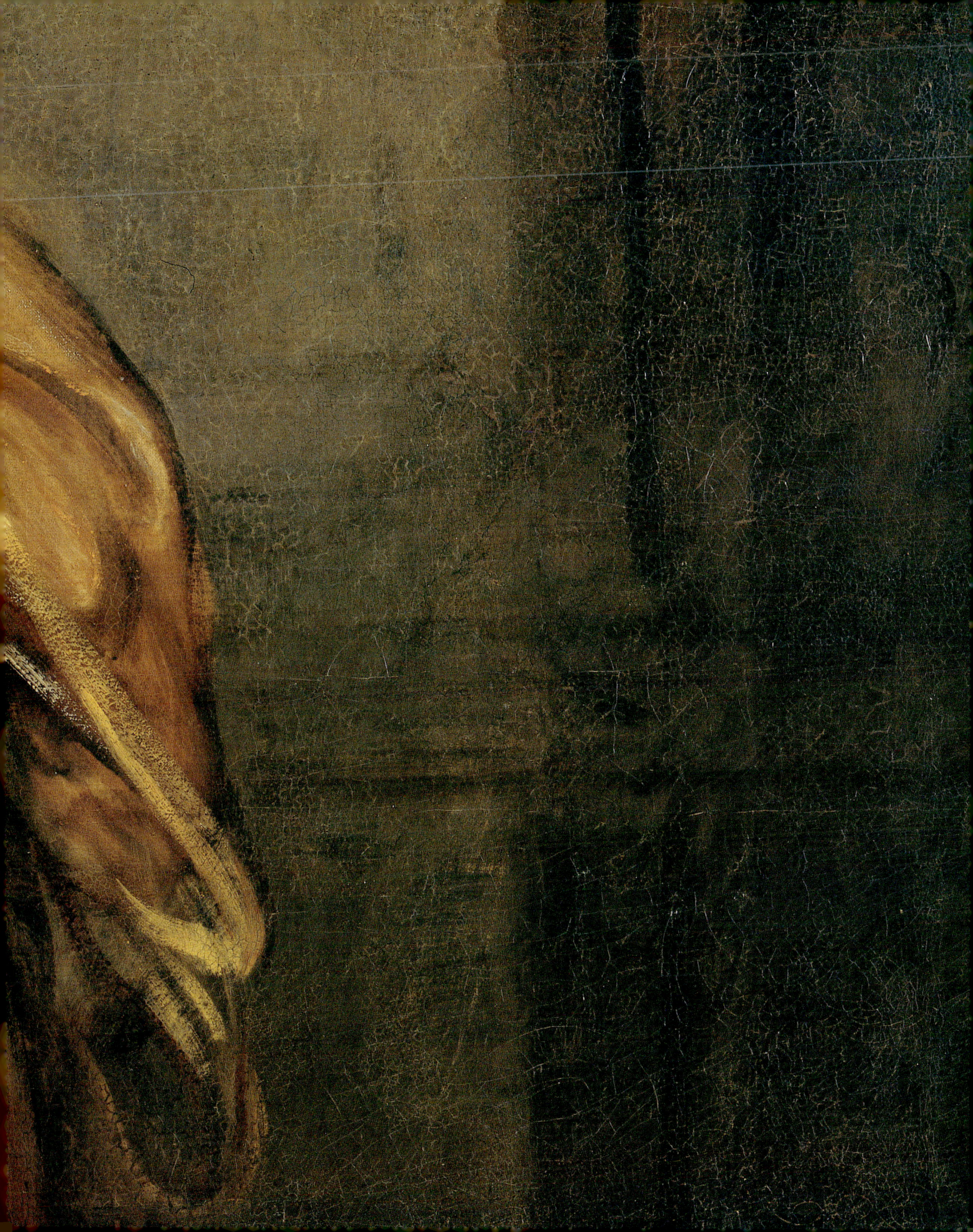

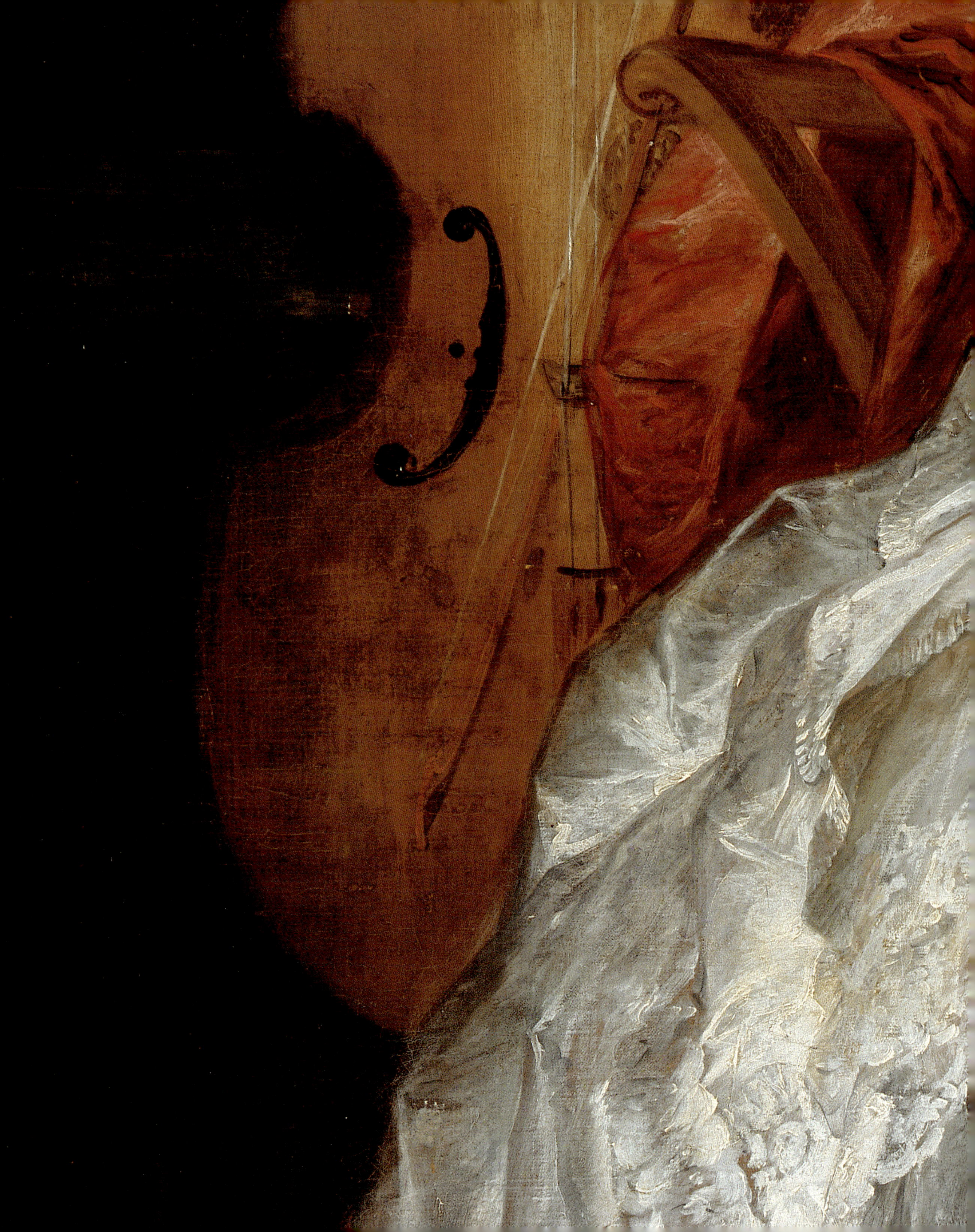

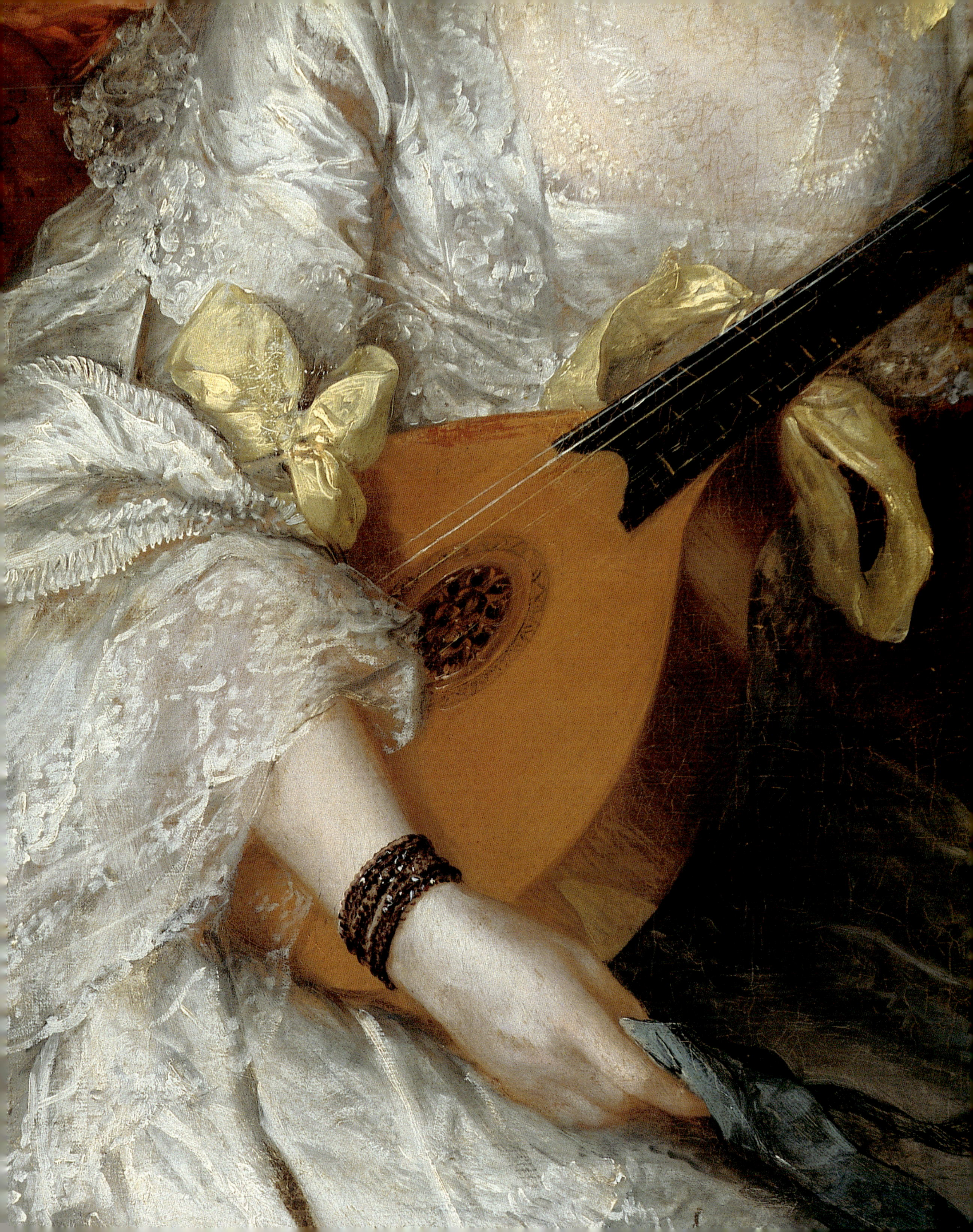

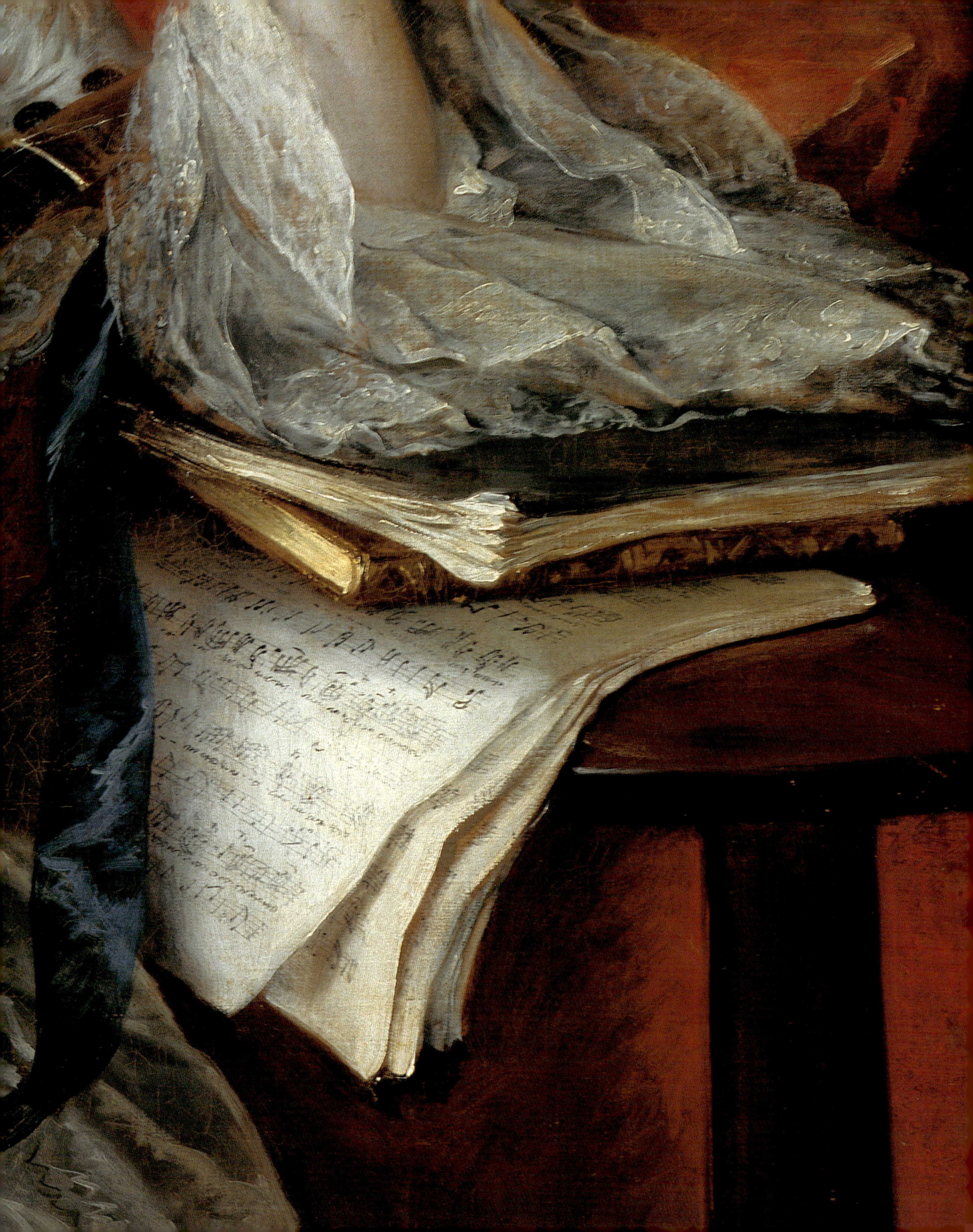

"A Most Extraordinary Figure, Handsome AND Bold" :

Gainsborough's Portrait of Ann Ford, 1760

By Aileen Ribeiro

Clothes, . . . though seemingly extraneous appendages, have entered into the very core of our existence as social beings.

J. C. FLÜGEL,
THE PSYCHOLOGY OF CLOTHES (1930)[1]

THE ENGLISH PSYCHOLOGIST John Flügel, Freudian in his belief that clothing carried sexual symbolism and that women's apparel in particular can often demonstrate a conflict between modesty and exhibitionism, knew that the study of dress had wider social and cultural implications. In the light of such views (but not exclusively), this essay examines the part played by appearance, costume, and pose in Gainsborough's famous portrait of Ann Ford and in other depictions of "modern" eighteenth-century women by the artist and his contemporaries. In the eighteenth century (most notably in the middle decades, around the time of the Ford portrait, a period of relative uniformity in elite, formal fashion), appearance was crucial to class and status. The art of dressing well was thought an important part of good manners, and essential to the general well-being of society.

Essays ON THE Art OF Pleasing

THE GENIUS OF GAINSBOROUGH is that when we look at his portrait of Ann Ford (PLATE 1), we see a beautiful and spirited woman in her early twenties, complemented and not overwhelmed by the stunning formal costume, a white silk satin *sacque* dress or *robe à la*

[1] John Carl Flügel, *The Psychology of Clothes* (London: Hogarth Press, 1930), 16.

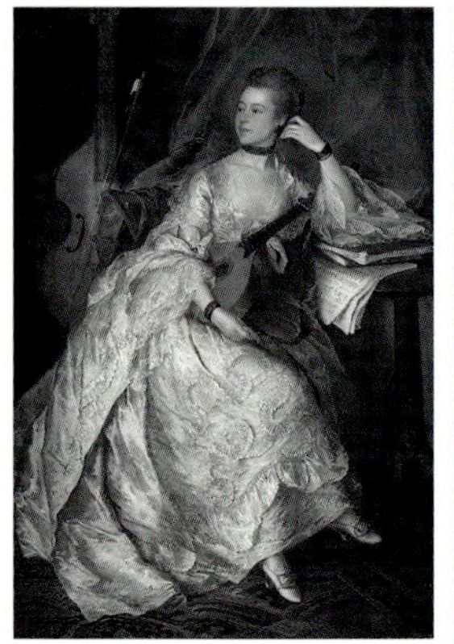

PLATE I
Ann Ford

française, characterized by flowing back drapery from the neckline to the hem, which can more clearly be seen in FIGURE 16. Both sitter *and* dress conform to the prevailing rococo aesthetic (or at least to the more muted English variant of the French mode), a series of gently curving serpentine lines, created by Ford's pose and the decorative aspects of the costume she wears. Down the sides of her dress snake robings — fabric decorations applied to the open edges of the bodice and skirt — of ruched silk, which also entwine along the front of the skirt ("petticoat" in contemporary parlance) above and below the scalloped flounce a few inches above the hem. In the mid-eighteenth century the number of *types* of dress was relatively small, so the trimmings *on* the dress and accessories worn *with* it achieved individuality in appearance. With this and the limitations of pose created by the structure of the costume, and by convention, in mind, we should beware of identifying so-called studies for Ann Ford's portrait, as only two have been firmly identified, including a beautiful sketch in the British Museum (FIGURE 17).[2] The transformative art of the modiste in providing the perfect accessories to a stylish ensemble is evident in the treble lace flounces attached to the sleeves, the fine silk gauze shoulder mantle, the clever placing of yellow

FIGURE 16

THOMAS GAINSBOROUGH
Study for Seated Woman
1760 – 65
GRAPHITE ON PAPER
13-15/16 X 8-7/16 IN (35.4 X 21.4 CM)
BRITISH MUSEUM
(1895,0725.2)

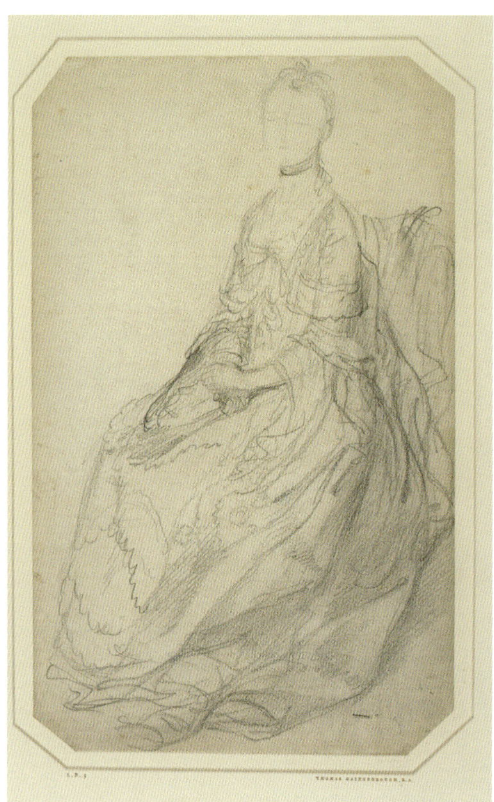
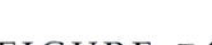

2
The other confirmed study for the portrait of Ann Ford is in the collection at Gainsborough's House, Sudbury. A number of drawings by Gainsborough have been associated with the portrait. These include two drawings at the Frick Collection (1913.3.06-7) described as "possibly

silk rIbbon knots to add a touch of color. And to emphasize the whiteness of the sitter's skin, her jewelry — necklace, clip-on earrings (snaps), and bracelets — is made of fine strands of black bugle (glass) beads, inexpensive and striking.[3] As was customary in such a gala outfit, the shoes matched the dress, so they are made of the same satin, with highish heels and with a large jeweled buckle (see the studies of shoes attributed to Gainsborough, FIGURES 18 AND 19).

Mid-eighteenth century writers on aesthetics, and specifically on beauty, were united in praise for the *pleasure* given by women's dress, for its variety, intricacy, smoothness, and curves. William Hogarth in his *Analysis of Beauty* (1753) praised the "pleasure of variety," and the "waving and serpentine lines" created by female costume.[4] In his famous *Philosophical Enquiry into the Origin of our Ideas of the Sublime and Beautiful* (1757), Edmund Burke admired "the winding surface, the unbroken continuance, the easy gradation of the beautiful," a sense of delicacy, of "mild" colors such as "weak whites," and smooth and shining materials.[5] Ann Ford's dress, with its "gentle winding contrasts" (Hogarth's phrase),[6] its shine and sparkle, also fulfills more specific rococo notions of the ideal feminine ensemble, such as Sir Joshua Reynolds's portrait of Suzanna Beckford of 1756 (FIGURE 20), where variety consists not just in the three-dimensional ornamentation of the dress and accessories, notably the shining blonde silk lace, but also in the wavy lines of a glittering watered silk.

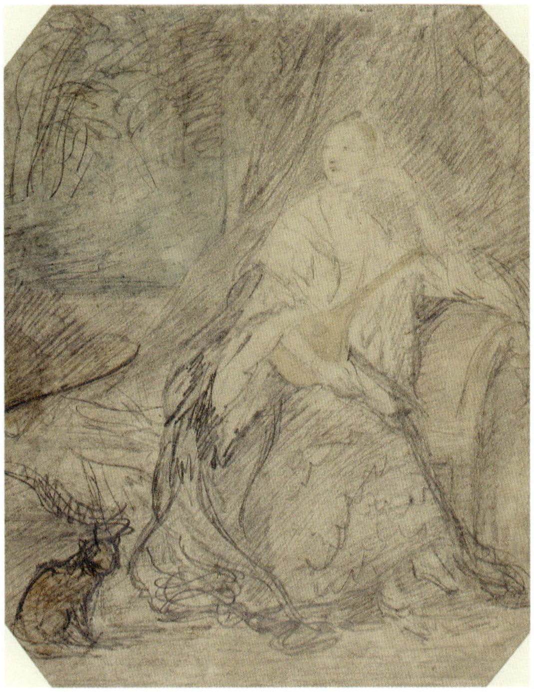

FIGURE 17

THOMAS GAINSBOROUGH
Study for Ann Ford
1760 – 65
WATERCOLOR AND GRAPHITE ON PAPER
13-3/16 X 10-1/8 IN (33.5 X 25.7 CM)
BRITISH MUSEUM
(1894,0612.11)

3
Bugle beads were very popular in this period, and were often mentioned in advertisements; for example, the John Johnson Collection (Bodleian Library, Oxford) has a trade card dated 1759 for a Matthew Pinnell, Haberdasher, at the New Exchange in the Strand, offering bugle earrings for sale.

4
William Hogarth, *The Analysis of Beauty* (1753), ed. Ronald Paulson (New Haven: Yale University Press, 1997), 20 and 35.

5
Edmund Burke, *A Philosophical Enquiry into the Origin of our Ideas of the Sublime and Beautiful* (London, 1757), 112 and 102.

6
Hogarth, *Analysis of Beauty*, 102.

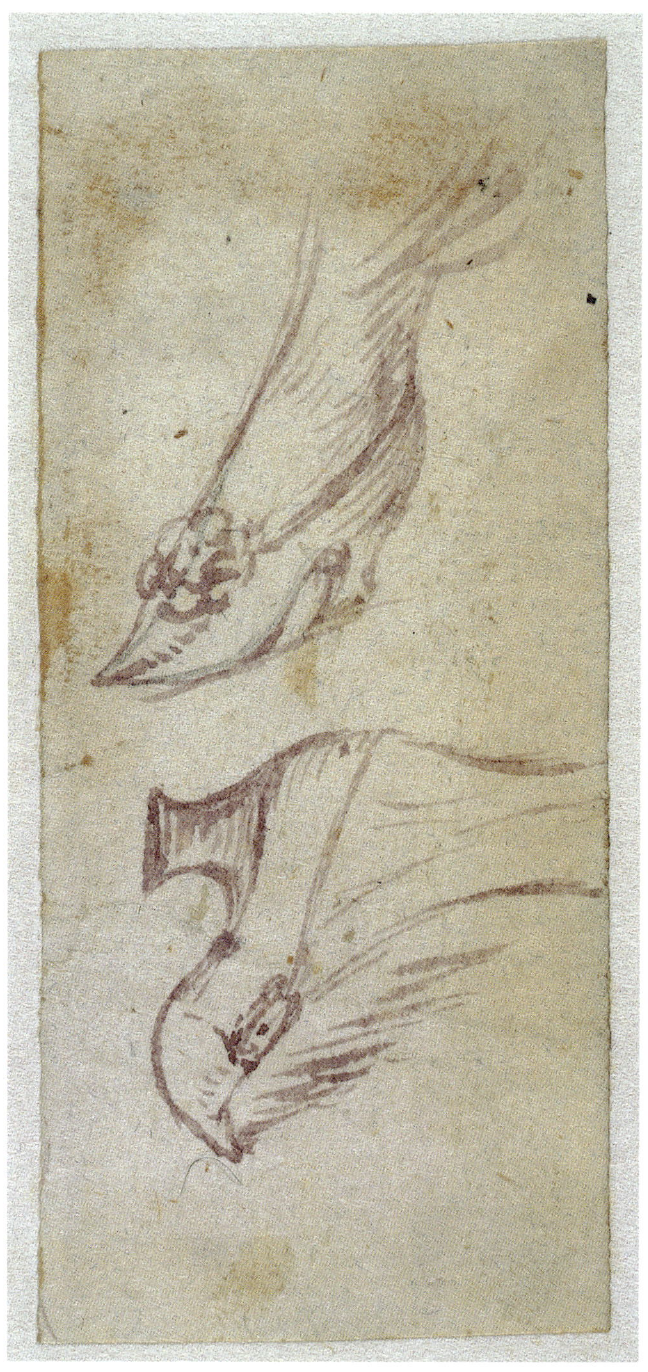

FIGURE 18

THOMAS GAINSBOROUGH (attr.)
Lady's Shoes
18TH CENTURY
PURPLE INK ON PAPER, 3-9/16 X 1-9/16 IN (9 X 4 CM)
THE COURTAULD INSTITUTE OF ART GALLERY, LONDON
SIR ROBERT CLERMONT WITT BEQUEST, 1952 (D.1952.RW.1193.50)

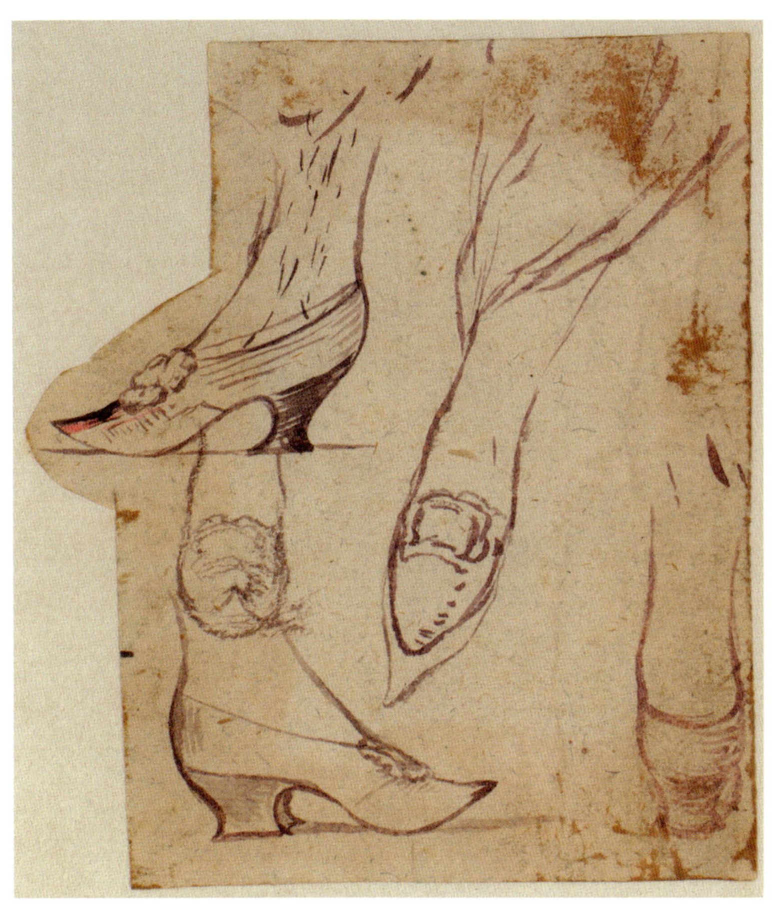

FIGURE 19

THOMAS GAINSBOROUGH (attr.)
Lady's Shoes
18TH CENTURY
PURPLE INK ON PAPER, 3-1/4 X 2-3/4 IN (8.2 X 7 CM)
THE COURTAULD INSTITUTE OF ART GALLERY, LONDON
SIR ROBERT CLERMONT WITT BEQUEST, 1952 (D.1952.RW.1193.53)

But whereas Beckford's is a cold and slightly haughty beauty, Ford's presence engages the attention by the liveliness of her face and manner. An anonymous work "on the Preservation of Health and Beauty" (1770) urged women to adopt a "life of gaiety conducted with temperance," for by so doing, "agreeable ideas . . . constantly engage the mind . . . animate the countenance, and preserve a lively complexion."[7] According to the philosopher of aesthetics Daniel Webb, a portrait should express the mind as well as present a likeness, and such expression should be "conveyed in the air of the head, and intelligence of the countenance."[8] As for Gainsborough, Thicknesse stated in 1770 that he was the only modern artist "who paints the mind . . . equally as strong as the countenance."[9] Both Beckford and Ford, however, conform to the critic André Rouquet's description of the ideal Englishwoman as represented in art: She "must have a fine white skin, a light complexion, a face rather oval than round, a nose somewhat longish, but of a fine turn, and like the antiques, her eyes large and not so sparkling as melting; her mouth graceful, without a smile, but rather of a pouting turn which gives it at once both grace and dignity; her hair clean and without powder . . . her shape tall and erect, her neck long and easy, her shoulders square and flat."[10]

Rouquet comments that portraiture "is the kind of painting the most encouraged, and consequently the most followed in England,"[11] a propensity that encouraged intense competition among artists, including Thomas Gainsborough, who moved to Bath in 1759, leasing a house on Abbey Street near the Pump Room. His friend

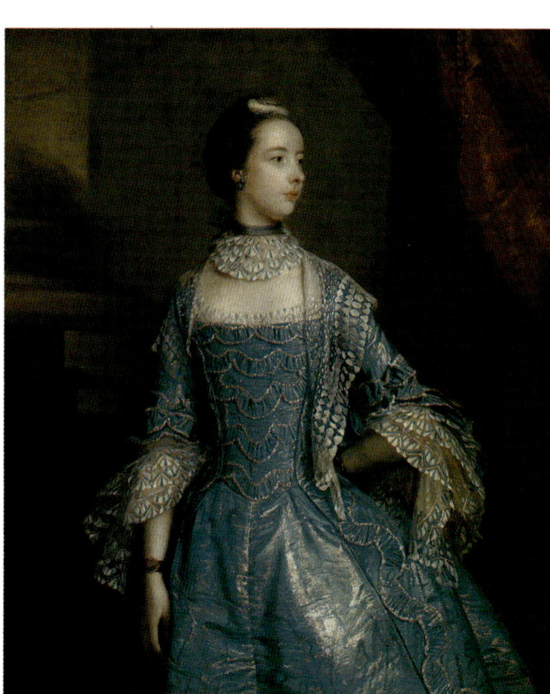

FIGURE 20

SIR JOSHUA REYNOLDS
Suzanna Beckford
1756
OIL ON CANVAS
50 X 40-1/4 IN (127 X 102.2 CM)
TATE
PURCHASED 1947 (NO5799)

7
Letters to the Ladies on the Preservation of Health and Beauty (London: Printed for Robinson and Roberts, 1770), 12.

8
Daniel Webb, *An Inquiry into the Beauties of Painting; and into the Merits of the most celebrated Painters, Ancient and Modern* (London: Printed for R. and J. Dodsley, 1760), 54.

9
Philip Thicknesse, *Sketches and Characters of the most Eminent and most Singular persons now Living* (London: Printed for John Wheble, 1770), 96.

10
André Rouquet, *The Present State of the Arts in England* (London: Printed for J. Nourse, 1755), 46–47. Rouquet, a Swiss miniature painter who spent most of his career in London, wrote this book to inform the French about English art.

11
Ibid., 33. Daniel Webb also noted the "extraordinary passion which the English have for portraits"; in his view, this passion prevented the English from developing the art of history painting. Webb, *An Inquiry into the Beauties of Painting*, 35.

14
Joyce Ellis, "On the Town: Women in Augustan England," *History Today* 45 (December 1995): 20. Ellis also notes that by 1801 (according to the census of that year), men were only 39 percent of the population in Bath.

15
John Brewer, " 'The Most Polite Age and the Most Vicious': Attitudes Towards Culture as a Commodity, 1660–1800," in *The Consumption of Culture 1600–1800: Image, Object, Text*, ed. John Brewer and Ann Bermingham (London: Routledge, 1995), 357.

16
Ann (Ford) Thicknesse, *The School for Fashion* (London: H. Reynell, 1800), 1:ix.

17
John Harold Plumb, *The Pursuit of Happiness: A View of Life in Georgian England* (New Haven: Yale Center for British Art, 1977), 18.

12
Philip Thicknesse, *A Sketch of the Life and Paintings of Thomas Gainsborough* (London, 1788), 4. This exaggeration of his importance in Gainsborough's success was typical of Thicknesse's self-promoting and combative nature. Contemporary comments and satires refer to his quarrelsomeness, such as the caricature below: Thomas Rowlandson (attr.), *Philip Quarrel the English Hermit and Beau Fidelle the mischievous she monkey famous for her skill on the viol de gamba*, 1790, etching, 13-3/4 x 10 1/16 in. (35 x 25.5 cm), British Museum (1868,0808.5963).

13
Susan Sloman, *Gainsborough in Bath* (New Haven: Yale University Press, 2002), 5.

and earliest biographer Philip Thicknesse claimed to have been the first to perceive the artist's genius, and "dragged him from the obscurity of a Country Town" (Ipswich) [12] to the fashionable elite watering place, "the most rapidly expanding social centre in England," [13] with its elegant streets, squares, and stylish assemblies.

Women in particular found that urban centers provided a freer life, more sophisticated entertainments, luxury shopping, and greater opportunities to display wealth, breeding, fine costume, and social accomplishments. Some historians have commented on the expansion of the female population in the larger towns of England during the long eighteenth century and the impact this had on social life and culture.[14] John Brewer, for example, finds an uneasiness among eighteenth-century critics that culture had become increasingly "feminized," as it moved away from "masculine values," however these were defined.[15] The "problem," to some extent, lay in the increased cultural presence of women, what Ann Ford herself refers to as "the potency of female influence in . . . civilized society," with all its opportunities for social emulation, for luxury, for life, to a greater or lesser extent, outside the formats of convention.[16] Women, in short, were on display, as Ford herself is in Gainsborough's portrait, not just as a woman of fashion but as a performer. For Gainsborough's depiction of musical instruments in this portrait — the English guitar she holds, and the viola da gamba hanging on the wall behind her — pays tribute to Ann Ford's fame as an accomplished musician and singer.

As J. H. Plumb notes: "England [was] one of the leading musical nations of the western world," not with regard to composers, but in providing opportunities for them, and for musicians and performers generally.[17] The ability to play a musical instrument was an accepted part of feminine education and behavior; according to the author of the conduct manual *The Polite Lady: or, A Course of Female Education* (1760), playing on the harpsichord,

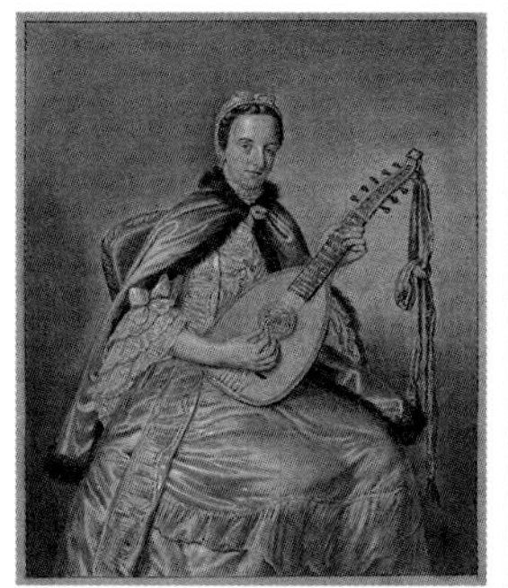

spinet, and guitar was a "most agreeable amusement."[18] The guitar was a relatively recent addition to English musical life, but soon "became a common feature of society paintings";[19] a portrait by William Hoare of the early 1760s (FIGURE 8) shows an unknown woman (once thought to be Ann Ford) in a white satin dress and fur-lined cloak, playing the guitar.[20] In Gainsborough's portrait, the sitter merely *holds* the guitar, suggesting, according to some writers, the controversy that surrounded women performing in public. In 1760 and 1761 Ford gave a series of subscription concerts in London, in spite of opposition from her father, who tried to forcibly prevent her. Richard Leppert claims that contemporaries saw women playing or singing in public as masculine and unnatural, the performer becoming "complex, astonishing, and more like a man."[21] This rather overwrought argument (especially in the light of the more nuanced relationship between the genders than the now outmoded "separation of spheres" would imply) is to some extent followed by Michael Rosenthal, who states, apropos the Gainsborough portrait, that Ford had "invaded a male sphere, which therefore implies impropriety," although, in a slightly contradictory way, he notes that she plays "an instrument associated mainly with women and domestic concerts."[22] It was admittedly difficult in the eighteenth century for women to lead professional lives, for their legal position was precarious: they were the property first of fathers and then of husbands. After her marriage to Philip Thicknesse in 1762, Ann Ford didn't play in public; the renowned soprano Elizabeth Linley ceased to give public performances after her marriage to Richard Brinsley Sheridan in 1773.

Dr. Johnson, deploring women's "public practice of any art," declared that female portraitists were especially to be criticized, because "staring in men's faces is very indelicate in a female."[23] The only exceptions were women on the stage, where a long tradition of "indelicacy" existed, and female authors of novels, "necessarily minor productions by unprofessional writers . . . [which] required less high literary ability than verse, criticism or scholarship."[24] A high public profile for a woman brought attention. Gainsborough used Ann Ford's portrait — his first lifesize, full-length portrait, and possibly commissioned by Philip Thicknesse — as a "showpicture" to attract potential customers. Such portraits, argues Susan Sloman, included those of contemporary celebrities and "those who had earned a certain notoriety through some real or imagined scandal in their private lives."[25] Ford's beauty and musical talents attracted the unwelcome attention of the Earl of Jersey, who tried, unsuccessfully, to make her his mistress: "Every Man who beholds you, must see Graces the most attractive, the most sweet, the most bewitching."[26]

18
The Polite Lady: or, A Course of Female Education. In a Series of Letters, from a Mother to her Daughter (London: Printed for J. Newberry, 1760), 21.

19
Philip Coggin, " 'This Easy and Agreeable Instrument': A History of the English Guittar [sic]," *Early Music* 15 (1987): 207.

20
Information from Susan Sloman.

21
Richard Leppert, *The Sight of Sound: Music, Representation, and the History of the Body* (Berkeley: University of California Press, 1995), 69. It is surely an exaggeration to state that a "well-bred woman who took music seriously constituted a threat to social boundaries" (70).

22
Michael Rosenthal, "Thomas Gainsborough's Ann Ford," *Art Bulletin* 80 (December 1998): 654.

23
Quoted in Katharine M. Rogers, *Feminism in Eighteenth-Century England* (Urbana: University of Illinois Press, 1982), 17.

24
Ibid, p. 23.

25
Sloman, *Gainsborough in Bath*, 73.

26
William Villiers, Earl of Jersey, *Letter to Miss F—d* (London, 1761), 19. As well as offering Ann Ford £800 to be his mistress, Lord Jersey sent her gifts, including a boar's head—which appears on the head of Philip Thicknesse in the caricature in note 12.

So what made Mrs. Delany say when she noticed, among what she calls the "splendid impositions" of Gainsborough's paintings in his studio in October 1760, the portrait of Ann Ford: "There I saw Miss Ford's picture — a whole length with her guitar, a most extraordinary figure, handsome and bold; but I should be sorry to have any one I loved set forth in such a manner"?[27] She didn't elaborate any further, and two days later George II died unexpectedly, a far more absorbing event for a woman who moved in court circles. It's unclear whether Mrs. Delany's "extraordinary figure" refers to the cross-legged pose of the sitter, a stance which some conduct manuals reported as being too "masculine," although it appears in a number of portraits. Perhaps she was taken aback by the striking, sweeping curve created partly by the costume, and partly by the angle at which Ford leans on the table, her left hand touching her hair. Art historians have tried to find implications of impropriety in the possible sources Gainsborough might have used for the pose. Gill Perry suggests it was "based on a combination of Roubiliac's statue of Handel in Vauxhall Gardens, and Hogarth's gambling aristocrat in *The Lady's Last Stake* of 1758–59, suggesting the singer's controversial invasion of a masculine realm."[28] A more plausible comment made by Sloman takes it to be "a reversed image of Sir Peter Lely's famous portrait of King Charles II's mistress Barbara Villiers, Countess of Castlemaine."[29]

Gainsborough's use of a strong diagonal emphasis in his portrait may have suggested itself by the placing of the guitar on the body. The actual playing of the instrument, according to Ann Ford's *Letters and Instructions for Playing on the Guitar* (ca. 1761), created a "becoming Attitude"; had the guitar been in fashion, she stated, "when the inimitable Hogarth wrote his ingenious *Analysis of Beauty,* I doubt not, but he would have shewn, that the Attitude this Instrument almost naturally throws the Performer in, is very graceful, and forms the Line of Beauty he so justly has exemplified; not to mention the Advantage which the Hands and Arms are seen in."[30] Feminine upbringing taught women to be aware of how their bodies had to be held in place and controlled by clothing — literally controlled, in fact, by the whalebone stays which were worn from a very young age, and which created the ideal body shape as the girl grew into adulthood, as we see from Gainsborough's portrait of his daughters Mary and Margaret (PLATE 2). Stays pushed back the shoulders and compressed the chest in what some critics of female dress (on health grounds) called "preposterous bondage";[31] they shaped and supported the figure, creating the slender line of the torso, and sometimes, especially when longer, more rigid, and heavily boned stays were worn under

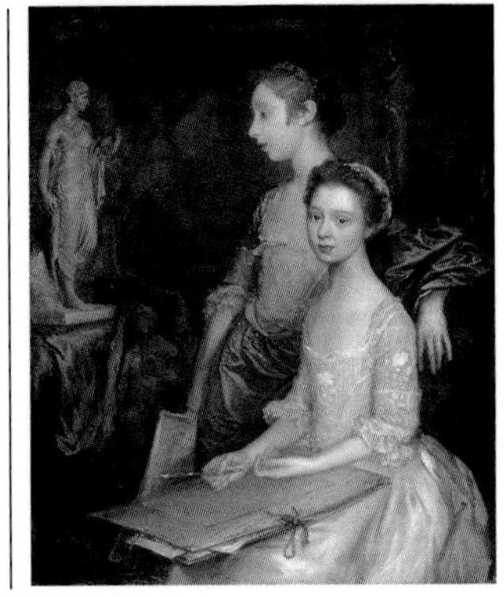

PLATE 2
Portrait of the Artist's Daughters

27
Mary Delany, *The Autobiography and Correspondence of Mary Granville, Mrs. Delany,* ed. Lady Llanover (London: Richard Bentley, 1861), 3:605.

28
Gill Perry, *Spectacular Flirtations: Viewing the Actress in British Art and Theatre 1768–1820* (New Haven: Yale University Press, 2007), 162.

29
Sloman, *Gainsborough in Bath,* 74.

30
Ann Ford, *Letters and Instructions for Playing on the Guitar* (London, ca. 1761), 3–4.

31
Letters to the Ladies, 67.

formal dress, making it uncomfortable to sit cross-legged, which is perhaps why Ann Ford leans to one side, and forward in her chair (so as not to crush the silk back drapery of her dress), thus presenting an elegant serpentine line.[32] "A good shape is the most striking article of English beauty, from which it is almost inseparable," claimed the French lawyer and man of letters Pierre-Jean Grosley on a visit to England in 1765, a state of affairs he put down to the "free and easy manner" in which children were brought up, not dressed, as was so often the case in his own country, as miniature adults.[33] "Shape" meant what one physician referred to as an "elegant form," which was just as important as "the attraction of a beautiful face."[34]

The notion of shape incorporated not just the perfect figure but also an elegant deportment. The introduction to *The Rudiments of Genteel Behavior* (1737) by the professional dancer and dancing master François Nivelon summed up the ideal deportment as the attainment of "a graceful Attitude, an agreeable Motion, an easy Air, and a genteel Behaviour," all of which could best be achieved through dance; dance and deportment were regarded as inseparable in the elite world.[35] According to Gallini's *Treatise on the Art of Dancing* (1762), a "graceful address" was best achieved by learning how to dance, which gave "delicacy and suppleness" to the figure and the set of the head. Dancing, moreover, derived "from the truth of nature," was the enemy of affectation and "false refinements"; it aimed to "bring forth the natural graces, and not to smother them with appearances of study and art."[36] It taught women an easy and unaffected gentility, not to be too stiff in their deportment (a stance which could denote the provincial), nor to adopt what the *World* (June 27, 1754) referred to as "the airs and movements of an Italian dancer at the theatre" (a tendency of the *un*genteel) — in short, how to achieve a happy medium in self-presentation.

"Let ev'ry Attitude and Gesture show/Becoming Graces, if you sit or go," urged Thomas Marriott in his *Female Conduct; being an Essay on the Art of Pleasing* (1759).[37] Dancing also taught women the practicalities of moving and sitting when formally dressed — as Ann Ford is in Gainsborough's portrait — in heavily boned stays, small hoops, and voluminous skirts; walking, too, required practice, and the dancing master taught a gliding walk with small steps. The language used in contemporary dance manuals often echoes that in works of art theory, notably with regard to the virtues of the natural and the graceful; Roger de Piles, for example, notes how the posture in a portrait "should be natural, expressive, vary'd," and emphasized the "necessity of Grace in Painting."[38]

32
Stays were made of heavy, stiffened linen or canvas in which strips of whalebone (actually baleen: flexible plates in the upper jaw of the whale) were inserted and seamed in. The English custom in the mid-eighteenth century was for wearing stays that were longer and more reinforced with "bones" than was the custom elsewhere in Europe. However, from the 1760s some English-women began to wear lighter stays in the French style. Indeed, on a visit to London in 1765 a French lawyer and literary man, Pierre-Jean Grosley, claimed that Englishwomen were less corseted than the French, wearing "a sort of whalebone waistcoat . . . keeping the body in a slight compression," and kept in place by ribbands over the shoulders. See Pierre-Jean Grosley, *A Tour to London: or, New Observations on England and its Inhabitants* (Dublin: Printed for Lockyer Davis, 1772), 2:22.

33
Ibid., 2:21. England at this time was a pioneer in simpler and more comfortable styles of dress for children.

34
Letters to the Ladies, 64.

35
François Nivelon, *The Rudiments of Genteel Behavior* (London, 1737), unpaginated introduction.

36
Giovanni Andrea Gallini, *A Treatise on the Art of Dancing* (London, 1762), 46 and passim.

37
Thomas Marriott, *Female Conduct: being an Essay on the Art of Pleasing* (London: W. Owen, 1759), 200.

38
Roger de Piles, *The Art of Painting* (London, 1754), 3 and 43.

According to Lord Chesterfield, Ann Ford was celebrated for her dancing, and Gainsborough's portrait suggests how much she had imbibed the best of terpsichorean philosophy. Linked to these ideals, contemporary advice to women in conduct manuals advised them to avoid the singular and the affected in dress:

> In dressing, aim not to be singular,
> Your Sense, in your Apparel, will appear;
> Ah! Let no bold Peculiar in your Mien,
> Nor Affection in your Dress be seen.[39]

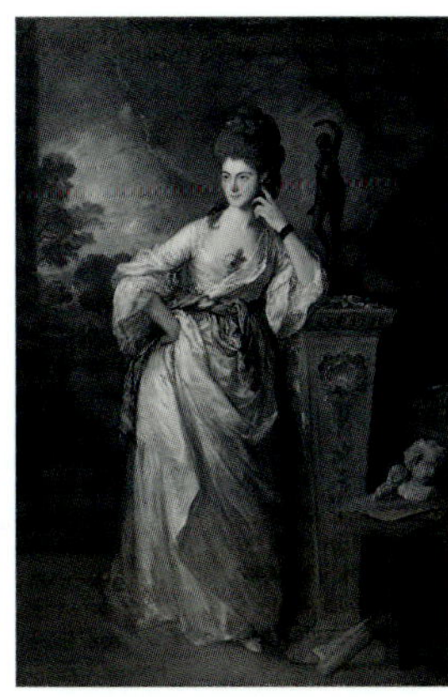

PLATE 3
*Penelope,
Viscountess Ligonier*

Mrs. Delany, ever prompt to detect any shortcomings in clothing, would have surely remarked on Ann Ford's dress if it had been inappropriate in any way. In fact, the slight ambiguity of Ford's status as a professional performer necessitated complete formality in dress, a world removed from, for example, the fanciful loose "bed-gown" worn by the actress and courtesan Nelly O'Brien in her portrait by Joshua Reynolds of the early 1760s (FIGURE 21).[40] Not being a member of the aristocracy, Ford couldn't be seen in the kind of elegantly raffish, fanciful wrapping gown Penelope, Viscountess Ligonier (soon to be as déclassée as O'Brien herself), wears in her portrait by Gainsborough (PLATE 3). In the 1750s

39
Marriott, *Female Conduct*, 61.

40
"Bed-gown" was the contemporary term for a plain, informal house-dress with a crossover front; originally a working-class item of clothing (often thigh-length), it was taken up by the fashionable world during the 1770s and 1780s as a "wrapping gown." The term bed-gown was also used to describe a similar type of invented dress in the studios of artists, like Reynolds, who employed the services of drapery painters.

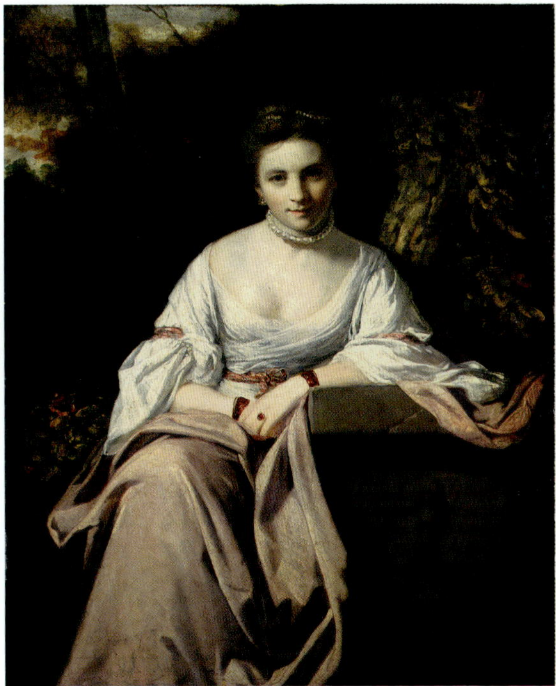

FIGURE 21

SIR JOSHUA REYNOLDS
Nelly O'Brien
CA. 1763 – 67
OIL ON CANVAS
49-1/4 X 39-7/16 IN (125.1 X 100.1 CM)
THE HUNTERIAN MUSEUM & ART GALLERY
UNIVERSITY OF GLASGOW
(GLAHA 43826)

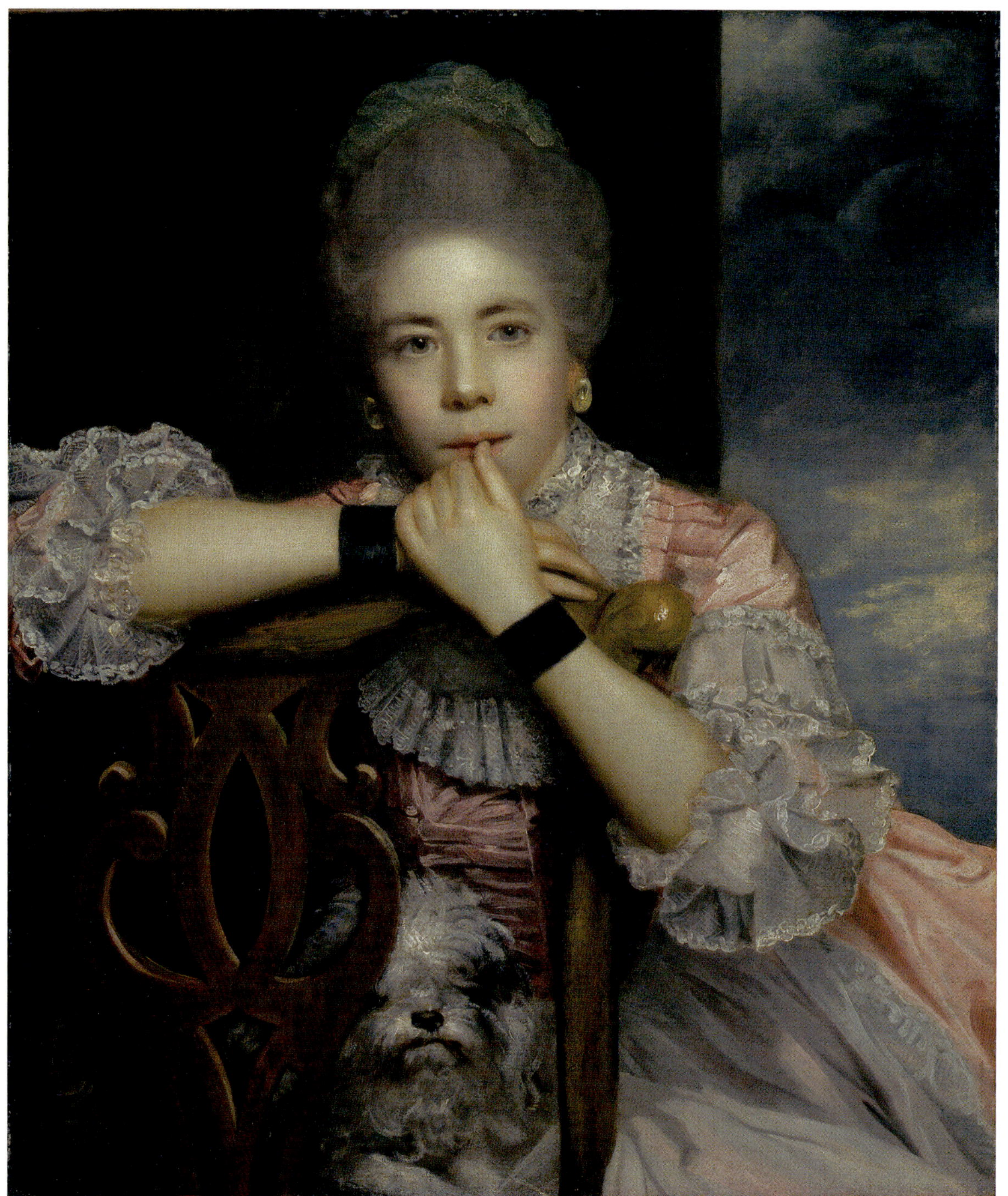

FIGURE 22

SIR JOSHUA REYNOLDS

Mrs. Abington as Miss Prue in 'Love for Love' by William Congreve

1771

OIL ON CANVAS, 30-1/4 x 25-1/8 IN (76.8 x 63.7 CM)

YALE CENTER FOR BRITISH ART

PAUL MELLON COLLECTION (B1977.14.67)

DETAIL APPEARS ON PAGES 128–129

some critics had deplored the fashion (blamed on the French) for female décolletage. The *World* (February 8, 1753) remarked that "shoulders . . . ivory necks . . . snowy breasts" were too much on display; more seductive still was the fashion for covering the breasts with "thinnest gauze" (we see such a transparent silk kerchief worn by Ann Ford), which will "enable the fancy to improve into beauty every thing it hides" (*World*, June 27, 1754).[41] Here, surely, is an example of what Flügel meant by a "conflict" (a happy one, in this case) between what Thomas Marriott calls a "modest Concealment" of charms and the desire to exhibit them, lightly veiled.[42] Alongside the vogue for such feminine display went the fashion — again from France, and in particular the Marquise de Pompadour — for the hair to be uncovered or with the tiniest and most insubstantial headdress. Again, the *World* pretended to be outraged at the "indecency of the modern headdress. Do the ladies intend to lay aside all modesty and go naked?" (May 7, 1754); "The fair part of the creation are shedding all covering of the head" (February 8, 1753). But the hair was never completely unadorned, and in Gainsborough's portrait, Ann Ford wears pearls, an appropriate style for the full dress she wears, which was presumably the outfit she wore for her performances.

We know that Mrs. Delany thought the portrait "bold," a term of disapproval, as it was for Thomas Marriott in his 1759 conduct manual, when, as noted above, he urged women to avoid a "bold Peculiar" in their "Mien." Presumably both critics disliked women to have the kind of direct and forceful look adopted by Ann Ford, which could be construed as "masculine." Indeed, the link between boldness and masculinity is made explicit in John Brown's well-known contribution to the luxury debate of the mid-eighteenth century, *An Estimate of the Manners and Principles of the Times* (1757), where he laments the amounts of time and money spent on dress and entertainments, which, he suggests, leave men "sunk into Effeminacy" and women "advanced into Boldness."[43] Paradoxically, Ford's face is *un*masculine in her use of cosmetics, notably the rouge she wears, a French taste described by André Rouquet as "the barbarous art of daubing one's cheeks with a glaring red," and increasingly fashionable in England by the late 1750s.[44] It may be that for added dramatic effect, Ann Ford wore makeup for her musical performances, thus creating — along with the turn of her head — the sense of boldness which Mrs. Delany found too pronounced. For boldness was a quality linked with the stage, and what, in the late nineteenth century, would be called a "professional beauty," a category analogous to a highly expensive courtesan. Gill Perry has recently elaborated on notions of the coquette and the flirt apropos the image of the actress both onstage and in painted portraits, defining her appearance as "flirtatious, beguiling or enthralling — as seducing or engaging the attention of the male and female audience."[45] The concept

41
The *Salisbury Journal* (1757) comments on the recent introduction of "gauze handkerchiefs [kerchiefs] . . . a fashion so ingeniously contriv'd as to preserve the appearance of decency"; such kerchiefs were "universally worn and admired." Quoted in Cecil Willett Cunnington and Phillis Cunnington, *Handbook of English Costume in the Eighteenth Century* (London: Plays, 1972), 326.

42
Marriott, *Female Conduct*, 62. Hogarth is in agreement, stating that "the body and limbs should all be cover'd, and little more than certain hints be given of them thro' the cloathing" (*Analysis of Beauty*, 40).

43
John Brown, *An Estimate of the Manners and Principles of the Times* (London: Printed for L. Davis and C. Reymers, 1757), 51.

44
Rouquet, *Present State of the Arts*, 48.

45
Perry, *Spectacular Flirtations*, 7.

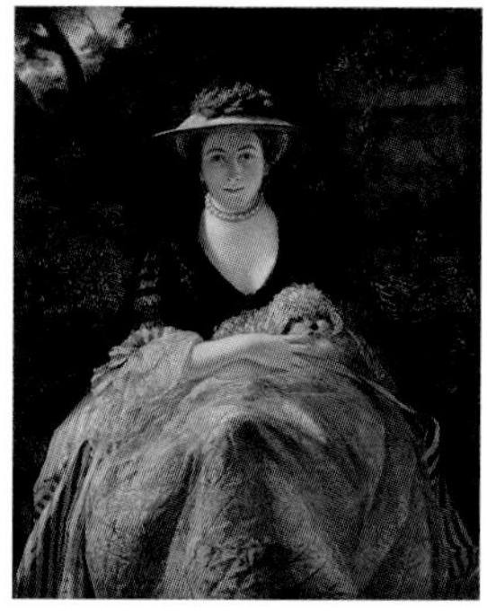

FIGURE 6
Miss Nelly O'Brien

of the flirt at its most obvious can be seen in Reynolds's 1771 portrait *Mrs. Abington as Miss Prue,* William Congreve's "silly, awkward, country girl" (although she was played and displayed here more as a coquette) in *Love for Love* (FIGURE 22); thumb to her mouth, and dressed in the latest high fashion, a glorious pink silk, she shimmers with sexual invitation and innuendo, as her part (and her own character) suggest.[46] As a fashion accessory, the same fluffy white Maltese dog appears in Reynolds's portrait *Miss Nelly O'Brien* in the Wallace Collection (FIGURE 6), but here the sitter's face is not that of the professional coquette, nor does it share the self-awareness of Ann Ford's gaze with her best profile to the camera; rather, it is a direct and intimate encounter with a close friend. This sense of the natural and unaffected, which Gainsborough rarely achieves in his pursuit of style and effect, is underlined by O'Brien's elegant but informal appearance, a beribboned straw hat partly shading the face, black lace shoulder mantle over a green-and-white-striped dress, which is open to reveal a peach-colored quilted skirt, and a gauzy silk apron; it's one of the great portraits of the eighteenth century.

" We Know
THE VERY Minds OF
People BY THEIR "
Dress.

WILLIAM HOGARTH,
THE ANALYSIS OF BEAUTY (1753)[47]

INSPIRED BY THE SUCCESS of his portrait of Ann Ford, Gainsborough's next two lifesize full-length portraits, painted in the early 1760s, followed similar lines, stylish exercises in elite fashion, but with the figures standing in a landscape. Such an outdoors setting is more appropriate to *Lady Howe* (Iveagh Bequest, Kenwood, London), whose straw hat gives her an Arcadian appearance as she steps out in a relatively informal kind of dress, tight to the waist, called a nightgown (here of a glazed silk called lustring), worn with an impractical but beautiful embroidered gauzy white apron, lifted slightly to one side, in a gesture reminiscent of Van Dyck.[48] The formal dress worn by Lady Alston (FIGURE 23), a white silk *robe à la française,* is somewhat at odds with the countryside in which she stands; perhaps for that reason the artist has caused her to bundle up her *sacque* dress under her arms at the waist, although it still trails on the ground. Gainsborough delights in the tactility of the fabrics of women's gowns; *Lady Alston,* in particular, is a tour de force in its depiction of the creamy white satin of the dress and the greeny-blue quilted silk of the skirt.[49]

46
Frances Abington was a milliner (a position regarded by some contemporaries as synonymous with prostitution) before going on the stage, and she was renowned for her sense of style, the fashions she wore being copied in high society. It was customary for well-known actresses to provide their own clothes for some roles where high fashion was de rigueur, and they were then reimbursed by the theater management. In the 1770s the accounts for the Drury Lane theater show that Abington was paid "£60 per annum for her clothes, apart from 'other general wardrobe expenditures', and by the early 1780s this had risen to £500 overall," a considerable sum at the time. See Aileen Ribeiro, "Costuming the Part: A Discourse of Fashion and Fiction in the Image of the Actress in England 1776–1812," in *Notorious Muse: The Actress in British Art and Culture 1776–1812,* ed. Robyn Asleson (New Haven: Yale University Press, 2003), 124.

47
Hogarth, *Analysis of Beauty,* 128.

48
"The starting point for Gainsborough's composition was the type of female full-length portrait which Van Dyck evolved during his second stay in England from 1632 until his death in 1641," the most important source being the portrait *Elizabeth Howard, Countess of Peterborough* (private collection); see Anne French, "Gainsborough's Portraits of Earl and Countess Howe," in *"The Earl and Countess Howe" by Gainsborough: A Bicentenary Exhibition* (Iveagh Bequest, Kenwood, London: English Heritage, 1988), 22.

49
On the grounds of costume and hairstyle, I would place the date of Gainsborough's portrait of Lady Alston ca. 1762–63, *after* that of Lady Howe.

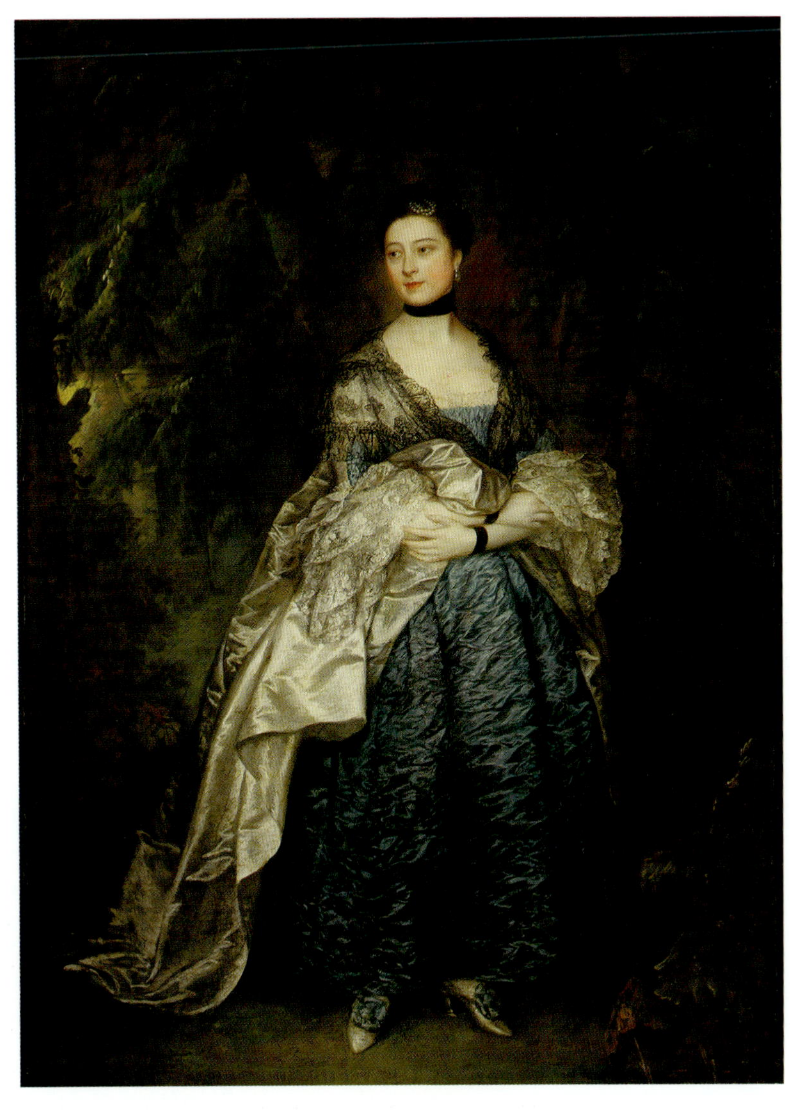

FIGURE 23

THOMAS GAINSBOROUGH
Lady Alston, Gertrude Durnford (1732 – 1807)
CA. 1760
OIL ON CANVAS
90 X 65-1/4 IN (228 X 166 CM)
LOUVRE, PARIS, FRANCE
(RF 1947-1)

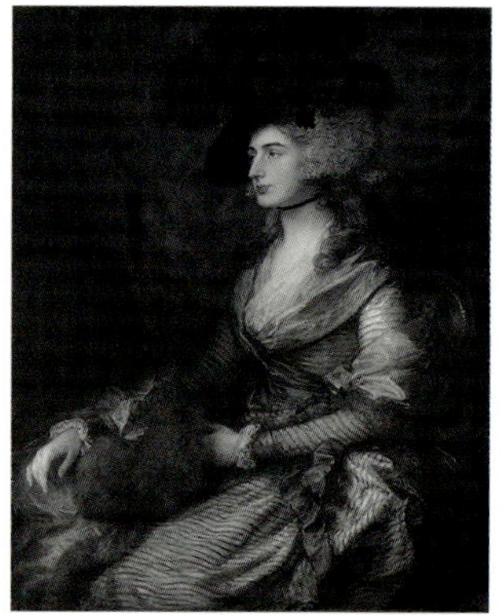

Rococo dress abhors a vacuum; it's the antithesis of plainness and simplicity, relishing movement, restlessness, the different ways light can be reflected in textiles, and the "pattern" created by playing with fabrics, which can be glazed, watered, pleated, ruched, beribboned, flounced, quilted — the varieties are endless. During the height of the rococo period in England (the 1750s and early 1760s), artists (Gainsborough included) seem to have preferred fashions made from fabrics treated in these ways as being more painterly than those made of woven patterns, where the repetition of detail might prove tedious to depict. An exception was sometimes made for the simpler striped silks that were very fashionable from the later 1760s (see the lustrous satin worn by Isabella, Viscountess Molyneux, later Countess of Sefton, FIGURE 24), right through into the 1780s, as in *Mrs. Siddons* (PLATE 9). Siddons, very much a leader of fashion, is depicted in a wrapping gown known as a *lévite* (a French style of dress, suitably theatrical in origin) of blue-and-white-striped silk, tied around the waist with a blue sash; she holds a fox-fur muff, and the same fur edges her yellow silk mantle, or pelisse.[50] Her face is thoughtful and composed under the spotlight of the artist's scrutiny, the line of her nose echoed by the sideways slant

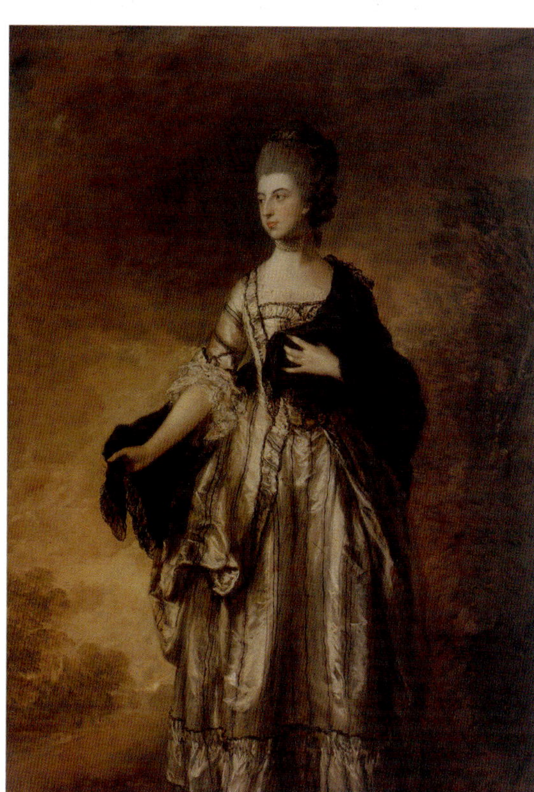

FIGURE 24

THOMAS GAINSBOROUGH
*Isabella, Viscountess Molyneux,
later Countess of Sefton*
1769
OIL ON CANVAS
92-15/16 X 61 IN (236 X 155 CM)
NATIONAL MUSEUMS LIVERPOOL
WALKER ART GALLERY
(WAG 8780)

50
See Aileen Ribeiro, *The Art of Dress: Fashion in England and France 1750–1820* (New Haven: Yale University Press, 1995), 73.

of her fashionable black hat trimmed with ostrich feathers and ribbons, placed on the wide stiff powdered hairstyle (the word "frizzled" was often used) of the early to mid-1780s.

Stripes were both fashionable and could sometimes be used to dramatic effect in stage costumes, as Gainsborough shows with *Giovanna Baccelli* (PLATE 7), in the dress she wore in the ballet *Les Amans Surpris*, performed at the King's Theatre in the Haymarket in 1781. A pert soubrette ensemble, it is composed of a white silk jacket and skirt, trimmed with wide blue stripes; an overskirt is looped up with matching blue ribbon bows, rather like a fashionable polonaise, and she holds out a gauzy silk apron.[51] Whereas Ann Ford is fashionable first and a performer second, Baccelli is seen as wholly professional in the liveliness of her movements, her expertly made up face, and most of all her short skirt, which provides the necessary freedom to dance, and which was an obvious source of attraction for a male audience. A contemporary image by Jean-Michel Moreau (le Jeune), *La Petite Loge* of ca. 1781 (FIGURE 25), shows a similar tight bodice, low décolletage, and looped-up skirt, worn by a dancer at the Paris Opéra, clearly subject to masculine approval and possible consumption. Actresses and dancers were thought to be free with their sexual favors. Sarah Siddons led a respectable private life, but this was regarded as unusual; Giovanna Baccelli, for example, was the established mistress of the Duke of Dorset.

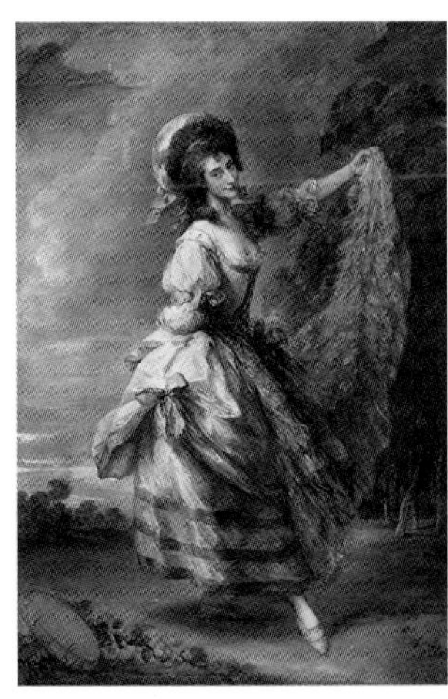

PLATE 7
Giovanna Baccelli

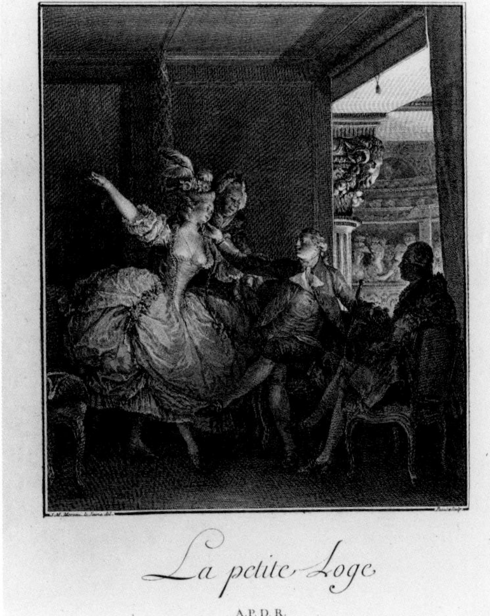

FIGURE 25

JEAN-MICHEL MOREAU (LE JEUNE)
(after)
La Petite Loge
CA. 1781
ENGRAVING BY C. E. PATAS
VICTORIA AND ALBERT MUSEUM
(E.483-1972)

51
A polonaise was a variant of the tight-fitting *robe à l'anglaise*, but the overskirt was lifted up by means of loops, buttons, ribbons, or tassels to form three swags of material. An early example of this style of dress can be seen in Gainsborough's portrait *Isabella, Viscountess Molyneux* (see FIGURE 24), but it was most popular during the 1770s and 1780s.

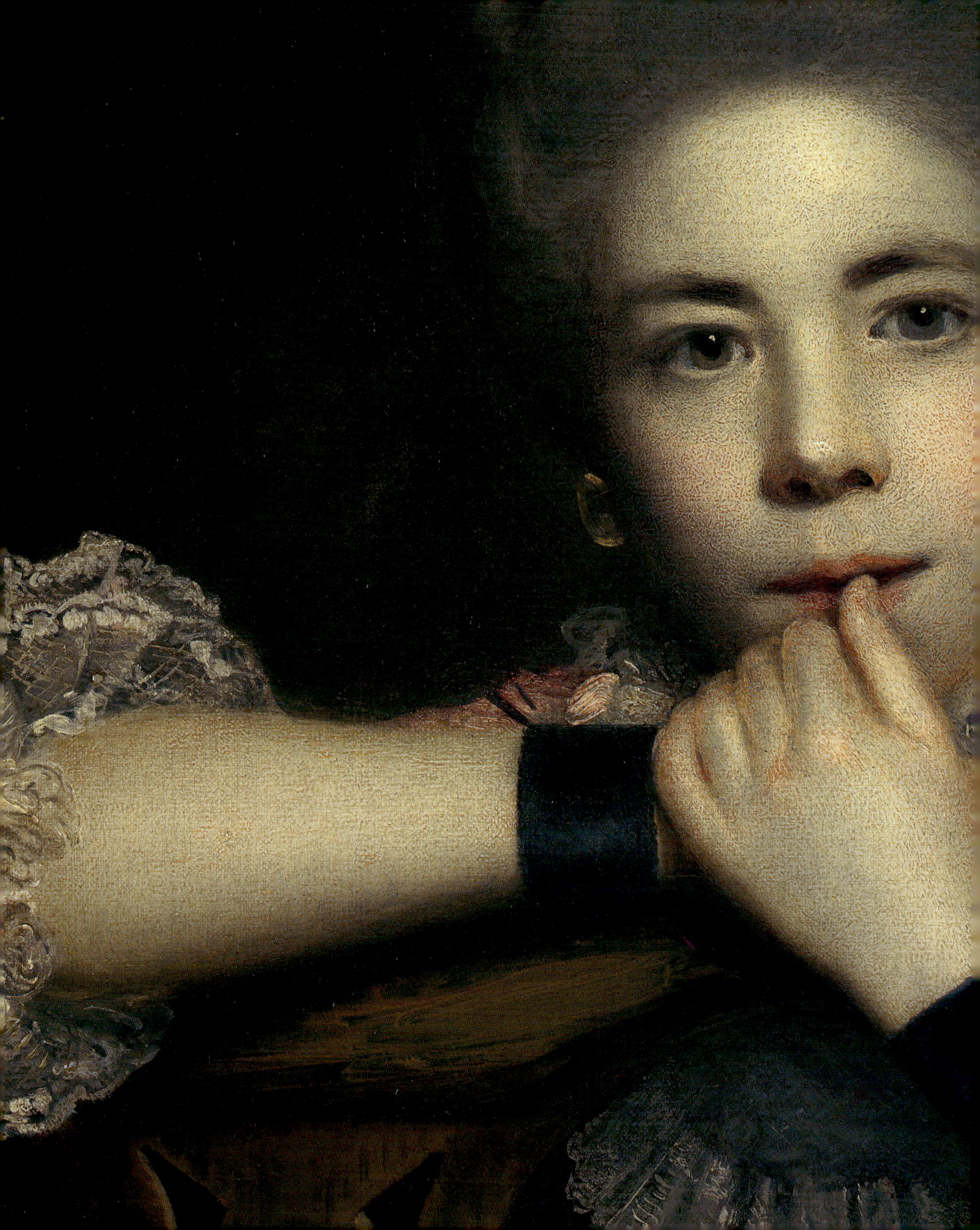

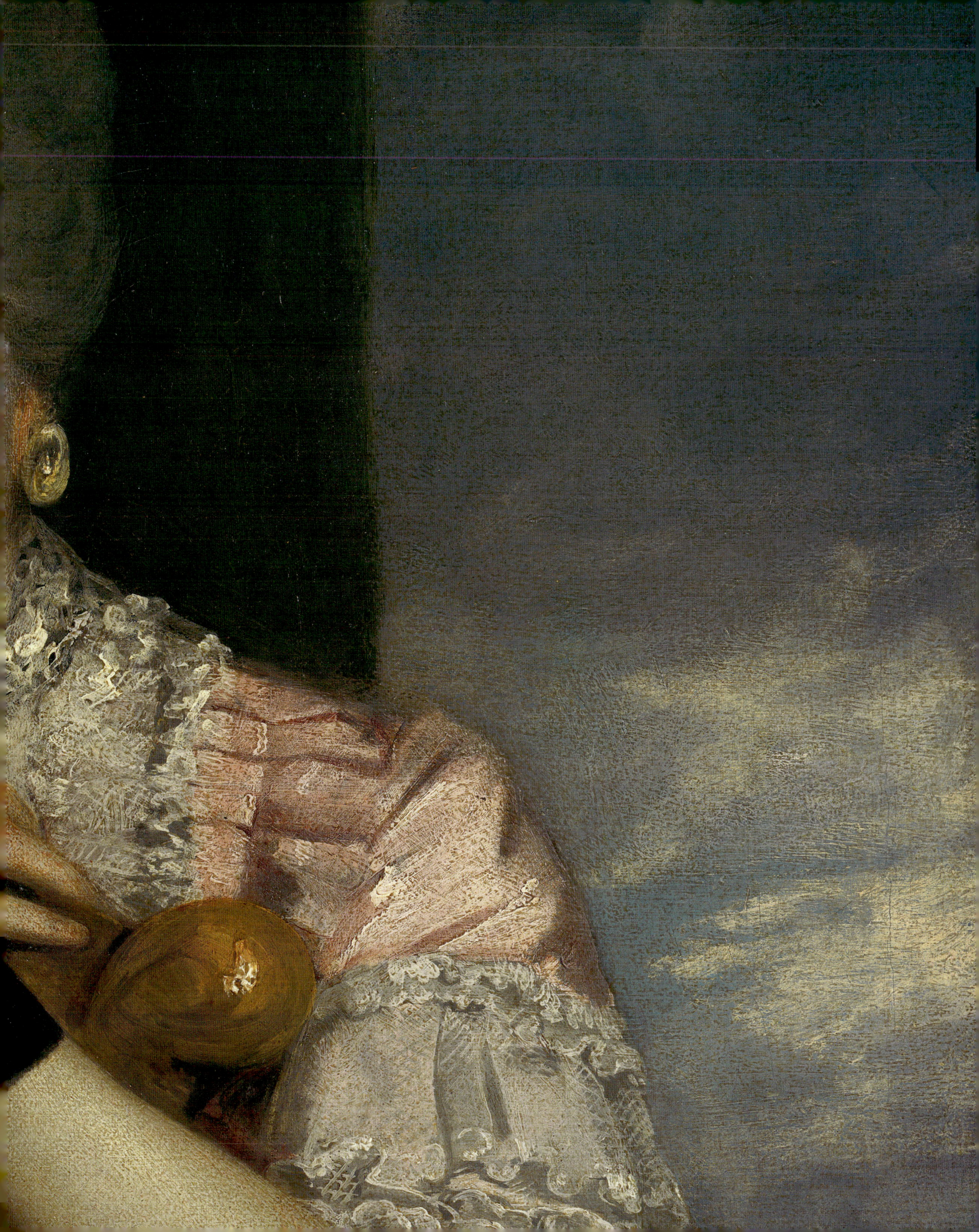

Compared to that of his great rival Reynolds, Gainsborough's range of feminine costume is relatively limited, indicating a preference for the decorative over the practical, more "masculine" styles such as the riding habit, adapted from the man's suit, which was all the rage in the 1780s. Critics, such as Elizabeth Montagu of Bath in 1780, complained that such quasi-masculine attire gave women the freedom to "strut and swagger about the streets," and could lead to the adoption of the kind of sexual libertinism that men enjoyed.[52] Thus the kind of dashing boldness of Reynolds's *Lady Worsley* (FIGURE 26) in her brilliant red riding habit adapted from the uniform of her husband's regiment, the Hampshire Militia, could be said to signal her unconventional behavior; she had many lovers and in 1782 was involved in a scandalous divorce case resulting from an affair with one of her husband's officers.

In some ways Reynolds and Gainsborough followed a similar trajectory in their portrait painting, from the detailed and precise depictions of real clothes in their early careers to more experimental images from the 1770s onward, often involving imaginary, fanciful costume. In Reynolds's case this was based primarily on theory, his admiration for history painting, and the urge to create "timeless" portraits (surely an oxymoron), inspired by a study of the Old Masters. In Gainsborough's case, one can only guess at the influences behind many of his portraits of the 1770s and 1780s; possibly they included emulation of his rival's Grand Style, or perhaps he worked out on his own account a "certain generalizing management" of the dress of his female sitters during these years, to arrive at his own idea of "modern truth."[53] For although Gainsborough claimed that contemporary dress aided likeness, and attacked the "ridiculous use of fancied Dresses in Portraits," a substantial number of his later portraits depict generalized versions of fashionable costume.[54] These include an early example, *Penelope, Viscountess Ligonier* (PLATE 3, exhibited at the Royal Academy in 1771), who wears a loosely draped fanciful version of the fashionable wrapping gown, of "white silk gauze over a shot silk of yellowish-pink,"[55] and tied with a fringed sash at the waist; it was described as a "graceful . . . fancied dress."[56] Soon after sitting for her portrait in the summer of 1770, Lady Ligonier had an affair with an Italian dramatist and fled to France, a liaison perhaps suggested by the statue of the dancing bacchante on top of the plinth, and the scallop shell, symbol of Venus.[57] Gainsborough also gently hints at her reputation by giving her a bold, assertive gaze and a pose where the skirt of her "fancied" gown is lifted up at one side, like the caftans seen in images of Turkish women in the harem.[58] The dress in the portrait has the blurred and shifting quality of Gainsborough's treatment of fabrics that is characteristic of his "impressionist" style.

52
"A quiet sober woman is a rarity in these times. How the misses waddle, and straddle, and strut, and swagger about the streets here, one arm akimbo, the other swinging," quoted in Aileen Ribeiro, *Dress and Morality* (Oxford: Berg, 2003), 114.

53
Ribeiro, *Art of Dress*, 26.

54
The Letters of Thomas Gainsborough, ed. John Hayes (London: Paul Mellon Centre for British Art, 2001), 88.

55
Information by Aileen Ribeiro as costume consultant in Robyn Asleson and Shelley M. Bennett, *British Paintings at the Huntington* (New Haven: Yale University Press, 2001), 136.

56
Ribeiro, *Art of Dress*, 26.

57
Catalogue entry by Christine Riding in Michael Rosenthal and Martin Myrone, *Gainsborough* (London: Tate Publishing, 2002), 116. Lady Ligonier is depicted as having been drawing sculpture, a practice more associated with male artists and students, although Gainsborough's daughters, 1764 (see PLATE 2), are shown "contemplating the statuette of the Farnese Flora." Rosenthal, "Thomas Gainsborough's Ann Ford," 658.

58
Such as the collection of prints after Jean-Baptiste Vanmour, published as the *Recueil de cent estampes représentant différentes nations du Levant*, 1714. European women living in Turkey adopted a version of Ottoman dress, as did visitors such as Lady Mary Wortley Montagu, who set the fashion for being painted *à la turque*. See Aileen Ribeiro, "Turquerie: Turkish Dress and English Fashion in the Eighteenth Century," *Connoisseur* 201 (May 1979): 16–23.

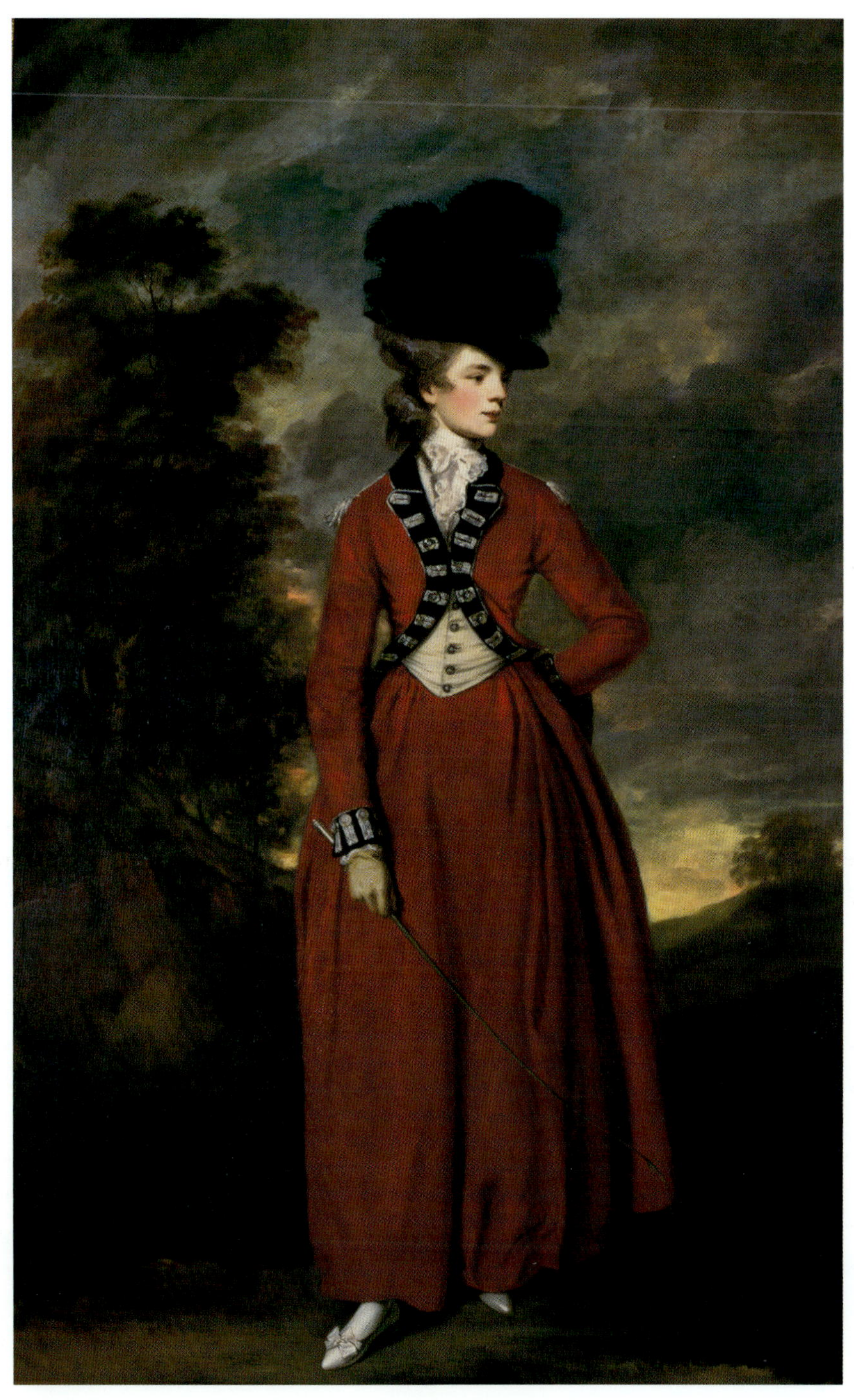

FIGURE 26

SIR JOSHUA REYNOLDS
Lady Worsley
1780
OIL ON CANVAS
92-15/16 X 56-11/16 IN (236 X 144 CM)
HAREWOOD HOUSE TRUST (HHTP:2001.1.43)

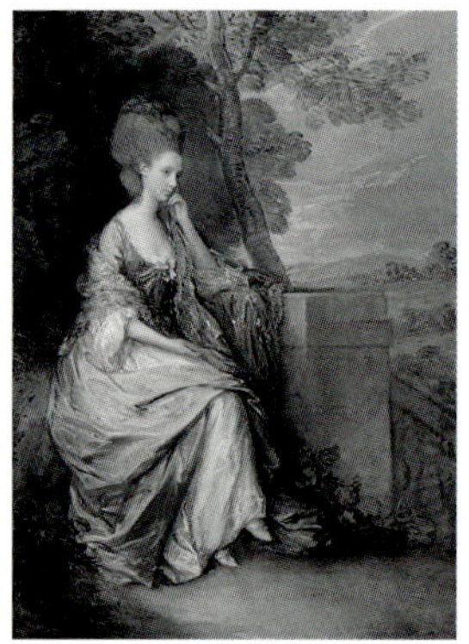

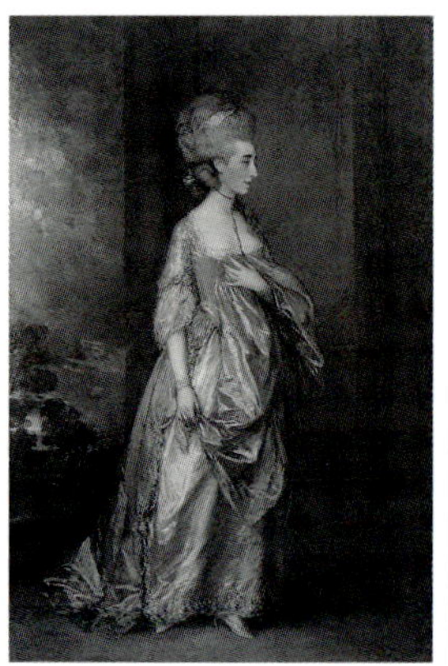

Helen Glanville remarks that the artist Ozias Humphry "describes the gloom of Gainsborough's painting room, in which both sitters and pictures *'were scarcely discernable'*, which enabled him to depict *'the masses and general forms'*, and leave out superfluous detail."[59] Humphry's comments were made during his acquaintance with Gainsborough in Bath in the early 1760s, but are especially applicable to his portraits in a later period, when his "fancied dresses" suggested only the main lines of costume at the expense of the fashionable details, and not the "exact resemblance" Glanville suggests.[60] *Anne, Countess of Chesterfield* (PLATE 5), for example, shows the sitter in a blue silk dress, a "simplified" version of the fashionable *robe à l'anglaise* (a fashionable style with a tight-fitting bodice, worn from the late 1770s and through the 1780s), worn over a white skirt and with a gauzy shawl draped over her shoulders. Around the same time, in *Mrs. Grace Dalrymple Elliott* (PLATE 6) the subject was depicted by Gainsborough also in a gown loosely based on the *robe à l'anglaise*: yellow satin over a white silk skirt; some of the back drapery of the train of her dress appears, not very convincingly, to be brought around to the front and clasped, mock-modestly, to her bosom. Faux modesty, for Mrs. Elliott was a well-known courtesan, numbering the Prince of Wales among her lovers. After her divorce in 1776, she became

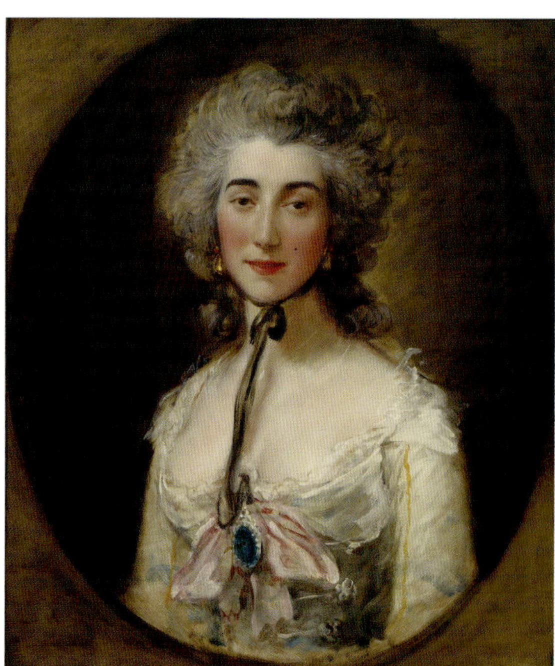

FIGURE 27

THOMAS GAINSBOROUGH
Grace Dalrymple Elliott
CA. 1782
OIL ON CANVAS
30-1/8 X 25 IN (76.52 X 63.5 CM)
THE FRICK COLLECTION
PURCHASED BY THE FRICK COLLECTION, 1946
(1946.1.153)

DETAIL APPEARS ON PAGE 141

59
Helen Glanville, "Gainsborough as Artist and Artisan," in *A Nest of Nightingales: Thomas Gainsborough and the Linley Sisters*, ed. Giles Waterfield (London: Dulwich Picture Gallery, 1988), 16.

60
Ibid., 17.

the mistress of the Earl of Cholmondeley, and it might be worth noting that the scalloped edge to her gown is reminiscent of a peeress's coronation robe, a hint perhaps that Elliott considered herself a virtual countess through this relationship, which later resulted in the birth of a daughter. Soon after this event, in 1782, Gainsborough painted another portrait of Elliott (FIGURE 27), a half-length, but this time in a real costume, blue stripes on cream silk; the black ribbon around her neck draws attention to her painted face and slightly parted lips.

The gauzy silks and muslins newly in vogue for women in the 1780s perfectly suited Gainsborough; they were part of high fashion, and were also appropriate for the impressionist *suggestion* of dress, which often seems to merge into the landscape. Examples of these late "Arcadian" images by Gainsborough include *Mrs. Mary Robinson* (1781), an actress, and *Mrs. Richard Brinsley Sheridan* (1785–87), a singer. Mary "Perdita" Robinson (she gained the nickname after playing the part in Garrick's adaptation of Shakespeare's *Winter's Tale* in 1779,

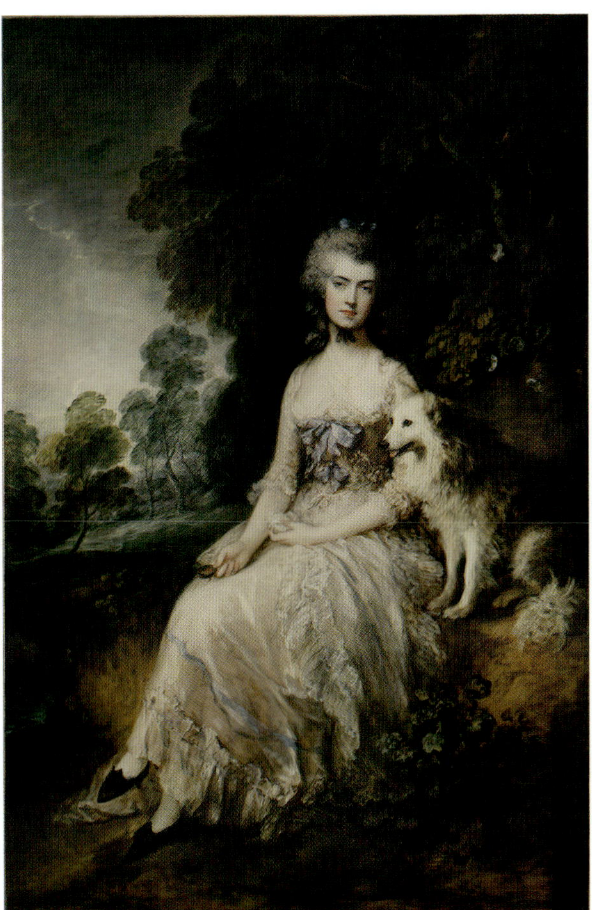

THOMAS GAINSBOROUGH
Mrs. Mary Robinson (Perdita)
1781
OIL ON CANVAS
92 X 60-1/4 IN (233.7 X 153 CM)
THE WALLACE COLLECTION
(P42)

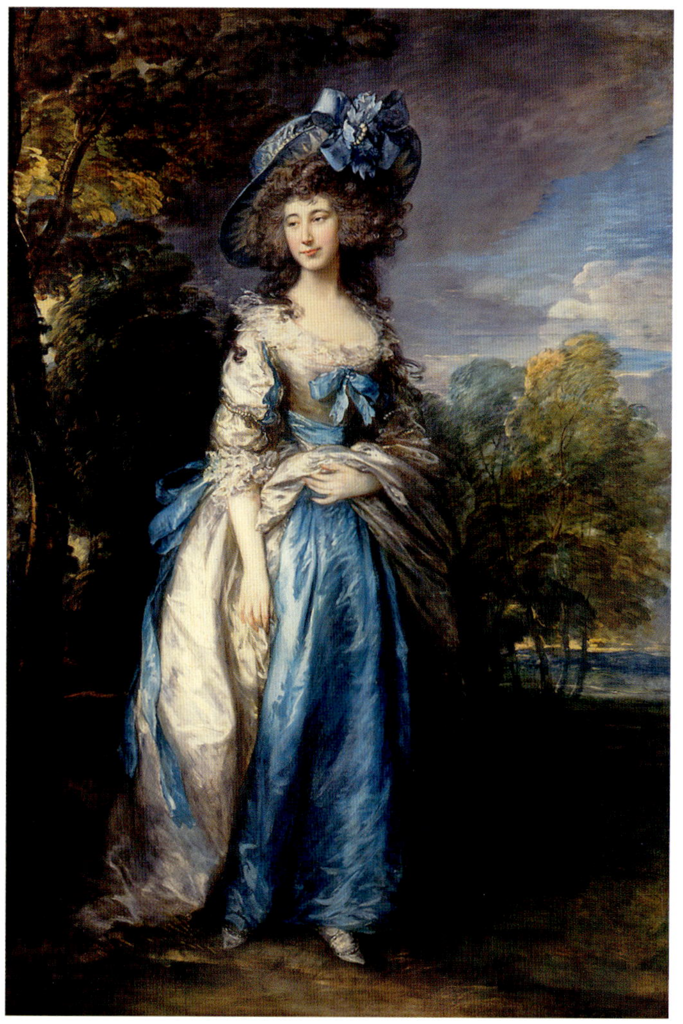

FIGURE 29

THOMAS GAINSBOROUGH
Sophia Charlotte, Lady Sheffield
1785 – 86
OIL ON CANVAS
89-1/2 X 58-3/4 IN (227.3 X 149.2 CM)
WADDESDON, THE ROTHSCHILD COLLECTION (NATIONAL TRUST)
(2260)

an event that led to her affair with the Prince of Wales) followed the established theater convention by which acting skill was allied to beauty and a sense of style. At the height of her fame, fashions were named after her, such as the Perdita chemise; the chemise, a style made popular by Marie-Antoinette, was based on the simple T-shaped fine muslin gown derived from the white linen shift that women wore next to the skin.[61] In Gainsborough's portrait (FIGURE 28), commissioned by the Prince of Wales (the miniature she holds is likely of him), Perdita wears a dress made from layers of floating, cobwebby silk, trimmed with blue ribbons;

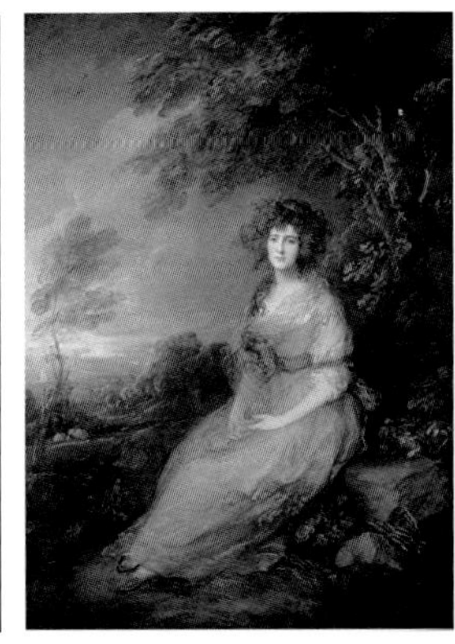

PLATE 10
Mrs. Richard Brinsley Sheridan

the airy pastoral effect of the costume seems appropriate for her most famous stage role. If Perdita Robinson exemplifies Gainsborough's ability to depict the reality of what, with its layers of hazy fabrics, can seem *un*real, the portrait of Elizabeth Linley Sheridan (PLATE 10) typifies the artist's depiction of a largely imaginary costume, more specifically Arcadian in spirit. The peach-colored dress ties with a green silk sash around the waist; the very short sleeves have a vandyked edge. It was Anthony Van Dyck who in the 1630s introduced the concept of the pastoral portrait into English art, with sartorial features such as the ribbons on the sleeves, a reference (more theatrical than real) of shepherd-ess costume. Mrs. Sheridan's hair, unraveling from its stiff, frizzed curls, blows about her face in sympathy with the insubstantial materials of her dress and the trees, which dominate the landscape.

The reference to Van Dyck in this image reminds us of the great vogue for his portraits in the eighteenth century. Gainsborough's *Sophia Charlotte, Lady Sheffield* of 1785–86 (FIGURE 29) is derived from Van Dyck's portrait of Elizabeth Howard, Countess of Peterborough (private collection), and shows Gainsborough's preference for blending elements of historical fantasy into fashionable dress: "The gown is a pale yellow silk *robe à l'anglaise* with a trailing overskirt; Gainsborough has added to the dress a central ribbon bow, pearls twining round the arms and edging the top of the bodice, and a gauzy Vandyke collar . . . The hat, a concoction of satin, ribbons and pearls, also shows the influence of van Dyck in the spiky, pointed appli-quéd silk on the underside of the brim."[62] Reverence for what was seen as the "romantic" period of Charles I, along with the great fondness for the masquerade in eighteenth-century England, helped to popularize the vogue for fancy-dress portraiture based on historic predecessors, particularly images by Van Dyck and his contemporaries. At a masquerade at Vauxhall Gardens in 1742, Horace Walpole noted, "quantities of pretty Vandykes and all kinds of old pictures walked out of their frames." In 1773, at a ball given by

61
See Paula Byrne, *Perdita: The Life of Mary Robinson* (London: HarperCollins, 2004), 203–4.

62
Ribeiro, *Art of Dress*, 74.

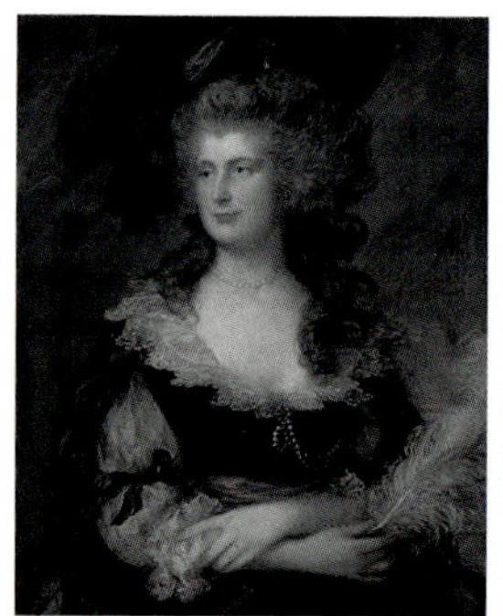

the French ambassador to London, Walpole remarked on the "Elizabethan" costume worn by a set of dancers, blue satin with blonde lace and high, stiffened collars: "collets montés à la reine Elizabeth."[63] This description recalls Gainsborough's portrait of Frances Duncombe (ca. 1777, FIGURE 30) in her stunning costume decorated with pearls, blue satin looped up *à la polonaise* over a white silk skirt; the feathered hat, the open lace collar, and the slashed sleeves of the dress allude to the early seventeenth century, and in particular to a portrait, ca. 1630–32, by Rubens of his second wife, Helena Fourment (FIGURE 31), attributed, until the mid-eighteenth century, to Van Dyck.[64] Fourment, in pastoral mode, wears a dress of black satin with bunched-up overskirt, transparent silk oversleeves tied with ribbon, a slightly raised collar, a brooch pinned to the center of the bodice with a jeweled chain looping over the shoulders, and a hat fastened up to one side with ostrich feathers. The Rubens portrait was an endless source of inspiration throughout the eighteenth century, both for actual masquerade costumes and as a studio prop. One of Gainsborough's closest versions of the Rubens portrait is *The Honorable Anne (Batson) Fane* (ca. 1786, PLATE 11). She wears a dress of black silk with an open lace-edged collar, ribbon tied over gauzy oversleeves, and loops of pearls descending from a brooch

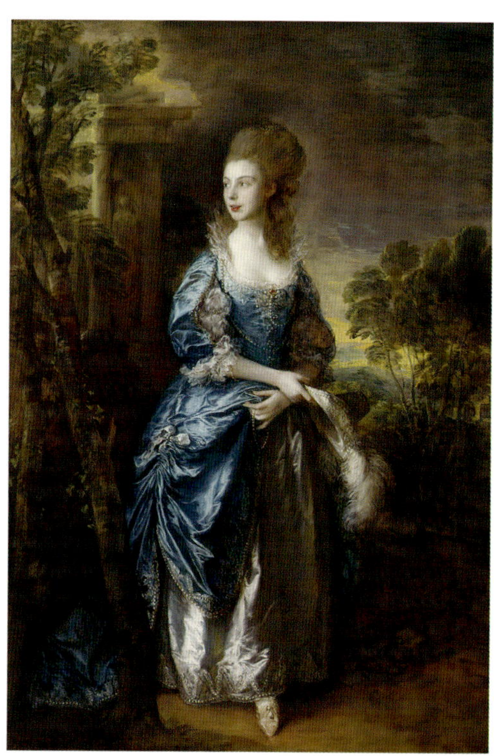

FIGURE 30

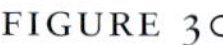

THOMAS GAINSBOROUGH
The Honorable Frances Duncombe
CA. 1777
OIL ON CANVAS
92-1/4 X 61-1/8 IN (234.32 X 155.26 CM)
THE FRICK COLLECTION
HENRY CLAY FRICK BEQUEST (1911.1.61)

63
Aileen Ribeiro, *Dress in Eighteenth-Century Europe 1715–1789* (New Haven: Yale University Press, 2002), 278; Ribeiro, *Art of Dress*, 192.

64
Ribeiro, *Art of Dress*, 193 and note 35, p. 243. The portrait was correctly attributed to Rubens in Thomas Jefferys's famous costume book *A Collection of the Dresses of Different Nations both Ancient and Modern* (London, 1757).

at the center of her bodice neckline. She carries a white ostrich feather as in the Rubens portrait, hands at waist in the same pose. Only the modest black beaver hat of the Rubens has morphed into the vast plumed and ribboned hat which was in the nineteenth century to become known as the Gainsborough hat; it sits on top of her equally large and majestic hairstyle. It's a striking image of a forceful and imposing woman, but completely lacks the fairytale quality of Gainsborough's great fancy-dress portraits of the 1770s, Frances Duncombe and Mary Graham (1777, National Gallery of Scotland). With Anne Fane's portrait the magic has vanished, and what we see is a rather tired and outmoded image. For it was in the 1770s that Gainsborough was painting at the height of his skill and imagination, a period when historical themes in dress were assimilated into high fashion; the "Rubens wife" dress (as it is listed in masquerade accounts) provided a mixture of current styles (the polonaise overskirt, the hat that fashion magazines dubbed the Rubens hat) alongside aspects of the dress of an admired period close enough in time to be familiar through art and culture. With a mysterious alchemy, Gainsborough combined these two moods to create images of dreamy romanticism so that it becomes immaterial whether he depicts reality or fantasy in the ravishing portraits of Frances Duncombe and Mary Graham.

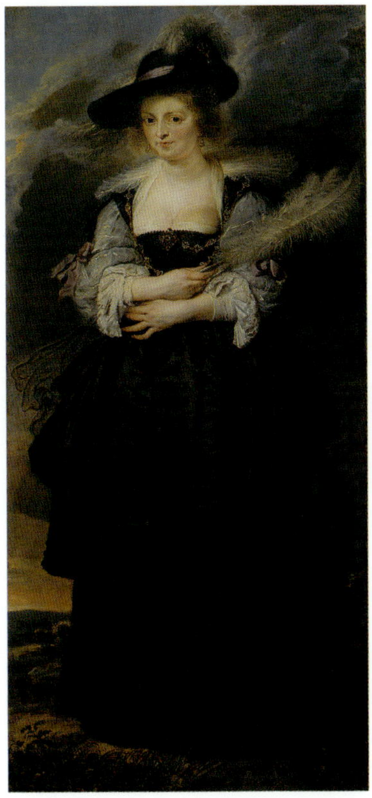

PETER PAUL RUBENS
Portrait of Helena Fourment
CA. 1630 – 32
OIL ON WOOD
73-1/4 X 33-7/16 IN (186 X 85 CM)
CALOUSTE GULBENKIAN MUSEUM
(959)

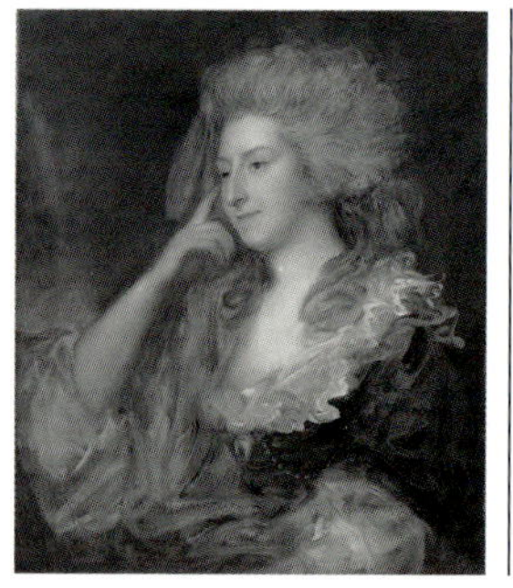

In 1777 Gainsborough also painted his elder daughter, Mary, à la Rubens's wife (FIGURE 32); although merely a faint shadow of the original portrait, it has a similar lyrical quality to the images of Frances Duncombe and Mary Graham. The emphasis here lies in the painting of his daughter's face, with its hectic coloring and nervous sensibility; the costume — a feathered hat, a dress with a soft frilled collar, and a pearl chain — is only vaguely sketched out. A similar sketchy and unfinished portrait is Gainsborough's *Mrs. Maria Anne Fitzherbert* (1784, PLATE 8), who in 1785 went through a form of wedding ceremony with the Prince of Wales (a marriage invalid under the 1772 Royal Marriages Act, which forbade the heir to the throne to marry a Catholic). The loosely painted dark brownish dress, the jewelry, and the frilled white collar tentatively suggest the costume of Rubens's wife, but the focus is on the sitter's large, powdered hair (the fat ringlets over her shoulders are rendered with a few squiggles of paint), and her sensible and intelligent face — she looks slightly amused at the gesture Gainsborough has given her of right forefinger pressed to her cheek. A few years later, Joshua Reynolds painted *Maria Anne Fitzherbert* (FIGURE 33), and the portrait is similar in feeling, with far less attention paid to the costume than to the face and hairstyle. In Reynolds's portrait, however, the frizzed and curled hair is depicted in more detail, and the face more attractive and engaged; the dress is quite indeterminate.

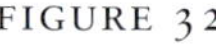

FIGURE 32

THOMAS GAINSBOROUGH
The Artist's Daughter Mary
1777
OIL ON CANVAS
30-1/2 X 25-1/2 IN (77.5 X 64.8 CM)
TATE
BEQUEATHED BY SIR OTTO BEIT, 1945
(NO5638)

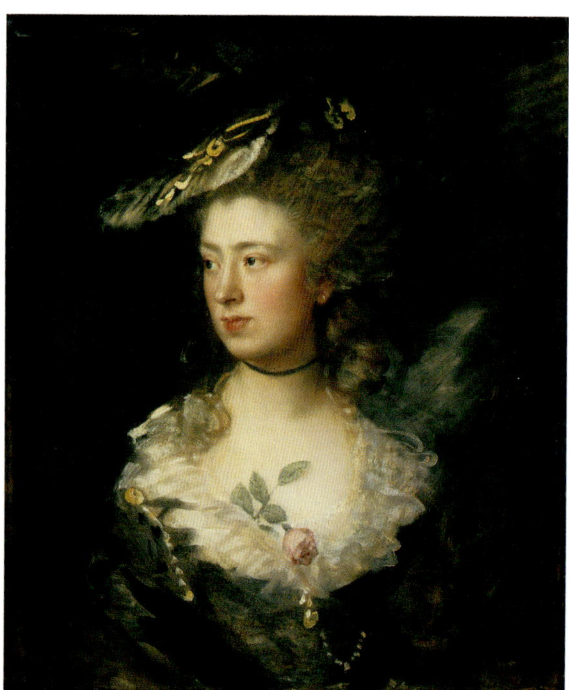

65
Valentine Morris, writing
from Antigua to Philip
Thicknesse in August
1773, thanks him for a
"pleasant & elegant"
painted silk gown sent by
Ann Thicknesse to his
wife. Thicknesse for-
warded this letter to a
friend with the words
"[Y]ou may see what a
figure Mrs Thicknesses
gown cut at Antigua."
Huntington MS TH 211.
Reference courtesy of
Susan Sloman. Painted
silks from China and
India were very fashion-
able in the 1770s, and
inspired talented ama-
teurs such as Ann Thick-
nesse to create their own
versions.

66
Thicknesse, School for
Fashion, 1:vii and viii.

67
Simone de Beauvoir,
The Second Sex, trans.
H. M. Parshley (London:
Jonathan Cape, 1953),
506 and 508.

CONCLUSION:

The Triumph

OF

Appearance

WOMEN HAVE ALWAYS HAD a complex relationship with fashion, which is linked so intimately with their sense of being. Attitudes can vary from a total engagement with fashion in youth to a more censorious viewpoint as a woman grows older. Ann Ford, for example, so stylish and involved with dress and appearance as a young woman,[65] later declared that fashion was a "tyrant," encouraging profligacy and misery when it dictated lives and manners; yet — a typically ambiguous attitude toward the subject — she acknowledges the "genius" of fashion.[66] Flügel in *The Psychology of Clothes* saw women's pleasure in decoration as a narcissistic aspect of their existence. Simone de Beauvoir in *The Second Sex*, a discourse on how femininity is constructed through dress, is largely in agreement with this assessment, declaring that woman has an erotic relationship with her clothes: "the feathers, pearls, brocades and silks she blends with her flesh," for "what she treasures is herself adorned."[67] Famously, of course, Beauvoir sees what she calls "ornamental attire" as making "woman into idol," an idea approved of by Baudelaire but one *she* deplored as making her into a male creation: "paralyzed by inconvenient clothing and by the rules of propriety — then

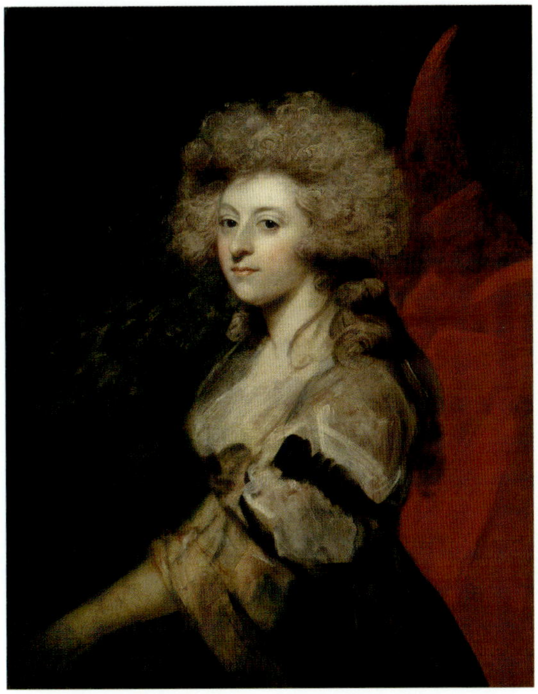

FIGURE 33

SIR JOSHUA REYNOLDS
Maria Anne Fitzherbert (née Smythe)
1786 – 88
OIL ON CANVAS
36 X 28 IN (91.4 X 71.1 CM)
NATIONAL PORTRAIT GALLERY, LONDON
LENT BY TWEED INVESTMENTS LTD., 1976
(L162)

woman's body seems to man to be his property, his thing." Is this how we are to see Gainsborough's Ann Ford, as — Beauvoir again — "narcissism in concrete form . . . a uniform and an adornment"?[68] The art historian Ann Bermingham seems to decry the eighteenth-century woman's "self-absorbed delight in her own appearance," and specifically "the musician's desire to appear beautiful to herself is ultimately directed to the desiring gaze of the beholder," a possible reference to Gainsborough's portrait of Ann Ford.[69] But it is ahistorical to attribute *our* ideas of dress to those living in past eras, to claim, as Bermingham does, that fashion's "emphasis on the female body as a surface of changing appearances . . . cut against the idea of the body as an expression of inner character or psychological essence."[70]

Social identity is, of course, constructed via dress and pose, but this fact was true for both genders in the eighteenth century: men were equally subject to the "tyrant of Fashion." Even though their clothing seemed to change less frequently, the details and nuances of *style* were as dictatorial as female dress codes. But in the new feminine culture of the period, which, as Rémy G. Saisselin suggests, relied on pleasure, on "the cultivation of the agreeable arts," more attention was devoted to the appearance of women and therefore to their clothes and hairstyles; from the 1770s, illustrated journals regularly reported female fashions. Saisselin claims that fashion was more about appearance than rank, seeing Gainsborough as an innovator, with his portraits of women in particular, in the creation of "pure appearance, what we call an *image*."[71] While Saisselin's argument apropos appearance as image isn't altogether clear, there is clearly a case for seeing in Gainsborough's great portraits of "professional" and "modern" women, beginning with Ann Ford, some downplaying of social status in favor of the triumph of fashionable appearance.

68
Ibid., 176 and 505.

69
Ann Bermingham,
"Elegant Females and
Gentlemen Connoisseurs:
The Commerce in Culture and Self-Image in
Eighteenth-Century England," in Brewer and
Bermingham, *Consumption of Culture*, 500–501.

70
Ann Bermingham,
"The Picturesque and
Ready-to-Wear Femininity," in *The Politics of
the Picturesque: Literature, Landscape and
Aesthetics Since 1700*, ed.
Stephen Copley and
Peter Garside (Cambridge: Cambridge
University Press, 1994),
106.

71
Rémy Saisselin, *The
Enlightenment Against
the Baroque: Economics
and Aesthetics in the
Eighteenth Century*
(Berkeley: University of
California Press, 1992),
124.

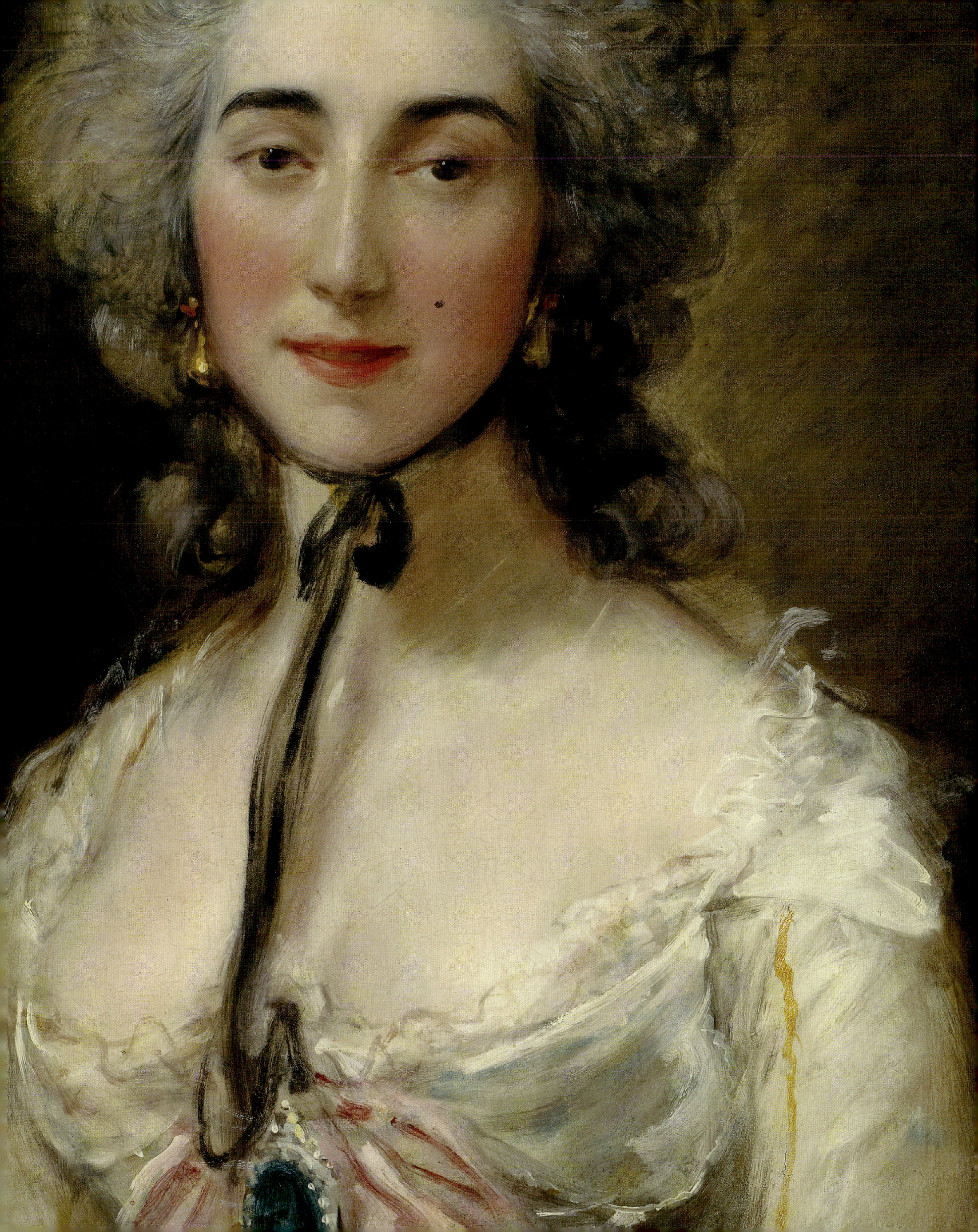

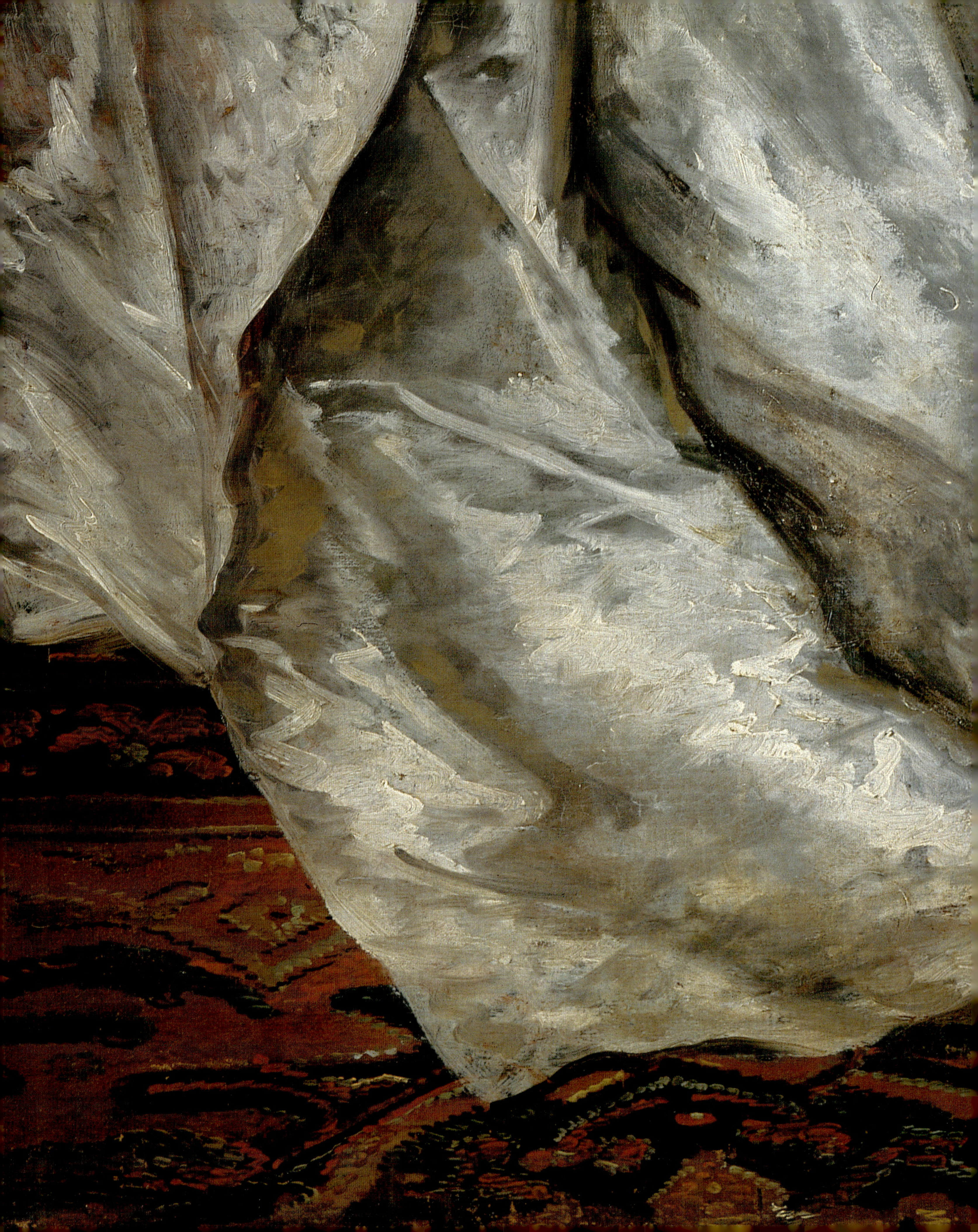

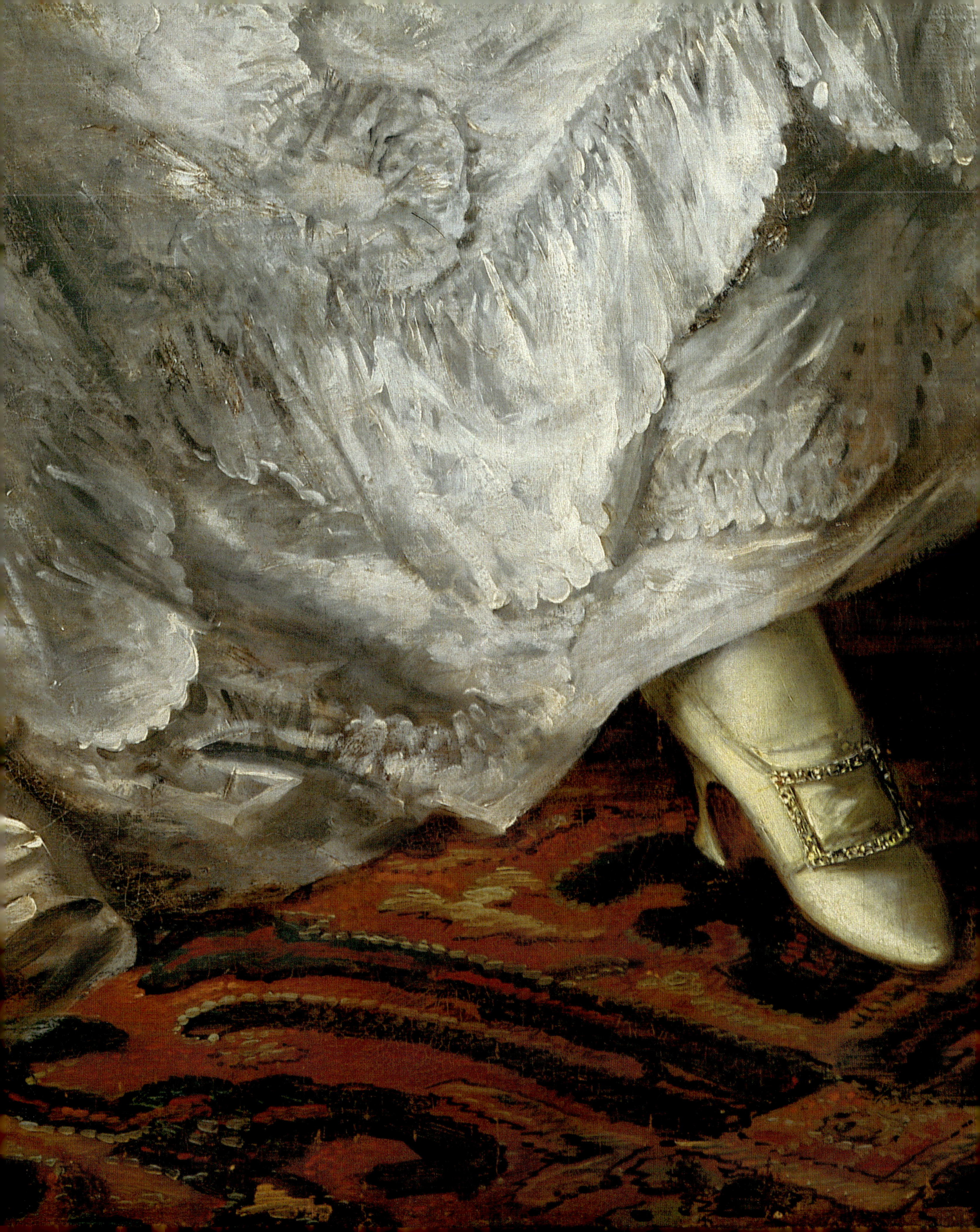

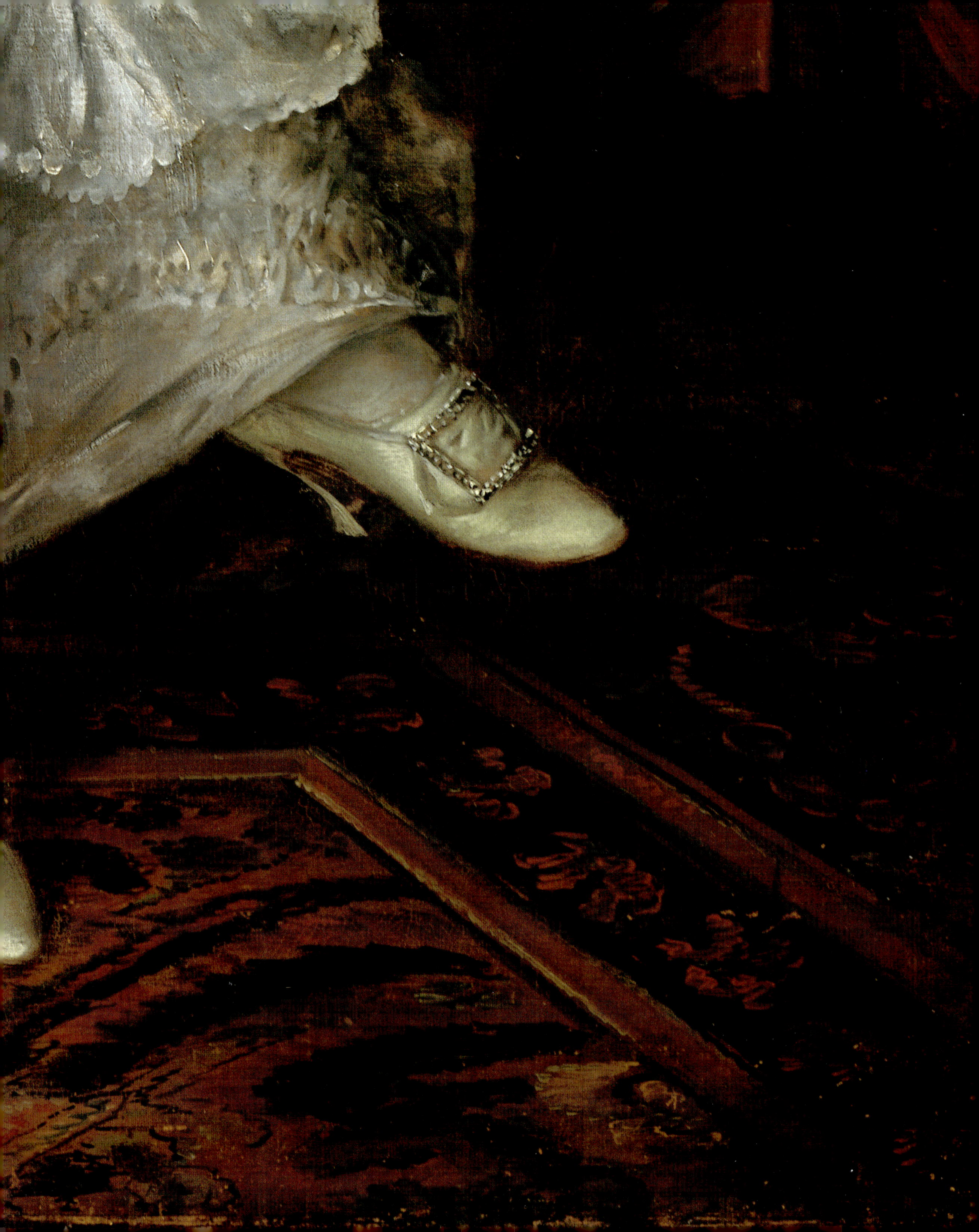

" Virtue IN A Vicious Age " :

Fashioning Feminine Identity in Eighteenth-Century London

"Censorious folly; noisy party-rage;
The thousand tongues with which she must engage
Who dares have virtue in a vicious age."

LADY MARY WORTLEY MONTAGU,
"CONSTANTINOPLE TO —" [1]

By Amber Ludwig

THE EIGHTEENTH CENTURY'S preoccupation with identity is not too far removed from our own twenty-first-century obsession. Though the standards for what constituted an acceptable or admirable identity differed from today's, people in the eighteenth century were interested in fashioning a public image to communicate their most worthy and interesting characteristics. In a time without our variety of means of communication — the Web, television, radio — choices for conveying one's public identity to a large audience were limited to written statements and painted or printed images. Women, in particular, were vulnerable to criticism in the patriarchal eighteenth century, and as they were often — then as now — judged on their appearance, portraiture was the natural choice for expressing and contesting a woman's character. Women who transgressed societal norms were particularly at risk for defamation and reports of scandal, and their portraits often negotiated the precarious social place they occupied.

Lady Mary Wortley Montagu, the author of the above verse, was one of these transgressive women. She traveled extensively and was a successful writer, with many of her works both acclaimed and condemned during her lifetime.[2] In these final three lines of her poem "Constantinople To —," Montagu creates an image of crowded drawing rooms filled with wildly foolish people the

[1]
Lady Mary Wortley Montagu, "Constantinople To—," in *A New Miscellany*, ed. Anthony Hammond (London: Printed for T. Jauncy, 1720), lines 107–9.

[2]
Alexander Pope (1688–1744), in particular, denigrated Montagu's work and her lifestyle, especially after she rebuffed his sexual advances. See Cynthia Lowenthal, *Lady Mary Wortley Montagu and the Eighteenth-Century Familiar Letter* (Athens: University of Georgia Press, 1994).

speaker must interact with. Presumably, the "thousand tongues with which she must engage" are ready to condemn nontraditional women like Montagu who transcend the established boundaries of their sex. Such was the reality of eighteenth-century London for many women, not just Montagu. Actresses like Sarah Siddons and Mary Robinson had to combat the negative associations of their chosen career. Women with disreputable pasts and dreams of grandeur, like Emma Hamilton, faced great social obstacles when marrying or loving men beyond their station in life. Thomas Gainsborough feared for his daughters' future in the "vicious" eighteenth century, and his portraits of them reflect his anxiety. For all these women, portraiture served as a line of defense against the "thousand tongues."

The poem's concluding image of "censorious folly" and "noisy party-rage" contrasts with the bucolic vision at the beginning of the poem:

> Give me, great God! said I, a little farm,
> In summer shady, and in winter warm;
> Where a clear spring gives birth to murm'ring brooks,
> By nature gliding down the mossy rocks.
> Not artfully by leaden pipes convey'd,
> Or greatly falling in a forc'd cascade,
> Pure and unsully'd winding thro' the shade.
> All-bounteous Heaven has added to my prayer
> A softer climate, and a purer air.[3]

The speaker implores God to provide her with a rural paradise, absent of artifice in its landscape and, presumably, in its inhabitants. Montagu seems to have enjoyed this kind of respite from the difficulties of life in England when she lived in Constantinople from 1716 to 1718. She accompanied her husband, the ambassador and diplomat Edward Wortley Montagu, on the seven-month journey to Constantinople, and though the poem idealizes Montagu's home away from home, her other writings reveal that despite the freedoms Turkey afforded her, the country had its own models of femininity. As an Englishwoman abroad, Montagu now had two sets of cultural standards to follow.

Neither Western nor Near Eastern culture fully respected women's intellectual curiosity or achievement in the eighteenth century. As a child, Montagu taught herself languages and studied various forms of poetry and prose in her father's

3
Montagu, "Constantinople To—," lines 1–9.

well-appointed library; women were not allowed a formal education. The result of her education and travel was the publication of *The Turkish Embassy Letters* in 1763, one year after her death. In an early, unpublished collection of the letters, Montagu's friend and fellow writer Mary Astell praised the writings in an effort to provide their author with proper admiration during her lifetime.

> If these Letters appear hereafter, when I am in my grave,
> let this attend them, in testimony to posterity that among her
> contemporaries, one woman at least was just to her merit. . . .
> I confess I am malicious enough to desire that the world should see
> to how much better purpose the LADIES travel than their LORDS; and that,
> whilst it is surfeited with *male* Travels, all in the same tone, and stuffed
> with the same trifles, a lady has the skill to strike out a new path, and to
> embellish a worn-out subject with variety of fresh and elegant entertainment.
> . . . Let us freely own the superiority of this sublime genius
> as I do in the sincerity of my soul; pleased that a *woman* triumphs,
> and proud to follow in her train.[4]

Montagu's travel to and study of the Ottoman Empire made her an outsider among most of her female peers, while also challenging the intellectual authority of many Englishmen in positions of power.[5] Though her writings strongly and pointedly assert her intelligence, portraits of Montagu demonstrate her delicate negotiation of power to fashion a nonthreatening identity acceptable to both Western and Near Eastern audiences. In short, the portraits simultaneously diffuse and emphasize the power she attained through her travel and exploration.[6]

Jonathan Richardson, who worked several generations before Gainsborough, painted Montagu in Turkish dress around 1725, almost a decade after her return from the Levant (FIGURE 34). Montagu presents herself to the viewer in a vaguely Eastern costume with a turbanlike headdress. The representation is one of colonial power and exotic sexuality: Eastern dress worn decoratively on a porcelain-skinned European accompanied by a young African boy. Montagu dominates the low horizon line, and a picturesque scene of Constantinople fades into the sunset. The work is painted in the tradition of grand manner portraits of the seventeenth century, a stylistic convention that continued well into the nineteenth century, and quotes the *Marchesa Elena Grimaldi Cattaneo* (FIGURE 35) of Anthony Van Dyck. Unlike the Marchesa, who is dressed in Western-style clothing of the seventeenth century, Montagu dons a white silk foundation garment called a *salvar*, over which is a close-fitting *anteri* cinched by a jeweled

4
Mary Astell, preface to *The Turkish Embassy Letters* by Lady Mary Wortley Montagu (1724). See also George Paston, *Lady Mary Wortley Montagu and her Times* (New York: G. P. Putnam, 1907), 313.

5
Anne McClintock, *Imperial Leather: Race, Gender, and Sexuality in the Colonial Conquest* (New York: Routledge, 1995), 24.

6
Marcia Pointon, *Hanging the Head: Portraiture and Social Formation in Eighteenth-Century England* (New Haven: Yale University Press, 1993), 141–57.

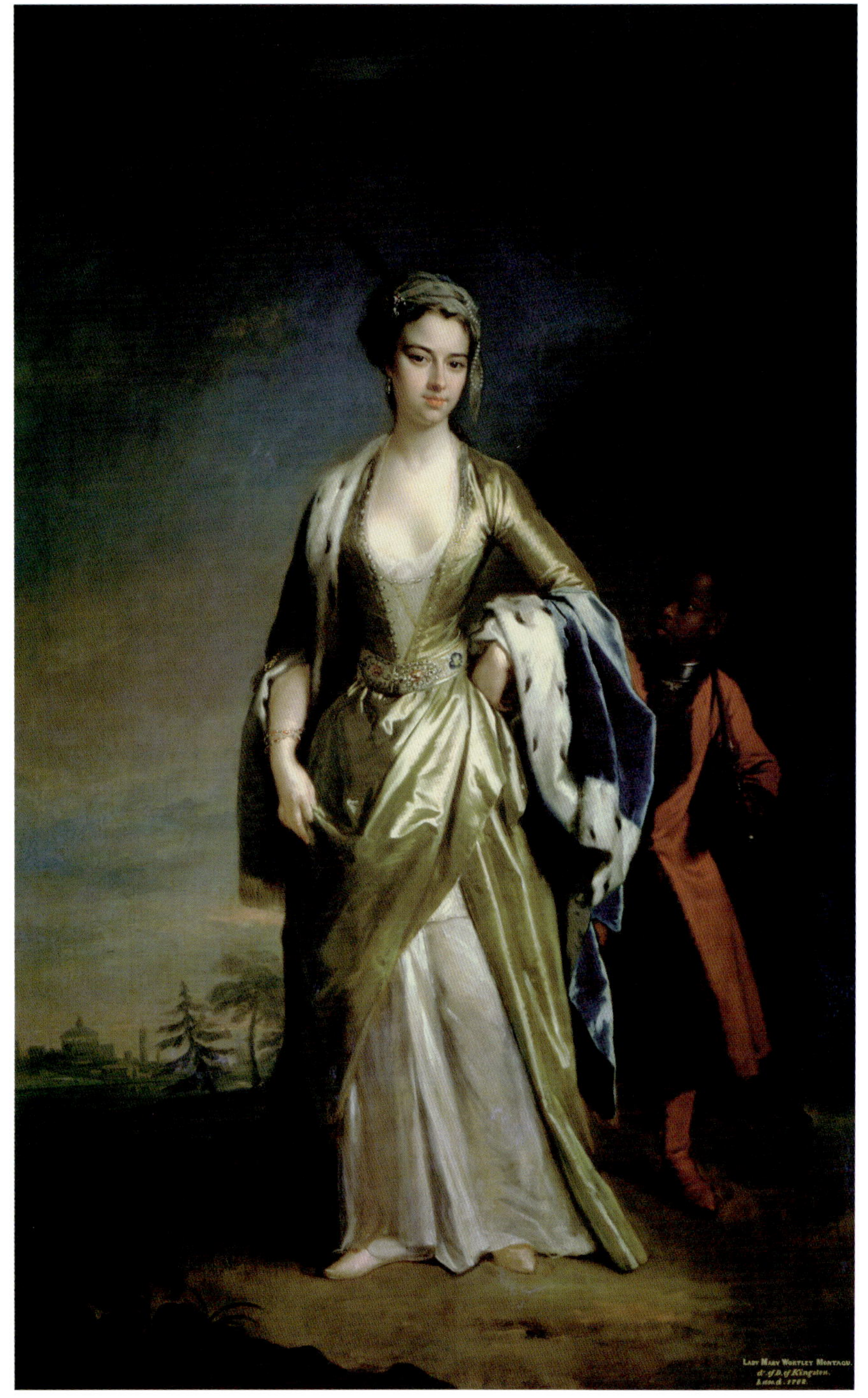

FIGURE 34

JONATHAN RICHARDSON (attr.)
Lady Mary Wortley Montagu
CA. 1725
OIL ON CANVAS
94-1/8 X 57 IN (239 X 144.8 CM)
PRIVATE COLLECTION

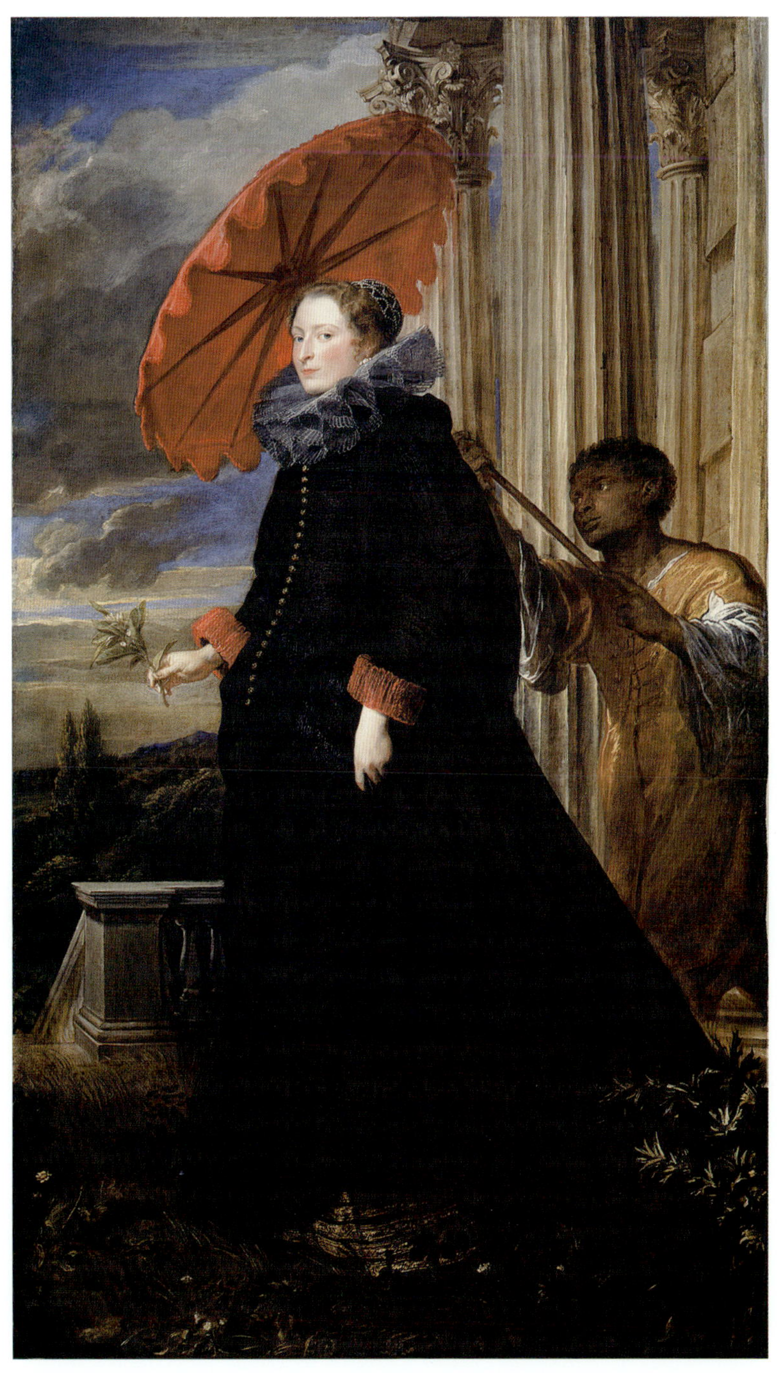

FIGURE 35

SIR ANTHONY VAN DYCK
Marchesa Elena Grimaldi Cattaneo
1623
OIL ON CANVAS
95-5/8 X 54-1/2 IN (242.9 X 138.5 CM)
NATIONAL GALLERY OF ART, WASHINGTON
WIDENER COLLECTION (1942.9.92)

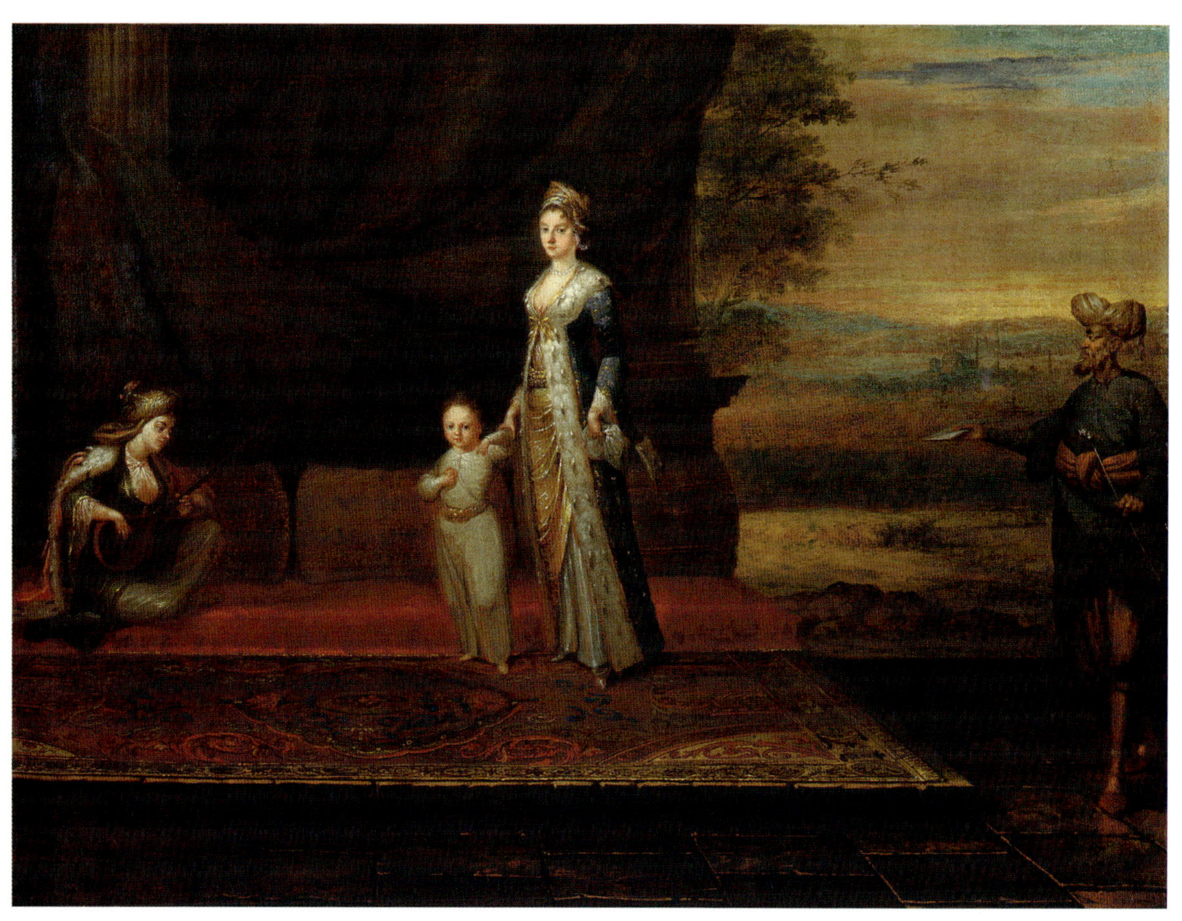

FIGURE 36

JEAN-BAPTISTE VANMOUR
Lady Mary Wortley Montagu and her Son, Edward Wortley Montagu,
and attendants
CA. 1717
OIL ON CANVAS
27-1/4 X 35-3/4 IN (69.3 X 90.9 CM)
NATIONAL PORTRAIT GALLERY, LONDON
PURCHASED, 1958 (3924)

belt. Her ermine-lined coat, called a *kirk*, contributes to the imperial tone of the portrait.

The art historian Marcia Pointon indicates that Montagu's costume differs in specific details from popular engravings of Turkish dress and what she describes herself wearing in Constantinople.[7] Her stiff satin *anteri* is gold rather than the typical patterned white-and-gold damask, and the plunging neckline barely conceals her breasts. In proper eighteenth-century Turkish dress, a woman would have most likely worn a piece of sheer fabric over her décolletage and under the *anteri*. It is unclear from the Richardson portrait whether Montagu's *salvar* is a skirt, rather than a pair of the trouserlike drawers that Turkish women — and Montagu while in Constantinople — wore in the eighteenth century.[8] This ambiguity allows Montagu to separate herself from Muslim women, whom as a colonial Briton she dominated, and also from men. Her slim waist and curvaceous hips convey a sexual and idealized femininity that British viewers would have expected and appreciated in 1725.[9]

Montagu's assertion of a mixed cultural identity was not something she initiated only after returning to England. During her stay in Constantinople, Montagu herself likely commissioned from Jean-Baptiste Vanmour, Painter-in-Ordinary to the Sultan, a double portrait with her son (FIGURE 36).[10] The work, which shows mother and son in Turkish dress, affirms Montagu's place in society by representing a woman in the traditional role of mother. The portrait, complete with Montagu's stern, controlling gaze, also suggests the subject's fertility, a faculty conferred upon women alone. The high value Ottoman society put on fertility and child rearing as important female virtues was very different from the attitude toward birth in Britain at the start of the eighteenth century. The more "natural" theories of child rearing espoused by John Locke in *Some Thoughts Concerning Education* (1693) had yet to become popular, and Jean-Jacques Rousseau's *Emile, ou l'éducation* wasn't published until 1762. During the eighteenth century, it was common for upper-class Englishwomen to give birth and then immediately hire a wetnurse and nanny to care for the children.[11]

Turkish women exhibited a certain amount of scorn for this approach to motherhood, since in their culture a woman's worth was often tied to her ability to produce and raise many children. In a letter, Montagu expresses her frustration with the Turkish view.

7
Ibid., 145.

8
Pointon describes the *salvar* as a skirt in the Richardson portrait, rather than trousers, but I believe it is ambiguous. Ibid., 145.

9
This work is particularly idealized considering that Montagu's face was marred by smallpox as a child. She was left with scars and lost her eyelashes and eyebrows.

10
Pointon, *Hanging the Head*, 149. Vanmour was in the Ottoman Empire by 1699 and, from 1725, was Painter-in-Ordinary to the Sultan. His time in Constantinople overlaps with Montagu's; thus one can reasonably assume that this work was, at least in part, painted from life.

11
For an extended discussion of childhood in eighteenth-century Britain, see James Christen Steward, *The New Child: British Art and the Origins of Modern Childhood, 1730–1830* (Seattle: University of Washington Press, 1995).

> [T]hey reason that the
> End of the Creation of Woman is to encrease and Multiply,
> and she is only properly employ'd in the Works of her calling
> when she is bringing children or takeing care of 'em,
> which are all the Virtues that God expects from her; and indeed
> their way of Life, which shuts them out of all public commerce,
> does not permit them any other.[12]

In not being pregnant and having only one child, Montagu was further separated from these women, contributing to her status as an outsider. When she became pregnant in Constantinople with her second child, Montagu realized the acceptance and approval she could gain from her Turkish peers.

> I am at this present writing not very much . . . ,
> my head being wholly fill'd with the preparations necessary
> for the Encrease of my family, which I expect every day.
> You may easily guess at my uneasie Situation; but I am, however,
> in some degree comforted by the glory that accrues to me from it,
> and a reflection to the contempt I shou'd otherwise fall under. . . .
> [I]n this country 'tis more despicable to be marry'd and not fruitfull,
> than 'tis with us to be fruitfull before Marriage.[13]

After the birth of her daughter, she continues the comparison between the Near Eastern and Western perspectives regarding birth.

> In this country, it is just as necessary to show proofs of youth,
> to be recognized among beauties, as it is to show proofs of Nobility
> to be admitted among the Knights of Malta. I was very angry
> at this necessity; but, noticing that people looked at me
> with a great air of contempt, I finaly [sic] complied with the fashion,
> and I lay in like the others.[14]

These dismissive comments are about as much as Montagu ever wrote on the subject of her own pregnancy. She experienced the anxiety and marginalization of being different from the majority of women in the Ottoman Empire. Even if her British correspondents shared her own feelings about childbirth and marriage, those who constituted her physical environment held different values. The culturally dominant attitude toward what was considered women's "natural" role

12
Lady Mary Wortley Montagu, May 29, 1717, *The Complete Letters of Lady Mary Wortley Montagu*, ed. Robert Halsband (Oxford: Clarendon Press, 1966), 1:363.

13
Ibid., Jan. 4, 1718, 1:372.

14
Ibid., April 1718, 1:403–4.

may have encouraged Montagu to commission a portrait with her son by her side in an effort to demonstrate her maternal qualities.

Though Vanmour's portrait of Montagu with her son attempts to communicate her similarity to Turkish women, the work cannot help asserting her colonial power within the traditional role of mother. She is positioned between a woman playing a *tehegour* at the left and a man delivering a letter at the right of the composition. The musician associates Montagu with the pleasures of the rich cultural life afforded to her during her time in the Ottoman Empire. The man delivering the letter, as Pointon contends, is a reminder of Montagu's more professional role as a correspondent.[15] Since the viewer is not allowed to know the information contained in the letter, Montagu maintains power despite being the object of the viewer's gaze.[16] The letter also implies the idea of travel, since the missive is probably from one of Montagu's many correspondents back in London. The work is strangely disjointed, with Montagu standing in the center of the composition, elevated on what appears to be a Hereke carpet.[17] The combination of business and pleasure, arts and letters, alongside traditional woman and powerful colonial communicates the complex identity Montagu assumed as a Briton in the Ottoman Empire.

Montagu's role as both mother and foreigner is also evident in her location and pose within this portrait. She physically occupies a space that is neither clearly outside nor inside. Classical columns and a large swag of cloth separate the open air from the covered patio, so that she is neither a woman protected within the domestic sphere nor a colonial engaged in political or economic endeavors. The presence of the man with a letter, however, hints that she is involved in something other than raising her child, which, according to her correspondence mentioned above, is undoubtedly correct. Perhaps further signaling her apathy toward motherhood, Montagu grasps her son's elbow aggressively, which hints at a controlling and unsympathetic relationship between parent and child. Montagu seems to hover between a symbolic East, represented by the romantic sunset and generic background with a mosque at the right (or east) of the picture, and a more civilized West, indicated by the enclosed space with the woman playing the *tehegour* at the left (or west) of the composition. Montagu's Europeanized clothing also places her in a sphere similar to, but ultimately different from, those Turkish women with whom she associated during her stay in Constantinople.

15
Pointon, *Hanging the Head*, 156–57.

16
Ibid., 157.

17
My thanks to Professor Bruce Redford for making this identification.

Aristocratic women with intellectual ambitions were not the only objects of scorn in the "vicious age" of the eighteenth century. Actresses, too, were acutely aware of the need to establish a reputation that clearly announced their principled decency. Long associated with provocative self-display and prostitution, the actress fought an uphill public relations battle in the second half of the eighteenth century. William Hogarth, one of Gainsborough's immediate predecessors, satirized the profession in the engraving *Strolling Actresses Dressing in a Barn* (FIGURE 37).[18] A theatrical troupe prepares for a performance of *The Devil to Pay in Heaven*, as indicated by the playbill near the bottom left of the composition. A ragtag band of actresses practice their parts and dress for the show. At the center of the chaos, the woman playing the role of Diana, the chaste goddess of the hunt, stares at the viewer as she assumes an exaggerated pose. Unlike the virgin goddess of Roman mythology, the actress exudes sexuality. Her come-hither gaze invites the viewer to look at her body in its state of undress. The hoopskirt has fallen from her hips to expose her stockings and an expanse of thigh, and her chemise plunges open, revealing her breast. The tattered underclothes contrast with her bejeweled hairstyle and comely face. At far right, Juno, queen of the gods and goddesses, is rehearsing. Her costume is in a similar state of disrepair, and the troupe's personification of Night darns a hole in Juno's stocking. Throughout the print, Hogarth draws the viewer's attention to the disparity between the fantasy of the performance and the reality of the situation. Onstage, these women become immortal goddesses and are not encumbered by the limitations of modern society. Lest audiences be deceived by the art of acting, Hogarth shows the mediocre truth of these women's lives: threadbare costumes, painted faces and stage sets, and a dilapidated barn for a dressing room.

Sarah Siddons, the preeminent actress of the eighteenth century, employed portraiture to craft an image of virtuous femininity in opposition to the general belief that actresses were not far removed from prostitutes. Siddons was born into a middle-class family of actors, the Kembles, and began her career as a provincial traveling player with them, first performing onstage around the age of eleven.[19] At nineteen she married a fellow actor, William Siddons, against her parents' wishes but returned to the stage with her father's troupe one month later. The early 1780s saw success for Siddons at London's Drury Lane after a less than triumphant appearance there in late 1775. It is during this early period of success that the actress realized the power of the portrait. The artist William Hamilton painted the first portrait of the actress in 1780 and exhibited it at the Royal Academy with little fanfare, but by May 1783, crowds were filling Hamilton's studio to see another portrait of Siddons in character.

18
Sean Shesgreen, ed., *Engravings by Hogarth* (New York: Dover Publications, 1973), no. 46. See also Ronald Paulson, *Hogarth's Graphic Works* (New Haven: Yale University Press, 1989).

19
For a thorough biography and chronology of Sarah Siddons's life, see Robyn Asleson, ed., *A Passion for Performance: Sarah Siddons and Her Portraitists* (Los Angeles: Getty Publications, 1999). This exhibition catalogue also contains an excellent bibliography relating to Sarah Siddons and portraits of actors and actresses in the eighteenth century.

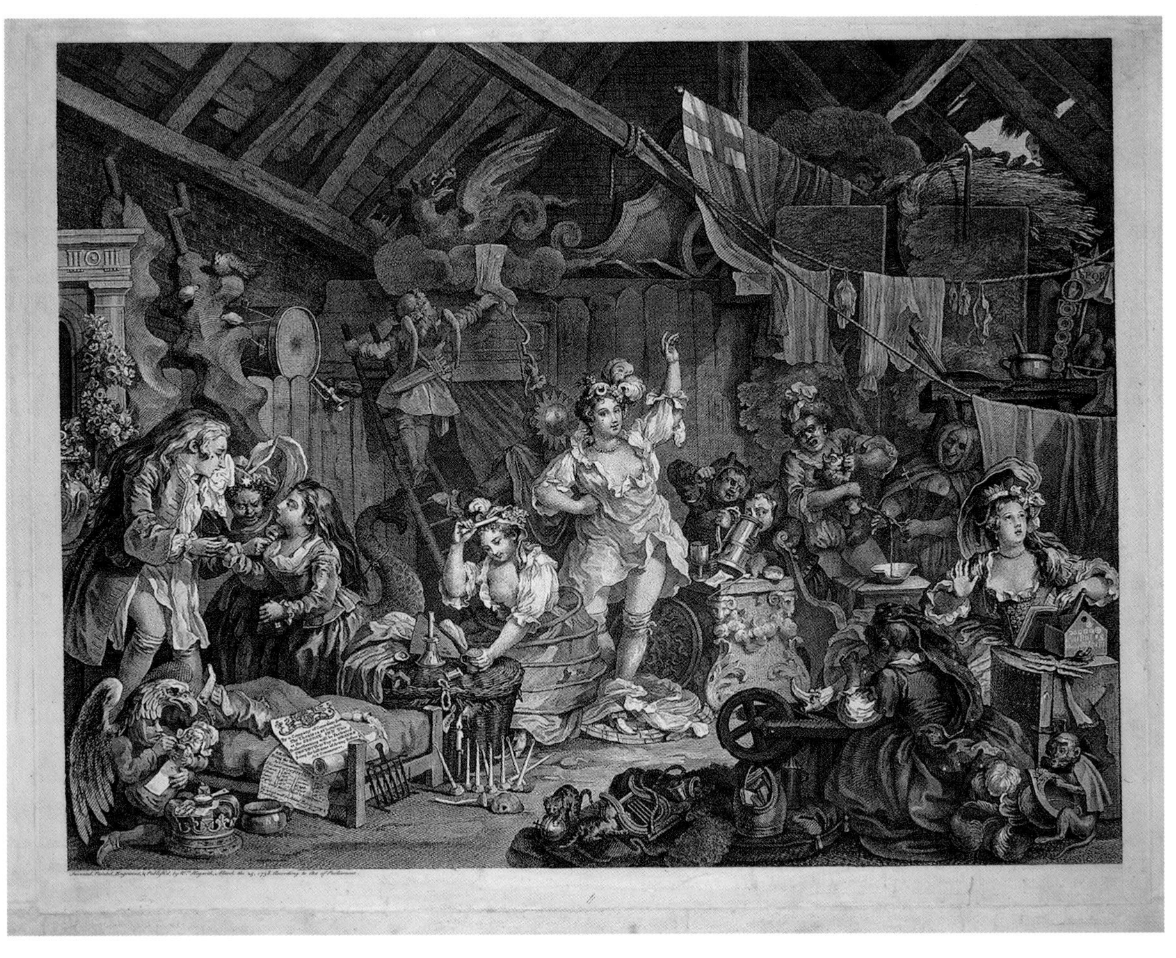

FIGURE 37

WILLIAM HOGARTH
Strolling Actresses Dressing in a Barn
1738
ETCHING
17-1/2 X 22-3/16 IN (44.5 X 56.3 CM)
BRITISH MUSEUM
(1857, 1857,0509.12)

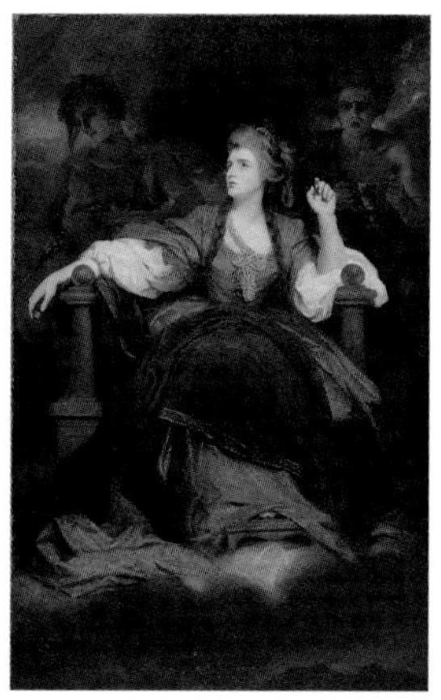

Thomas Beach also exhibited portraits of her at the Society of British Artists. The portraits, which depict Siddons in roles contemporary audiences came to associate with her, essentially served as advertisements for her performances and her talent as a tragedienne, while simultaneously bringing renown to the artists themselves. Sir Joshua Reynolds, Gainsborough's greatest rival, realized early in his career that celebrity sitters such as Siddons could bring attention to his portrait practice, and he eventually created an informal gallery in his studio of portraits of contemporary personalities.[20] Consequently, at the same time Hamilton and Beach were exhibiting their portraits of her, the actress began sitting at Reynolds's studio for what would become her iconic image, *Sarah (Kemble) Siddons as the Tragic Muse* (FIGURE 10).

Siddons's dramatic posture in Reynolds's portrait resembles the poses assumed by the subjects in Hogarth's *Strolling Actresses Dressing in a Barn*. Unlike Hogarth, however, Reynolds merges seamlessly the sitter and her timeless personification.[21] The actress's face — notably her distinctive nose, about which Gainsborough reputedly exclaimed "Confound the nose, there's no end to it" when he painted her portrait in 1785 — is recognizable, and her costume is generalized so as to suggest both antiquity and contemporary fashion.[22] Reynolds advocated this technique in portraits, particularly those of women, in order to lend the subject an air of grandeur. In his *Discourses*, the artist writes on his theory of portraiture:

> He therefore who in his practice of portrait-painting wishes to
> dignify his subject, which we will suppose to be a lady,
> will not paint her in the modern dress, the familiarity of which
> alone is sufficient to destroy all dignity. He takes care
> that his work shall correspond to those ideas and that
> imagination which he knows will regulate the judgment of others;
> and therefore dresses his figure something with the general air
> of the antique for the sake of dignity, and preserves something
> of the modern for the sake of likeness.[23]

Reynolds's portrait of Siddons follows the artist's own instructions to students and was so successful in communicating the essence of her talent that the painting was exhibited onstage alongside its subject, who imitated herself in the painting.[24] The relationship between the artist and the actress was mutually

---

20
For more information on Reynolds and his relationships with celebrities, see Martin Postle, ed., *Joshua Reynolds: The Creation of Celebrity* (London: Tate Publishing, 2005).

21
The portrait follows in the popular tradition of showing women in the guises of goddesses or personifications. See Andrew Wilton, *The Swagger Portrait: Grand Manner Portraiture in Britain from Van Dyck to Augustus John, 1630–1930* (London: Tate Gallery, 1992). Wilton argues that portraits of women in the late eighteenth century were necessarily more imaginative and inventive than those of men. A man's value was inherent in his social role of patriarch, and the impersonation of an idea or classical character was not required. Women were empty vessels to be filled with meaning, and actresses were particularly adroit at assuming roles, whether onstage or on canvas.

22
William Vaughan, *Gainsborough* (New York: Thames and Hudson, 2002), 179.

23
Sir Joshua Reynolds, *Discourses on Art*, ed. Stephen O. Mitchell, Library of Liberal Arts (New York: Bobbs-Merrill, 1965), 115–16.

24
William van Lennep,
ed., *Reminiscences of
Sarah Kemble Siddons,
1773–1785* (Cambridge,
Mass.: Widener Library,
1942), 16. In her
Reminiscences, Siddons
takes credit for the
posture she assumes.
"When I attended him
for the first sitting, after
many more gratifying
encomiums than I dare
repeat, he took me
by the hand, saying,
'Ascend your undisputed
throne and graciously
bestow upon me some
good idea of the Tragic
Muse.' " In doing so,
she presents herself
as naturally able to
communicate the essence
of tragedy. It has been
noted in various other
places, however, that
Reynolds contributed
equally, if not more, to
the noble manner of the
work, copying the pose
of the prophet Isaiah
from Michelangelo's Sis-
tine ceiling. See Asleson,
Passion for Performance,
69–73.

25
Reynolds, *Discourses*,
116.

26
Mary Robinson,
*Memoirs of the Late
Mrs. Robinson, Written
by Herself*, 2 vols.
(London: Printed for
Richard Phillips by C.
Mercier, 1803), 1:2.

27
John Ingamells, *Mrs.
Robinson and Her
Portraits* (London:
Trustees of the Wallace
Collection, 1978), 8.

28
Ibid., 11.

beneficial. Reynolds received exposure through the work's exhi-bition and subsequent reproduction in prints, while Siddons's public image finally had an appropriately majestic emblem.

Like his rival, Gainsborough associated himself with performers, including Siddons, but his portraits are not imbued, as Reynolds phrases it, with "the general air of the antique for the sake of dignity."[25] Gainsborough's portraits focus on the individual-ity of the sitter, and his likenesses of actresses underscore their particular identities rather than their profession. Gainsborough's portrait of Siddons (PLATE 9), thoughtfully analyzed by Benedict Leca in this catalogue, shows the actress not as one of the characters she made famous but as a lady of means, dressed in fashionable and luxurious clothing. The actress Mrs. Mary Robinson, a contemporary of Siddons, sat for Gainsborough a few years before Siddons, and the result is a strikingly beautiful and melancholy full-length portrait (FIGURE 28). Robinson, like Montagu, was also a writer, and, by the end of her life, she shared Montagu's cynicism regarding the viciousness of the eighteenth century, which she termed a "world of duplicity and sorrow."[26]

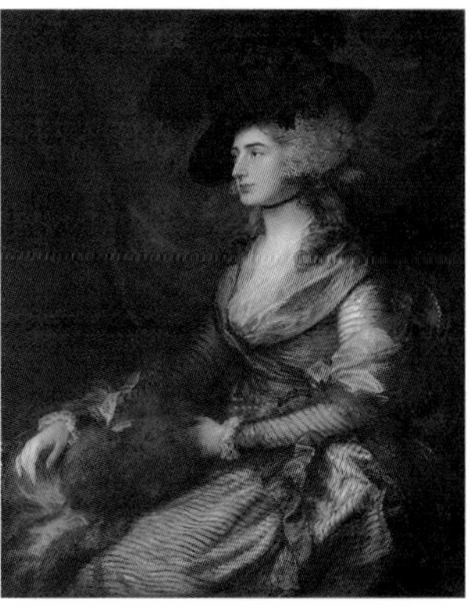

PLATE 9
Sarah Siddons

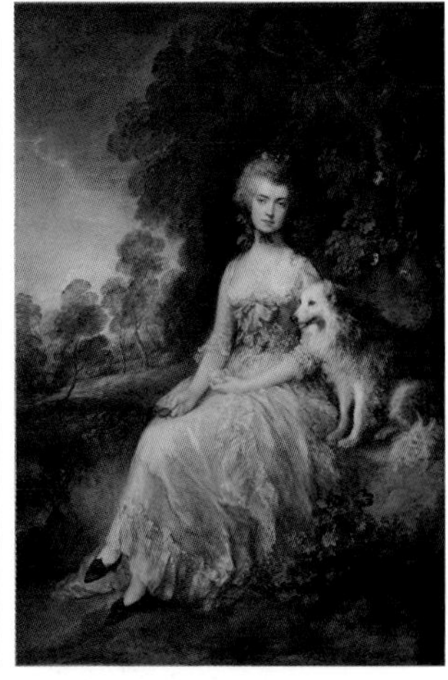

FIGURE 28
Mrs. Mary Robinson

Robinson made her stage debut as Juliet on December 10, 1776, after several years of hardship caused by her reckless husband. Thomas Robinson's debt and subsequent imprisonment compelled his wife to earn her own income. In addition to acting, Robinson published her first book of verse in the spring of 1775 with the patronage of the Duchess of Devonshire.[27] Her fame reached its height at the end of 1779 with a royal command per-formance of *The Winter's Tale*. The seventeen-year-old Prince of Wales, who had accompanied the king and queen to the play, was completely taken with Robinson's performance as Perdita and began to send her almost daily letters signed as her character's lover, Florizel.[28] By the spring of 1780, the two had begun meeting secretly at Kew. In June 1780, the affair was publicly known and commemorated with a satirical print published by A. Hamilton Jr. in the *Town and Country Magazine* (FIGURE 38). In the print, the couple gaze adoringly at each other, despite the symbolic confines of the oval frames. Robinson soon renounced her acting career, trusting the prince to abide by his promises to care for her financially. When the affair ended less than a year after it began, Robinson was left in debt and without a steady means of income. Adding insult to injury, she was now the butt of public jokes, rather than being the toast of the town. Another anonymous print — one of many — shows a bust-length caricature of the Prince of Wales as Florizel and Robinson as Perdita (FIGURE 39). The faces are joined along a vertical axis to create a composite portrait. At the left, a small caricature of George III, the prince's father, exclaims "Oh! My Son My Son." At the right, bust-length caricatures of Robinson's other lovers sit on a shelf supported by a stag-horned portrait of Thomas Robinson, under which is inscribed "King of Cuckolds."

Understandably, Mary Robinson was devastated after the end of the short-lived affair, especially since the prince's new lover was a Mrs. Armstead, former personal maid to Robinson.[29] Rather than retire into obscurity, Robinson continued life in the public sphere, engaging her critics and former lover through portraits. In 1781, the year after the affair, she sat for four portraits by the most revered portraitists of the eighteenth century, and the *Public Advertiser* took note: "The *Perdita* has been particularly successful in the commerce of this Year. How immense must have been her *Imports* and *Exports* is cognisable from this one Circumstance: she has sate for her Picture four times, viz. twice to *Romney*, once to *Gainsborough*, and once to *Sir Joshua Reynolds*!"[30] Gainsborough's

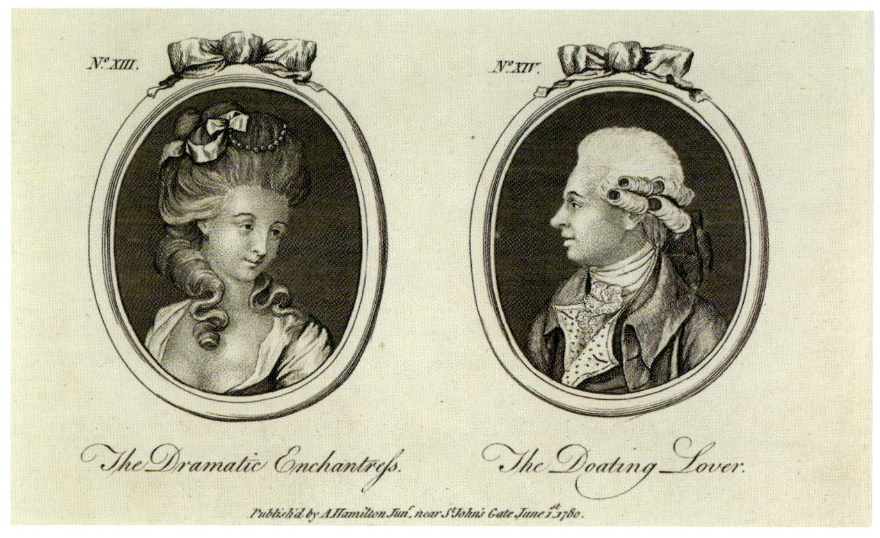

FIGURE 38

A. HAMILTON, JR. (publisher)
The Dramatic Enchantress/The Doating Lover
1780
ETCHING
4-1/8 X 6-7/8 IN (10.5 X 17.5 CM)
BRITISH MUSEUM (1948,0217.30)

29
Ibid., 14.

30
Public Advertiser,
April 19, 1782.
Quoted in Ingamells,
Mrs. Robinson, 30.

full-length portrait of Robinson is now generally agreed to be the most striking, though contemporary critics found it less than successful. The *Public Advertiser* disparaged it for "not being a likeness" and called the painting "one of his [Gainsborough's] Few Failures."[31]

The negative reception of the painting could be linked to its reproachful tone toward the Prince of Wales. Martin Levy has astutely argued that the portrait, "rather than being a depiction of her during her love affair, is in fact a portrait of her after it had ended; and . . . its purpose is to rebuke the Prince for his failure to honour his obligations."[32] Robinson sits in a serene pastoral landscape, the type Gainsborough took such pleasure in painting. It is a fairly typical portrait composition — a beautiful young woman in the countryside — meant to convey the subject's artlessness and rejection of superficial society, a society the Prince of Wales embodied with his profligacy. Robinson appears in harmony with the

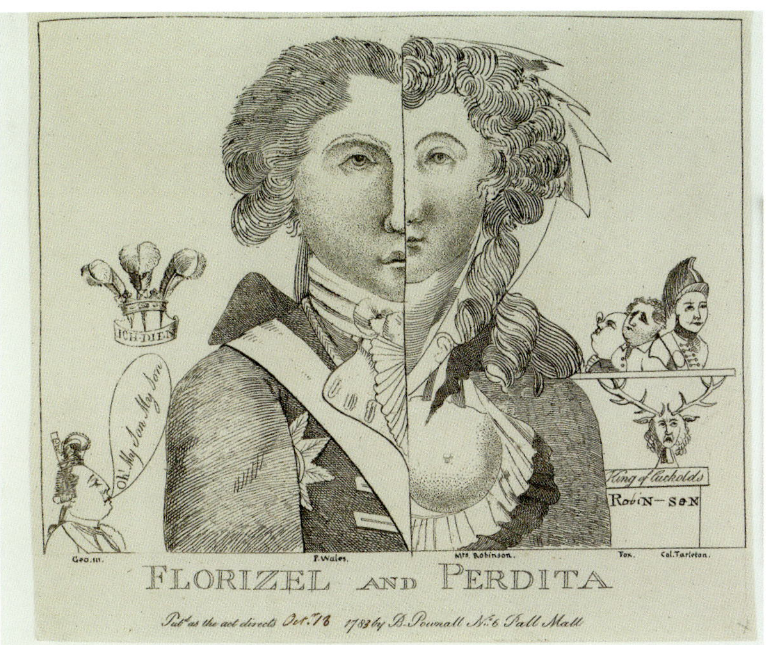

FIGURE 39

B. POWNALL (publisher)
Florizel and Perdita
1783
ETCHING
8-5/16 x 9-7/16 IN (21.1 x 23.9 CM)
BRITISH MUSEUM (1868,0808.5044)

31
Quoted in Ingamells, *Mrs. Robinson*, 31.

32
Martin Levy, "Gainsborough's *Mrs. Robinson*: A Portrait and its Context," *Apollo* 86 (September 1992): 154.

surrounding landscape; the delicate ruffles of her white dress complement the billowing trees and soft fur of her canine companion. She gazes out with a sincere and melancholy expression that makes the viewer feel as if he is sharing a private moment with her, despite the very public nature of the portrait.

In her hand, Robinson holds a miniature, which was considered a private token of affection in the eighteenth century. Though the portrait within the miniature is unclear, the subject is very likely the Prince of Wales.[33] The same year Gainsborough painted this portrait, Robinson was publicly seeking to make the prince accountable for his actions. In a series of items in the *Morning Herald*, Robinson's threats to her former lover are made explicit. One of these reads:

A certain *amour royal* is now totally at an end;
a separation has taken place *a thoro* for more than three weeks,
and a *settlement* worthy of such a *sultana* is the only thing
now wanting to break off all intercourse whatever.
Mrs. R—n thinking the adjustment of this part of the divorce
too essential to be trifled with, has roundly written to her once *ardent lover*,
"that if her establishment is not duly arranged within the space of
fourteen days from the commencement of the new year,
his — — must not be surprized, if he sees a full publication of
all those *seductory epistles* which alone estrange her from *virtue*
and the *marriage vow*!"[34]

Seen in this context, Gainsborough's beautiful portrait takes on a more aggressive tone. The inclusion of a handsome and attentive dog highlights the devotion the prince took for granted in his relationship with Robinson. In the case of the relationship between Robinson and the Prince of Wales, the silent art of portraiture plays the role of Montagu's "thousand tongues" in this "vicious age."

Like Robinson, Emma Hamilton lived a life often defined by her relationships to famous men. She began life as Amy Lyon, daughter of an illiterate Cheshire smith, and eventually gained international fame and notoriety through her many portraits, classically inspired performances, and affairs with powerful men. In the twenty-first century, people know her best as the lover of Horatio Nelson and wife of Sir William Hamilton. Her rise to fame began in a relatively serene manner, especially compared to how the rest of her life transpired. Her first serious lover, Charles Greville, insisted on her living a frugal and domestic life in

33
Ibid., 153. Robinson treasured a very similar object that the prince presented to her during one of their meetings at Kew. The miniature portrait of the prince was placed in a small case in which he had placed a heart-shaped piece of paper. The paper read "*Je ne change qu'en mourant*" and "Unalterable to my Perdita through life." Robinson had the miniature set in diamonds and always carried it with her. It was still in her possession just before her death.

34
Morning Herald, Jan. 5, 1781. Quoted in Levy, "Gainsborough's *Mrs. Robinson*," 154.

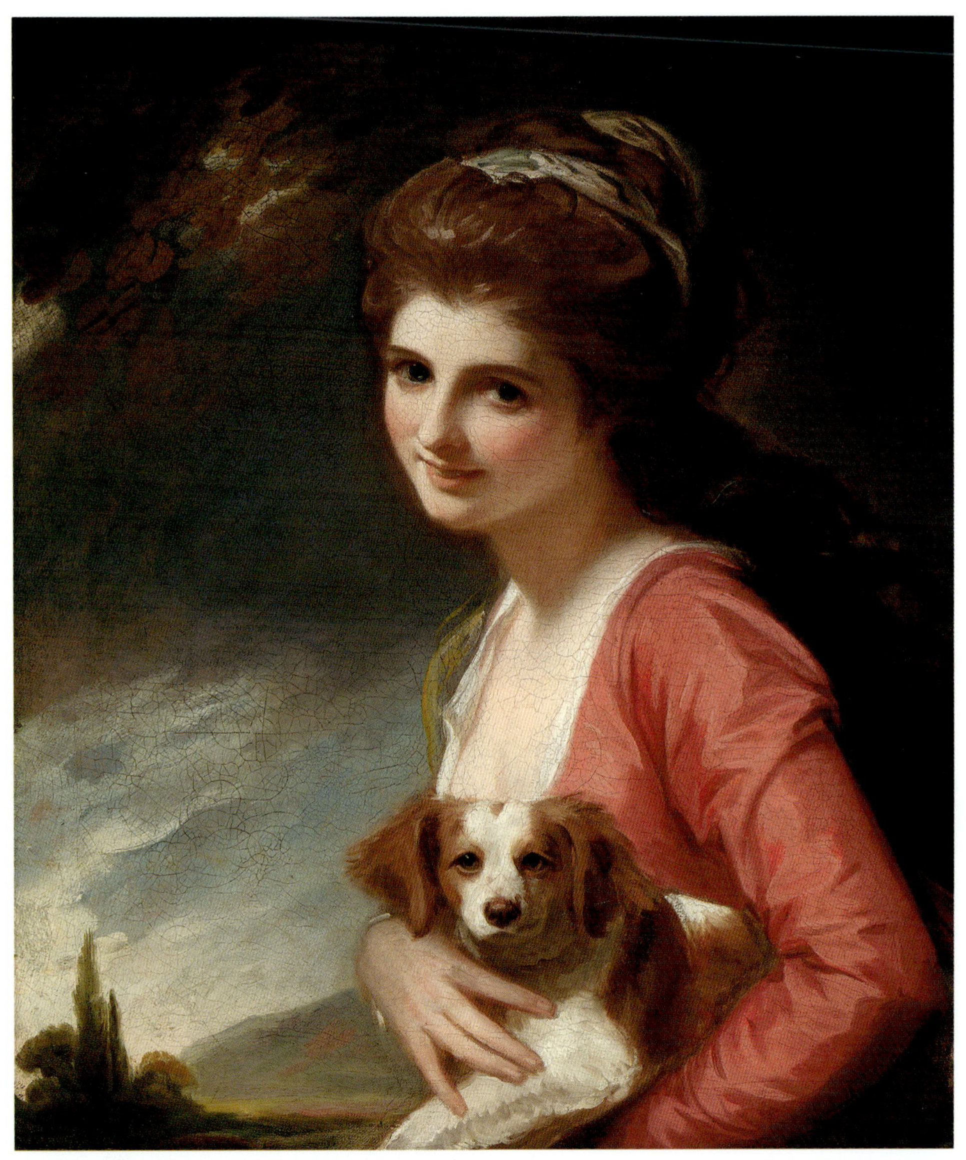

GEORGE ROMNEY
Lady Hamilton as 'Nature'
1782
OIL ON CANVAS
29-7/8 X 24-3/4 IN (75.88 X 62.87 CM)
THE FRICK COLLECTION
HENRY CLAY FRICK BEQUEST (1904.1.103)

the house he provided for her in an undeveloped section of London and advised her to adopt the name Mrs. Emma Hart. Greville, Sir William Hamilton's nephew, had a great interest in art and collecting, and the young Emma was the perfect model for artists. George Romney, one of the most fashionable portraitists of the late eighteenth century, painted Mrs. Emma Hart for the first time in 1782 (FIGURE 40).

Visits to Romney's studio in stylish Cavendish Square were some of the only instances when Greville allowed Emma to go out in public. By the beginning of 1782, when she began sitting for Romney, Greville had effectively restrained Emma's buoyant personality after an embarrassing scene at Ranelagh Gardens, a social gathering place in London. According to the anonymous author of the 1815 *Memoirs of Lady Hamilton,*

> Ambitious of displaying his conquest to the world of fashion,
> the lover conducted the lovely Emma, dressed out in a very elegant style,
> to Ranelagh, which was then the favourite theatre of gayety and gallantry.
> Here her form and agility attracted universal attention, and excited
> so much admiration that for once she gave way to a natural impulse;
> and to increase the applause with which she had been flattered,
> she gave the company some delightful specimens of her
> unrivalled powers both in musical expression, and flexibility of action.
> The consequence of all this was, as might be expected, that a convulsive
> sensation of astonishment and rapture ran through the whole assembly,
> whose plaudits proved so intoxicating to the object of them,
> that she redoubled her exertions and called forth
> renewed peals of applause.[35]

Greville reprimanded his mistress for her unseemly public display, and Emma quickly adopted the more discreet manner her protector preferred. That first Romney portrait of Emma from 1782, now known as *Lady Hamilton as 'Nature,'* reflects the attitude of devotion and innocence Greville wanted in his young lover. Her life before Greville, complete with a child born out of wedlock, reports of naked table dancing at parties, and perhaps a stint working as a nude model in Dr. Graham's Temple of Health, was wild, and a painting like *Nature* seeks to conceal her past. Through social performances — publicly in Ranelagh Gardens and more privately in Romney's studio — Emma was learning what it meant to be a woman in eighteenth-century London.

35
Anonymous, *Memoirs of Lady Hamilton with Illustrative Anecdotes of Many of her Most Particular Friends and Distinguished Contemporaries* (New York: David Huntington, 1815), 37–38.

Nature shows Emma frolicking in a windswept landscape in a red dress, a loyal dog resting in her arms and symbolizing her own fidelity to a master. The pose of the picture was commonly used for portrait commissions in the mid-eighteenth century, and Romney used the same posture in an earlier portrait of the Honorable Henrietta Stanley, the future Lady Horton (FIGURE 41).[36] As evidenced by the comparison, Emma imitates and enters the world of polite society through the means of portraiture. Henrietta Stanley, on the other hand, was born into the world of the nobility and was readily accepted by her peers. Her performance of femininity would have been ingrained into her actions from the earliest age, contributing to a more consistent presentation. The environment in the Stanley portrait is tranquil and serene, suggesting that the subject's personality matches it. In the portrait of Emma, a breeze blows gently through her hair, and she moves gracefully through the countryside in a bright red dress, all of which only hint at her spirited personality. Emma engages the viewer with a doe-eyed gaze, her chin demurely tilting downward. This is an image of a woman who acquiesces to her lover's desires. As the one who commissioned this work, Greville wanted Romney to create an image of what he wanted his youthful lover to become.

36
Ian Jenkins and Kim Sloan, *Vases and Volcanoes: Sir William Hamilton and His Collection* (London: British Museum, 1996), 269.

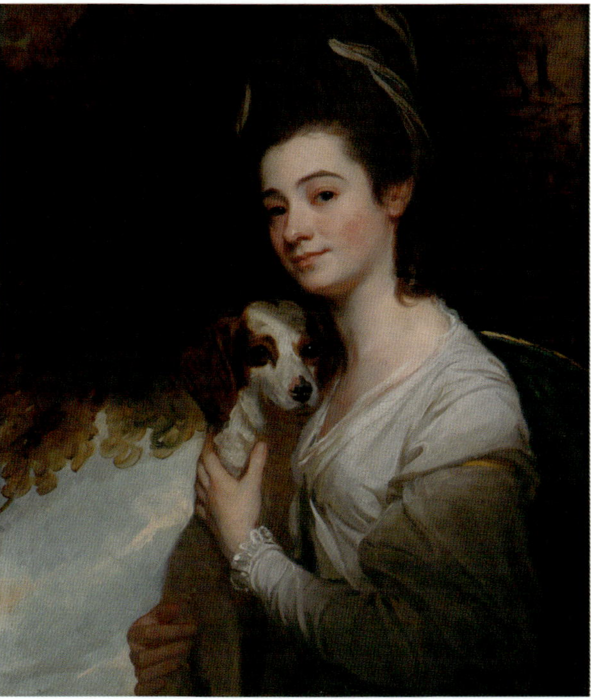

FIGURE 41

GEORGE ROMNEY
*Henrietta Stanley,
later Lady Horton*
1777
OIL ON CANVAS
29-1/2 X 24 IN (75 X 61 CM)
THE DERBY COLLECTION

The genre of portrait painting helped Emma create a believable identity, at least visually. If the gender-constituting acts illustrated in the portraits had been performed onstage, audiences could, as the feminist theorist Judith Butler explains in an essay on gender construction, "de-realize the act, make acting into something quite distinct from what is real."[37] Romney's portrait of Emma as "Nature," conversely, blurs the line between reality and role playing, making the portrait a more powerful act of identity construction. The portrait is a lasting and relatively public substitute for the absent subject. The likeness presents an identity fit for public consumption, with the hope that the actual subject will eventually follow suit. The art historian Mary Sheriff, invoking Butler's theoretical work, writes, "[I]mitation and identification occasion [a] sort of layered, and (apparently) contradictory subject."[38] Essentially, the subject's identity becomes a series of roles played for a particular audience.

In 1791, Emma Hart became Emma, Lady Hamilton. Romney commemorated this transformation in a work once known as *Lady Hamilton as an Ambassadress* (FIGURE 42). The title refers to Sir William Hamilton's role as a British diplomat in Naples and demonstrates the identity his wife claimed for herself later in life as a co-emissary during the war that engulfed Europe in the final years of the eighteenth century. The portrait is the last likeness Romney painted of Lady Hamilton, his most influential sitter. The composition closely resembles formal Grand Tour portraits popular in the eighteenth century, which superficially commemorated the aristocratic young British gentleman's extended journey through Europe. The trip served to educate young men in the ways of the (Western) world and to polish the future leaders of England. Portraits made during the Grand Tour verified the traveler's cultural authority and, as Bruce Redford states in *Venice and the Grand Tour*, "functioned as a visual curriculum vitae — a way of proclaiming accomplishments, articulating allegiances, and consolidating status."[39]

Before her 1791 marriage to Sir William, little was expected of Emma in terms of manners and education, but as the new Lady Hamilton, her social responsibilities increased, as did society's expectations of her. It was important for the Hamiltons to have visual confirmation of Emma's new position in Sir William's life. The change in her status is evident in Romney's *Lady Hamilton*, which he began on her wedding day. The work is the most formal portrait of Emma any artist ever painted. She assumes no character or personification, as she did in Romney's earlier portrait, since her role as Sir William's wife has been made official. In this portrait, Emma sits demurely with her body facing a window,

37
Judith Butler, "Performative Acts and Gender Constitution: An Essay in Phenomenology and Feminist Theory," in *The Feminism and Visual Culture Reader*, ed. Amelia Jones (New York: Routledge, 2003), 398.

38
Mary Sheriff, *The Exceptional Woman: Elisabeth Vigée-Lebrun and the Cultural Politics of Art* (Chicago: University of Chicago Press, 1996), 9.

39
Bruce Redford, *Venice and the Grand Tour* (New Haven: Yale University Press, 1996), 81. See also Jeremy Black, *Italy and the Grand Tour* (New Haven: Yale University Press, 2003), and Jeremy Black, *The British Abroad: The Grand Tour in the Eighteenth Century* (Stroud, England: Sutton, 2003).

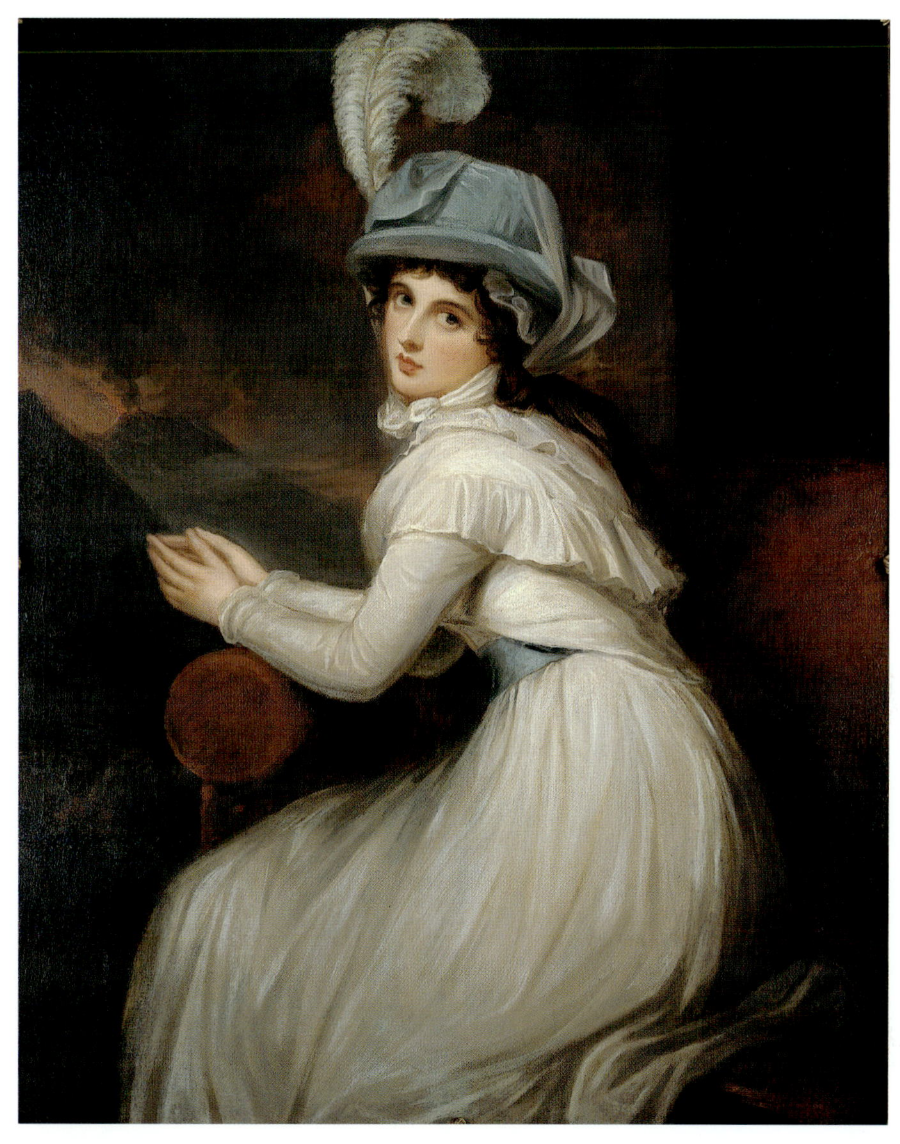

FIGURE 42

GEORGE ROMNEY
Lady Hamilton
1791
OIL ON CANVAS
62-5/8 X 52-3/8 IN (159.1 X 133.1 CM)
THE BLANTON MUSEUM OF ART
THE UNIVERSITY OF TEXAS AT AUSTIN
BEQUEST OF JACK G. TAYLOR, 1991 (1991.108)

through which the viewer sees a sublime Vesuvius smoking and discharging fire. She does not share the same exterior space with the volcano, as she does in other portraits from before her marriage, but occupies a location presumably inside her and Sir William's villa in Naples. Emma looks away from the volcano toward the viewer with a softly serious expression on her face. The dark red couch sets off her white dress, which some biographers have hypothesized is her wedding gown.[40] The work closely follows the visual model of a Grand Tour portrait: a richly attired central subject in a well-appointed interior with a specific signifier of a foreign location.

Few Grand Tour portraits of women exist. The Grand Tourist was usually a young, single man traveling abroad for the first time. When women traveled, it was almost always with their husbands and usually on a wedding tour. Edgar Peters Bowron and Peter Björn Kerber note in their monograph on Pompeo Batoni, the preeminent Grand Tour portraitist, that even when he undertook a portrait of an English female traveler, he "usually discarded the customary Grand Tour trappings."[41] Batoni's *Lady Mary Fox, later Baroness Holland* is typical of his female portraits, which make up only one-tenth of his oeuvre (FIGURE 43).[42] Commissioned during Baroness Holland's wedding tour in March 1767, the portrait depicts the sitter against a dramatic red curtain, which sets off her gray

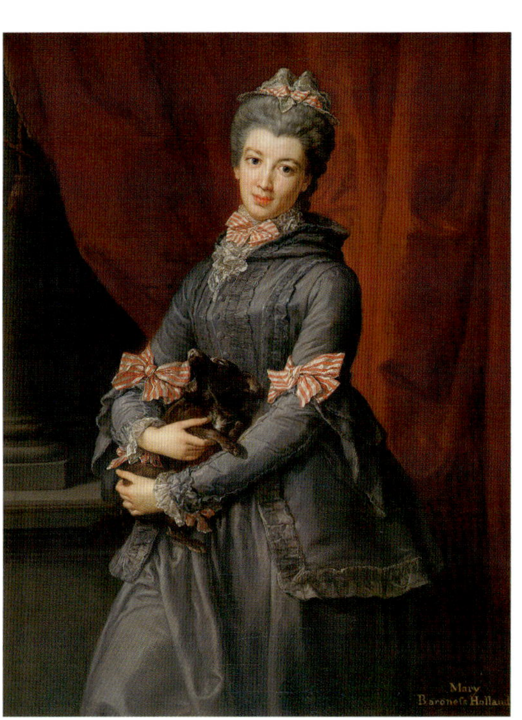

FIGURE 43

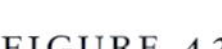

POMPEO BATONI
*Lady Mary Fox,
later Baroness Holland (1746–78)*
1767 – 68
OIL ON CANVAS
48 X 36 IN (121.9 X 91.4 CM)
THE HON. MRS. TOWNSHEND
MELBURY HOUSE, DORSET

40
Flora Fraser, *Beloved Emma: The Life of Emma, Lady Hamilton* (London: John Murray, 2003), 160. Hugh Tours, *The Life and Letters of Emma Hamilton* (London: Victor Gollancz, 1963), 93. For more letters relating to Sir William, Lady Hamilton, and Lord Nelson, see *The Collection of Autograph Letters and Historical Documents formed by Alfred Morrison* (London: Printed for Private Circulation [by Strangeway & Sons]), 1883–97.

41
Edgar Peters Bowron and Peter Björn Kerber, *Pompeo Batoni: Prince of Painters in Eighteenth-Century Rome* (New Haven: Yale University Press, 2007), 70.

42
Ibid., 70.

traveling costume, known as a Brunswick, or German, habit.[43] The baroness's attire is the only indication that she is abroad. Despite the feminine attributes of the dress — ornately ruffled collar and cuffs, red and white bows — the design is adapted from a traditional masculine riding habit.[44] Enduring the rigors of eighteenth-century travel required a certain strength of constitution, and the clothing associated with female travelers gently suggests the so-called masculine toughness required of women abroad.

Accordingly, the idea of Emma as a Grand Tourist locates her in a male-dominated realm. The inclusion of an indicator of the Sublime, a theoretical idea relating to art and experience that inspires awe or terror in the viewer, such as Vesuvius also associates her with other masculine characteristics. Sheriff, summarizing W. J. T. Mitchell's work on Romantic aesthetics, points out that "sublimity signified in a 'masculine' mode because [it is] founded on ideas of pain, terror, vigorous exertion, and power."[45] For a male Grand Tourist in Naples, visiting Vesuvius was one of the most sublime features of the entire trip, and Lady Hamilton, of course, traversed its slopes and wrote to friends of her experiences.

> We was last night up Vesuvus at twelve a clock
> and in my life I never saw so fine a sight.
> The lava runs about five mile[s] down from the top,
> for the mountain is not burst as ignorant people say it is. . . .
> [T]here was the finest fountain of liquid fire
> falling down a great precipice & as it run down
> it sett fire to the trees and brush wood so that the mountain
> looked like one entire mountain of fire. . . .
> For me I was inraptured.
> I could have staid all night there . . .[46]

Lady Hamilton describes the magnificent sight with amazement and bravery, as well as a sense of superiority over those "ignorant people" who report that Vesuvius has erupted. As a firsthand visitor, she wields cultural power over others for one of the first times in her life, and Romney's portrait captures her close association with Vesuvius and its sublime power.[47] In the same letter, Lady Hamilton continues her haughty tone in describing the Neapolitan Prince Royal's visit to Vesuvius on the same evening:

43
Ibid., 71.

44
Ibid., 71.

45
Sheriff, *Exceptional Woman*, 257.

46
Quoted in Tours, *Life and Letters*, 78.

47
The artist Elisabeth Vigée-Lebrun climbed Vesuvius herself several times and even brought her daughter along on her second ascent. She, like Emma Hamilton, was impressed by its sublimity. As an artist in the eighteenth century, Vigée-Lebrun was accustomed to occupying a male-dominated realm. By climbing Vesuvius, Vigée-Lebrun contributed to her artistic authority in experiencing firsthand something many of her male contemporaries could only read about.

We met the Prince Royal on the mountain, but [h]is foolish tuters
onely took him up a little whay, and did not let him stay 3 minuets;
so, when we asked him how he liked it, he said Bella ma poca roba
when if the[y] had took him five hundred yards higher
he would have the noblest sublimest sight in the world,
but poor creatures, the[y] where frightened
out of their sences & glad to make a hasty retreat.
O I shall kill myselfe with laughing.[48]

Not only has Lady Hamilton experienced Vesuvius at a closer proximity and with greater nerve than (male) members of the royal family, she also brandishes enough cultural supremacy to laugh at the prince and his "foolish" tutors.

The portraits of Lady Hamilton by Romney illustrate the social transition occurring in the adult life of a young woman. Gainsborough, like Romney, specialized in visually expressing his female sitters' virtue and place in society. This occupation took on a highly personal quality for Gainsborough as he painted his daughters throughout their lives. The portraits of Mary and Margaret Gainsborough are intimate and unguarded, even when at their most formal, and communicate not just the girls' likenesses but also Gainsborough's own anxiety about their entrance into the society for which he worked. No eighteenth-century artist painted portraits of his young children as often as Gainsborough.[49] The early portraits of his daughters, such as *The Painter's Daughters Chasing a Butterfly* and *Portrait of the Artist's Daughters*, demonstrate the bravura handling of paint for which Gainsborough was and is still revered. The works are hauntingly beautiful and communicate the girls' vivacity, but there is a melancholy quality to them. They are not the typical images of a playful, ephemeral childhood; rather, the personal pictures of Gainsborough's daughters combine the transitory innocence of youth characteristic of child portraits with an almost preternatural awareness of the difficulties that awaited the young women.

Gainsborough fathered three children. His first daughter died in infancy and was buried at St. Andrew's, Holborn, on March 1, 1748. An early group portrait shows Gainsborough and his wife, Margaret, accompanied by a young child, probably a posthumous portrait of their infant daughter, also called Margaret (FIGURE 44). The child is wedged between Gainsborough and his wife, wrapped protectively in the folds of her mother's dress. The mother smiles thoughtfully, as if the presence or remembrance of her firstborn brings happiness. She does not appear wracked

48
Quoted in Tours, *Life and Letters*, 78, and John Cordy Jeaffreson, *Lady Hamilton and Lord Nelson* (New York: New Amsterdam Book Company, 1897), 137.

49
This could be true throughout the history of art, not just in the eighteenth century. Gainsborough's output may be rivaled only by that of Rembrandt, an artist very interested in intimate subjects taken from daily life, who used his son Titus as a model in several works.

with grief; rather, she seems to be agreeable and content. Gainsborough, on the other hand, though sitting elegantly on a rock, confronts the viewer with a serious, almost defiant expression. The chilly landscape, perhaps indicative of the winter of the lost child's life, contrasts eerily with the shimmering satins of the figures' costumes. In this group composition with a self-portrait, Gainsborough reveals sadness over his first daughter's untimely death and unease about his future as a father. The poetic handling of the heartrending subject demonstrates Gainsborough's sensitivity toward young people, which is seen in many of his portraits of children, but especially those of his two surviving daughters, Mary and another called Margaret.

From around 1755 to 1765, the artist explored representations of childhood in his art. That childhood is transitory, both specifically in Gainsborough's own life and more generally in eighteenth-century society, probably contributed to the artist's fascination with creating images of his daughters. The life of a child in the eighteenth century was certainly not an easy one, nor was its length predictable. Gainsborough probably experienced tragedy associated with childhood

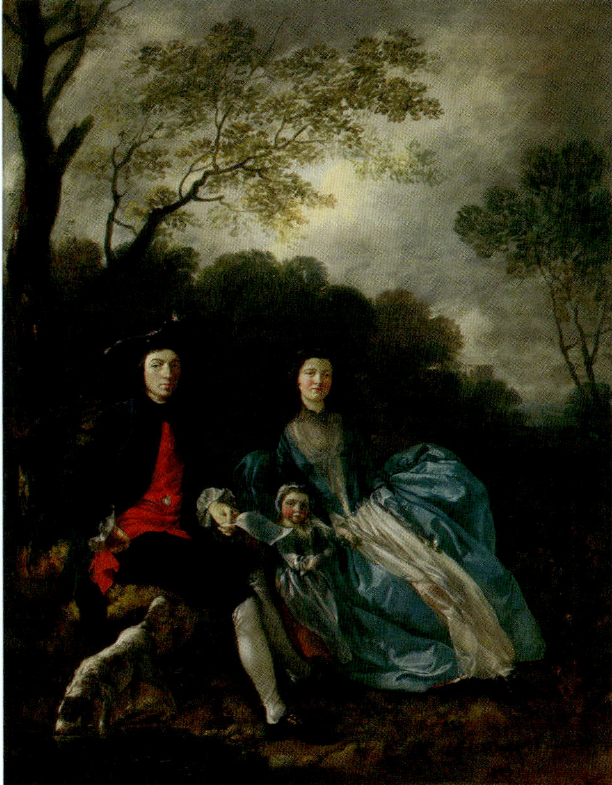

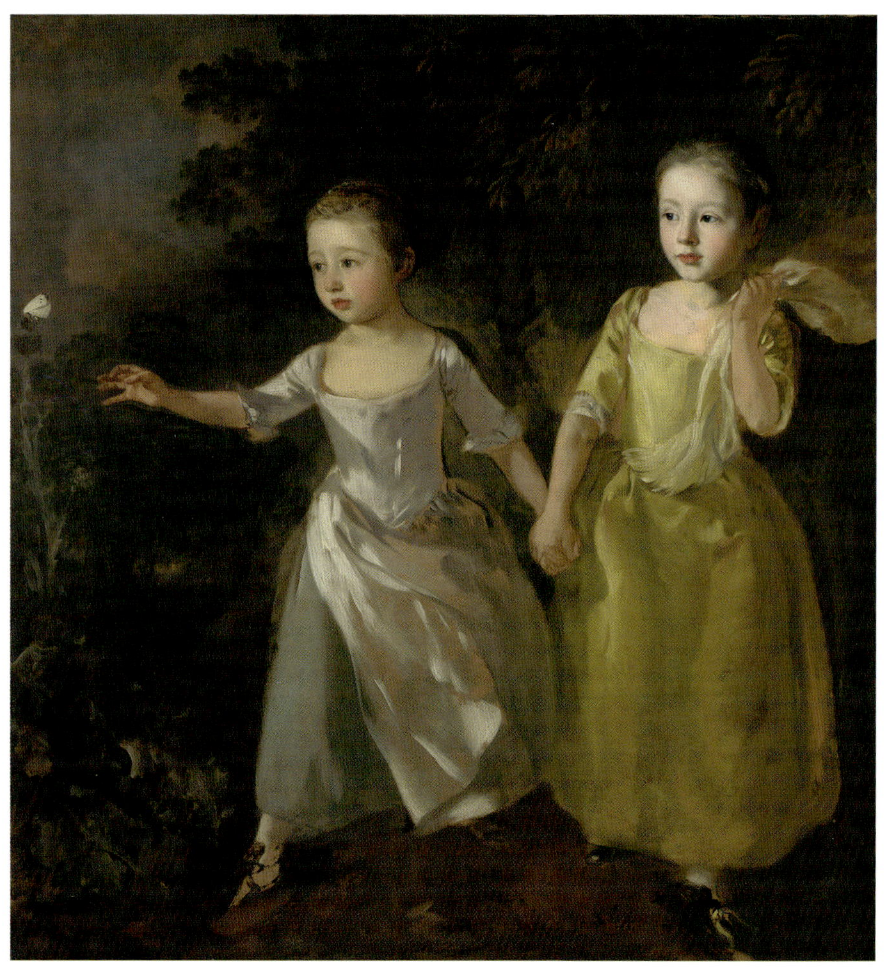

FIGURE 45

THOMAS GAINSBOROUGH
The Painter's Daughters Chasing a Butterfly
CA. 1756
OIL ON CANVAS
44-11/16 X 41-5/16 IN (113.5 X 105 CM)
NATIONAL GALLERY, LONDON
HENRY VAUGHAN BEQUEST, 1900 (NG1811)

even before the death of his first daughter. His older brother, Matthias, may have been killed as a child by falling on a fork as he was running with it in his hand.[50] It is also likely that many of Gainsborough's friends and acquaintances experienced the loss of children during and shortly after birth. Even royalty was not immune to such heartbreak. At the 1783 Royal Academy exhibition, Gainsborough exhibited a portrait study of the four-year-old Prince Octavius, who died just one week after the opening of the exhibition. A viewer wrote of the subject, "[B]looming in the natural health of Gainsborough's pencil, [he] seemed to say, 'I yet live! Look at me!' "[51] Gainsborough was surrounded by the death of children and often was in the business of creating child portraits that, as Pointon has noted, "fulfilled the role of an emotional insurance policy."[52]

In an early and unfinished double portrait of his daughters chasing a butterfly, Gainsborough explicitly depicts the transience of childhood, emphasizing the separation that will occur as the girls move out of childhood and into womanhood (FIGURE 45). The two girls run after a butterfly with hands joined. Their small, delicate bodies mirror the shape of the insect they covet. The butterfly, representative of ephemeral and superficial beauty, symbolically hovers over a thorny thistle plant at the left side of the composition, about to fly out of the picture plane. The traditional reading of this work identifies the image as an allegory against passing pleasures and vanity.[53] The young girls attempt to gratify their childish desires by seizing the butterfly, which will surely die and lose its luster upon capture. The younger girl, Margaret, more enthusiastically lunges for the object of desire, whereas Mary, the older of the two, looks more reservedly at the butterfly, holding her sister back. Such a difference in attitude indicates maturity and a corresponding ability to recognize the insignificance of vain pursuits.

Though eventually sold to a neighbor, *The Painter's Daughters Chasing a Butterfly* was never originally conceived for a patron, making Gainsborough not only the creator but also the primary viewer. As the main focus of the composition, the girls are subject to the gaze of the painter/viewer/father, who is overwhelmingly present, even 250 years later in the free, spontaneous handling of the paint. The presence of the artist signified by his mark makes Gainsborough another subject within the work. The father's presence in this allegorical forewarning is an anxious one, related not only to the loss of his first child, but to the problems his daughters will encounter in the future. That Gainsborough never finished this work is, perhaps, indicative of the strength of his anxiety.

50
Mrs. Arthur Bell, *Thomas Gainsborough: A Record of His Life and Works* (London: George Bell, 1897), 10. This is the only publication in which this assertion appears, and the original source of the anecdote remains unclear.

51
Quoted in Steward, *The New Child*, 97.

52
Pointon, *Hanging the Head*, 206.

53
Amal Asfour and Paul Williamson, *Gainsborough's Vision* (Liverpool: Liverpool University Press, 1999), 88–91. Vaughan, *Gainsborough*, 67–68.

As female children, Gainsborough's daughters — on canvas and in life — were in particular jeopardy. On canvas, the girls were subject not just to their father's gaze, but to the gazes of other men. Throughout their lives, Mary and Margaret would have to rely on men, first their father and then their husbands. In a letter from 1764 to a good friend, Gainsborough writes candidly of his apprehension about their futures.

[Y]ou must know
I'm upon a scheeme of learning them both to paint Landscape;
and that somewhat above the common Fan-mount stile.
I think them capable of it, if taken in time,
and with proper pains bestow'd. I don't mean to make them . . .
partly admired & partly laugh'd at at every Tea Table;
but in case of an Accident that they may do something for Bread . . .
I think (and indeed always did myself) that I had better do this
than make fine trumpery of them, and let them be led away with Vanity,
and ever subject to disappointment in the
wild Goose chase.[54]

The artist expresses several worries in this letter. He desires to impart a skill to his girls so that they may provide for themselves if he or another man cannot. In accordance with his role as father/protector, Gainsborough wants to ensure that his daughters, no matter the circumstances, are able to live comfortably. He fears they may fail in their art and become the butt of jokes, and here again the father asserts his need to shield his children from pain. He also desires to defend them against vanity and continued disappointment in the game of courtship. When Gainsborough wrote this letter, his daughters were on the threshold of womanhood, and he was certainly contemplating their futures and likely worried about what would become of them. In this way, the artist's anxiety moves out of its focus on the past — the girls, after all, have survived the dangers of eighteenth-century childhood by 1764 — and into the future, where their gender puts them further at risk.

Portrait of the Artist's Daughters shows Mary age thirteen and Margaret age twelve, with tools for drawing in front of a replica of the *Farnese Flora*, enacting the plans Gainsborough laid out in his letter (PLATE 2). Mary sits prettily in a white dress, looking at the viewer with a gentle expression on her face. Her younger sister Margaret stares intently at the statue. Gainsborough pairs the girls' budding femininity with examples of their education in the arts, emphasizing the worries stated in the letter. Mary and Margaret are both presented here

54
Thomas Gainsborough to James Unwin, March 1, 1764, *The Letters of Thomas Gainsborough*, ed. John Hayes (New Haven: Yale University Press, 2001), 25.

for the delectation of the viewer, their incipient womanliness underscored by their fashionable dress. They no longer wear the childish pinafores of *The Painter's Daughters Chasing a Butterfly*; the viewer is confronted instead with expanses of creamy porcelain skin exposed from developing breast to elegant neck to curving forehead.

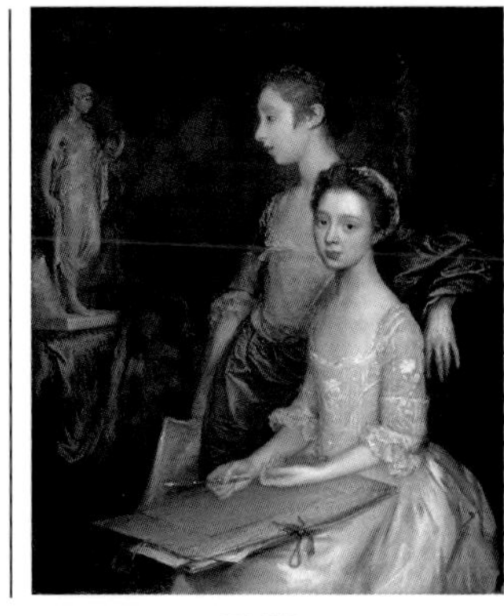

PLATE 2
Portrait of the Artist's Daughters

Similarly, the girls are no longer engaged in frivolous pursuits like chasing a butterfly but are shown enjoying more intellectual pursuits. There is a greater emphasis on the "object-ness" of the girls subjected to the viewer's gaze. Mary confronts the viewer who looks upon her, neither welcoming nor challenging him. She exists as an object for visual pleasure, despite Gainsborough's inclusion of drawing materials that attempt to assert her independence, in accordance with the letter quoted above. Margaret is occupied with her own consideration of a work of art, the *Farnese Flora*. Compositionally, the statue occupies the same spot as the butterfly in the earlier double portrait. Instead of lunging for the butterfly, Margaret contemplates a personification of flowers and spring and beholds the embodiment of what she and her sister will become: fertile women in the spring of their lives. Even as they display their skills in the arts, Mary and Margaret remain objects to be desired, and Margaret pointedly exhibits her own desire to assume the role of the *Farnese Flora*. The obstacles Gainsborough's daughters faced as women in this "vicious age" are not to be defeated simply by the acquisition of a marketable skill.

Despite their father's attempts to give them a sense of independence, however small, the young women simply wanted to marry well and lead the lives of ladies.[55] Complicating matters, mental illness ran in the family, and Mary, the elder daughter, became seriously ill in 1770.[56] As a result, she was never married, living at home until her death in 1826. Margaret did marry, though against her parents' wishes. Both daughters were fond of the talented musician Johann Christian Fischer, of whom Gainsborough painted a spectacular full-length portrait.[57] In a letter to his sister, Gainsborough anxiously writes, "I have detected a sly trick in Molly [Mary] by a sight I got of one of her letters, forsooth, to Mr. Fischer . . . [W]hile I had my eye upon Peggy [Margaret], the other slyboots, . . . has all along been the object. Oh, d—n him, he must take care how he trips me off the foot of all happiness."[58] Gainsborough's initial inclination — that Fischer fancied Margaret — was the correct one, but the match was troubled from the start. The marriage lasted just six months, with Margaret returning home and, like her sister, lapsing into periods of insanity. She died in 1820.

55
Vaughan, *Gainsborough*,
164.

56
Ibid., 162.

57
In the literature on
this painting, there are
discrepancies related
to the date. Mary and
Margaret may have met
Fischer as he was sitting
for the portrait, or the
work might have been
a symbol of Gainsbor-
ough's acceptance of
Fischer and Margaret's
union.

58
Gainsborough to Mary
Gibbon, Dec. 26, 1775,
Letters, 130.

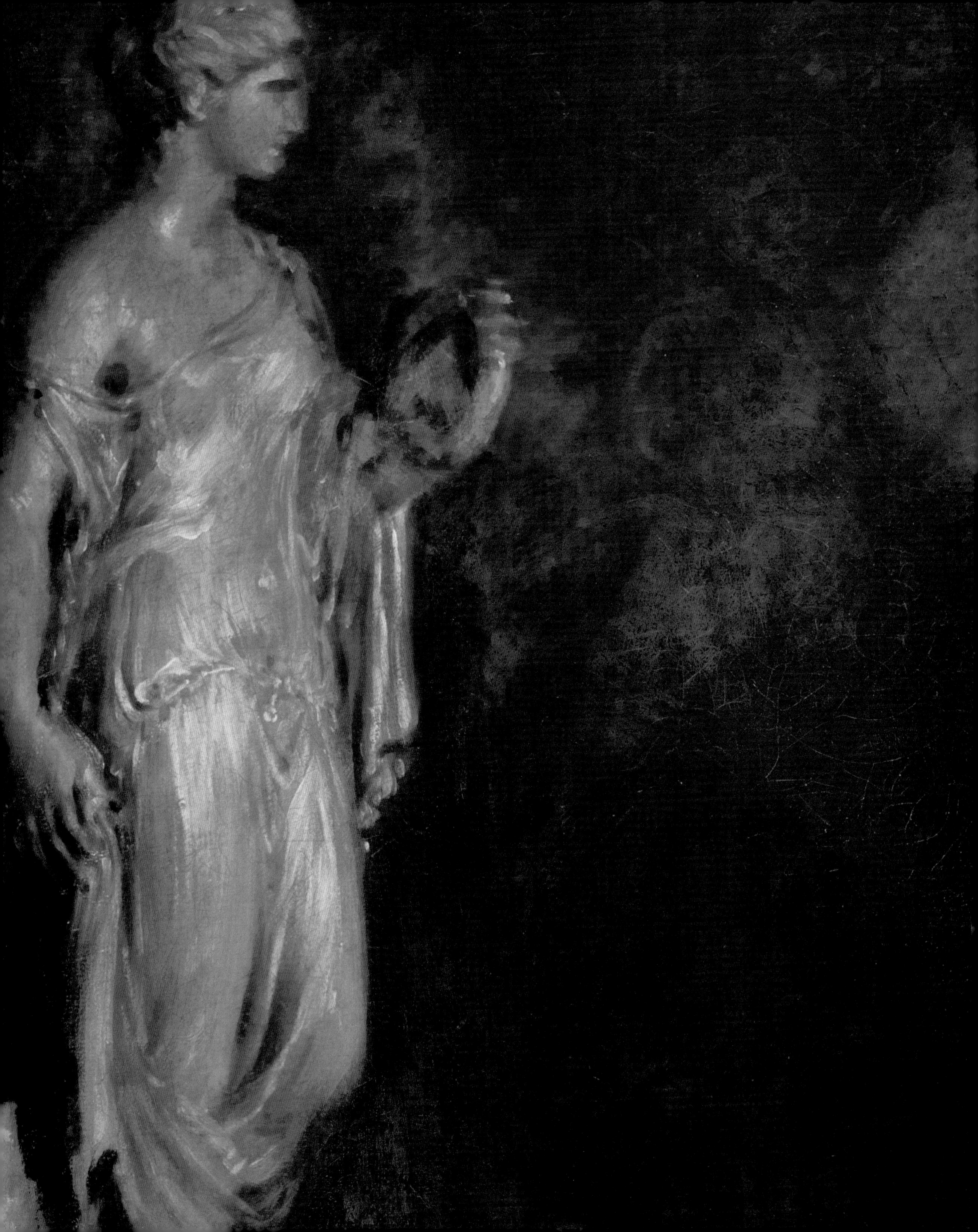

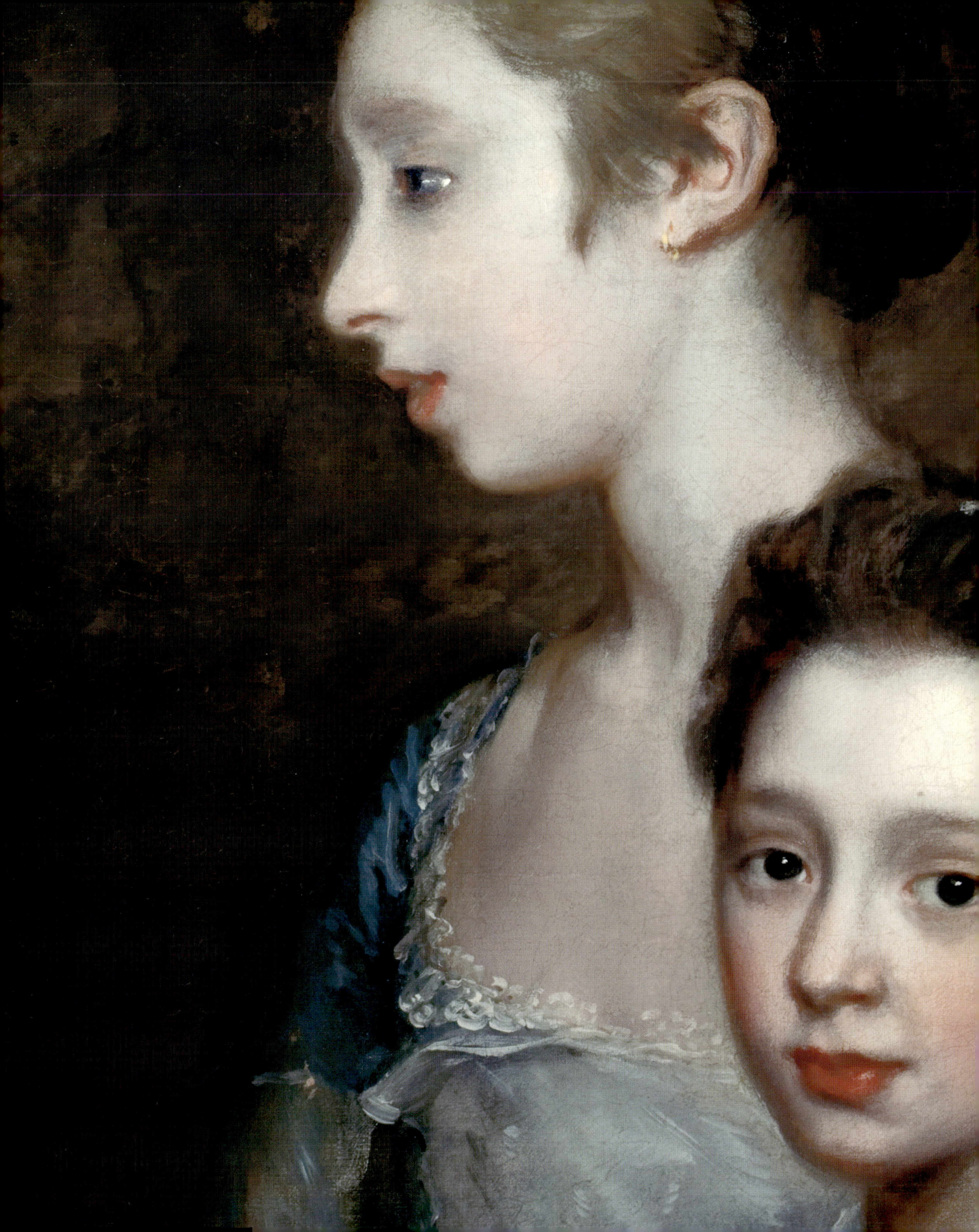

In the last double portrait Gainsborough ever painted of his daughters, Mary and Margaret stand in a typical Gainsborough landscape (FIGURE 46). He painted the work around 1770–74, at roughly the same time that Mary first experienced bouts of insanity. The two girls exhibit the same melancholic expressions of the earlier *Portrait of the Artist's Daughters*. Unlike the pose of the previous paintings, the girls seem unified, both addressing the viewer with confidence. As is obvious from their biographies, these women were hardly as self-assured as they are presented here. Gone are the truthful, intimate portraits of the period from 1755 to 1765. This painting is similar to many of Gainsborough's commissioned works, probably due to the daughters' desire to be in the upper echelon of society, like many of their father's patrons. The women depicted here ostensibly exist in a world where value is based on superficial standards and, as Gainsborough describes it, where ambition is channeled into "tea drinkings, dancings, husband huntings, and such."[59] Mary and Margaret's unified stance makes them appear somewhat cautious, as if seeking the protection of each other's presence. The sisters stand close together, and Margaret even crosses her hands guardedly in front of her body. The luxurious clothes they wear, the natural landscape, and the loyal dog at the right of the composition all communicate eighteenth-century feminine virtue, but the young women's bodies and unsmiling faces communicate their discomfort with their existence. Despite his anxiety and efforts, Gainsborough's daughters suffered the same ups and downs of life as many other eighteenth-century women.

"[N]othing is so delicate as the reputation of a woman: it is, at once, the most beautiful and the most brittle of all human things."[60] So states the Reverend Dr. Villars in Fanny Burney's epistolary novel *Evelina, or A Young Lady's Entrance into the World* from 1778. Villars is the guardian of Evelina, a young woman of uncertain parentage, who, after a series of humorous and embarrassing events, learns to navigate the complex expectations of eighteenth-century aristocratic society. Villars worries about Evelina's development outside his protective home. Her story, despite its comic exaggeration, characterizes eighteenth-century society's fascination with reputation and morality. Portraits were one way eighteenth-century women could communicate their virtue and status to a relatively wide audience. Gainsborough, like Villars, was certainly aware of his daughters' delicate reputations. Montagu, Siddons, Robinson, and Lady Hamilton did not have the support of worried guardians, but, as adults, they all recognized the need to assert a virtuous image to combat the viciousness of the age into which they were born.

59
Quoted in Vaughan, *Gainsborough*, 164.

60
Fanny Burney, *Evelina, or A Young Lady's Entrance into the World*, ed. Susan Kubica Howard, Broadview Literary Texts (Peterborough, Ontario: Broadview Press, 2000), 279.

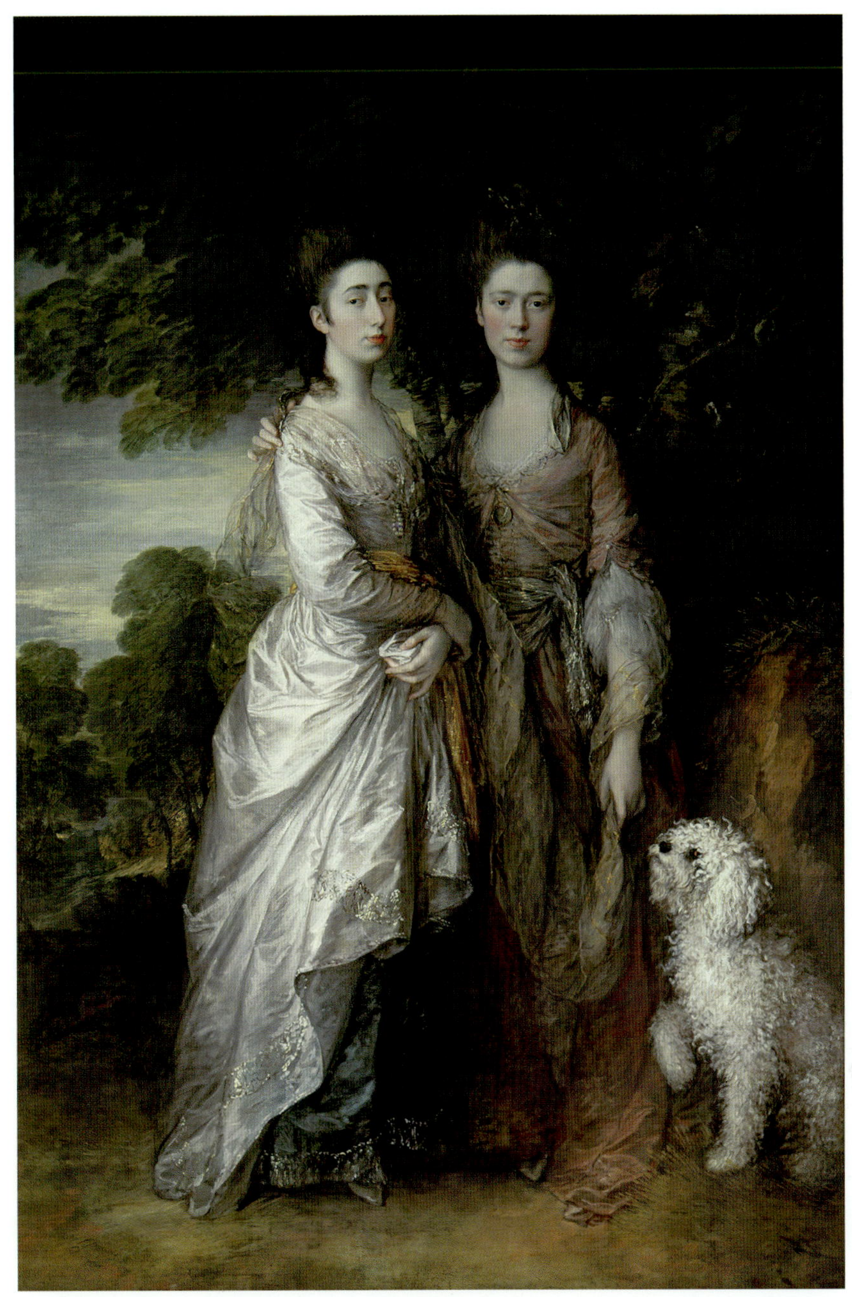

FIGURE 46

THOMAS GAINSBOROUGH
The Painter's Daughters
CA. 1770 – 74
OIL ON CANVAS
91 X 59 IN (231.1 X 149.9 CM)
PRIVATE COLLECTION

DETAIL APPEARS ON PAGE 181

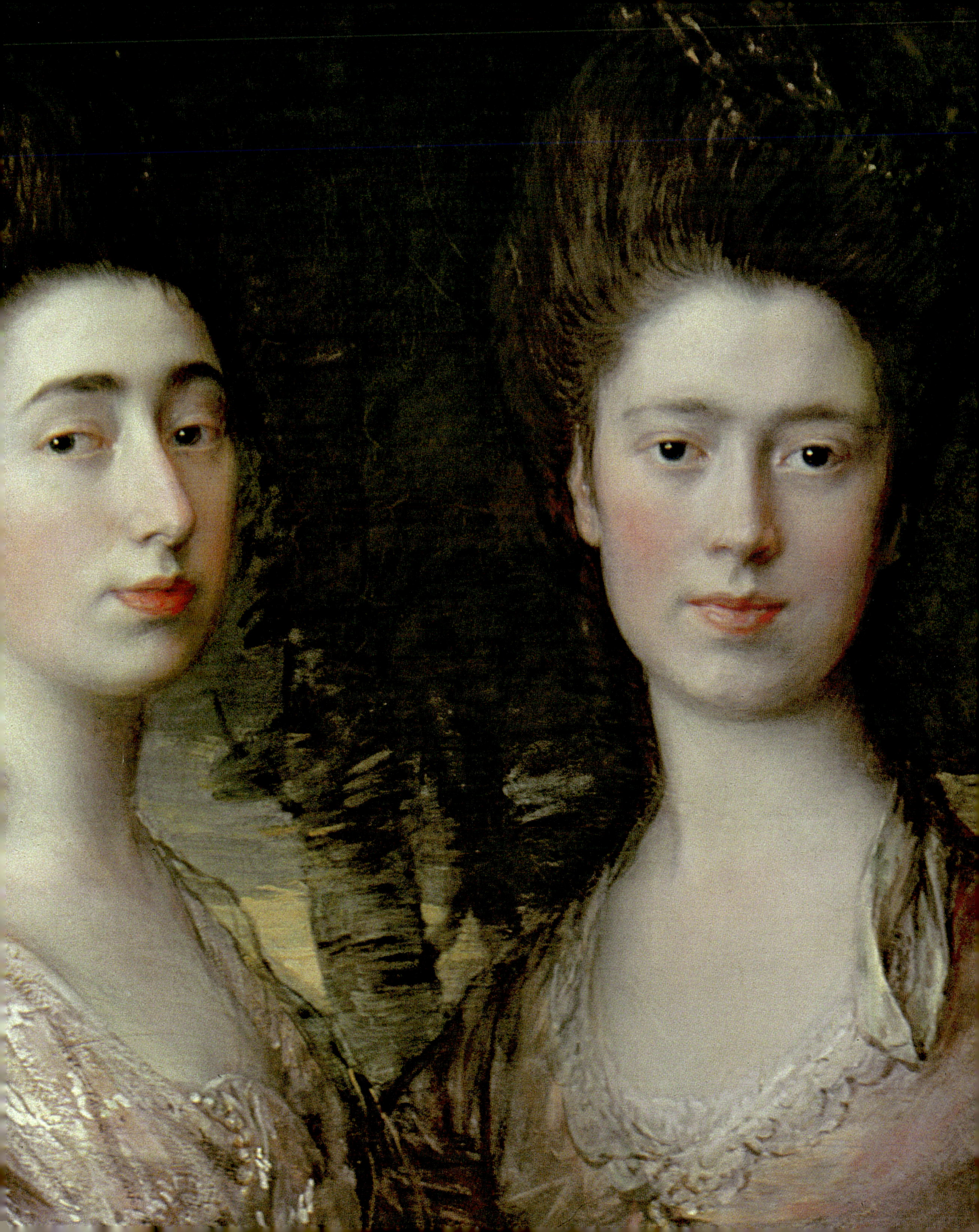

Bibliography

Primary Sources

Algarotti, Francesco. *Essay on Painting Written in Italian by Count Algarotti.* Dublin: T. & J. Whitehouse, 1765.

Anonymous. "Anecdotes of the late Mr. Gainsborough, the Portrait-Painter." In *The Beauties of Magazines, Reviews, and other Periodical Publications*, 2:65–70. Edinburgh: George Mudie, 1788.

———. "A Dictionary of Principles, and Terms of Art." In *The Artist's Repository and Drawing Magazine.* London, 1784–94, 3 vols.

———. *Memoirs of Lady Hamilton with Illustrative Anecdotes of Many of her Most Particular Friends and Distinguished Contemporaries.* New York: David Huntington, 1815.

———. "Mr. Gainsborough's Pictures." *Diary, or Woodfall's Register*, April 2, 1789.

———. "Mrs. Thicknesse." In *Public Characters.* London: Debrett, Fores, Hookham, and Robinson, 1806.

———. "On the Portrait of the Three Princesses, Painted by Thomas Gainsborough." In *An Asylum for Fugitive Pieces, in Prose and Verse, not in any other Collections*, 243–44. London: J. Debrett, 1785.

———. *The Polite Lady: or, A Course of Female Education. In a Series of Letters, from a Mother to her Daughter.* London: J. Newbery, 1760.

———. "Royal Academy Exhibition." *Morning Chronicle and London Advertiser*, April 25, 1778.

———. "Royal Academy Exhibition." *Morning Chronicle and London Advertiser*, May 25, 1778.

———. "Royal Academy Exhibition (review)." *Gazette and New Daily Advertiser* (London), May 1, 1782.

Astell, Mary. "Preface, by a Lady, Written in 1724." In *Letters of the Right Honourable Lady M__y W__y M__e: Written during her Travels in Europe, Asia, and Africa, to Persons of Distinction, Men of Letters, etc., in different Parts of Europe*, by Lady Mary Wortley Montagu, 1:4–7. London: A. Homer, 1764.

Bromley, Robert Anthony. *A Philosophical and Critical History of the Fine Arts, Painting, Sculpture, and Architecture.* London: Philanthropic Press, 1793.

Brown, John. *An Estimate of the Manners and Principles of the Times.* London: Printed for L. Davis and C. Reymers, 1757.

Burke, Edmund. *A Philosophical Enquiry into the Origin of our Ideas of the Sublime and Beautiful.* London, 1757.

Condillac, Etienne Bonnot de. *Traité des sensations, à Madame la Comtesse de Vassé, par M. L'Abbé de Condillac, de L'Académie Royale de Berlin.* Paris, 1754.

Delany, Mary. *The Autobiography and Correspondence of Mary Granville, Mrs. Delany.* Edited by Lady Llanover. London: Richard Bentley, 1861.

Fielding, Henry. *Tom Jones.* London, 1749.

Ford, Ann. *Letters and Instructions for Playing on the Guitar.* London, ca. 1761.

Gallini, Giovanni Andrea. *A Treatise on the Art of Dancing.* London, 1762.

Grosley, Pierre-Jean. *A Tour to London: or, New Observations on England and its Inhabitants.* Dublin, 1772.

Horde, Thomas. *The Empirick; an Entertainment in two acts.* Oxford: W. Jackson and Co., ca. 1785.

Jackson, William. "Character of Gainsborough." *The New Annual Register, or General Repository of History, Politics, and Literature for the Year 1798.* London: S. Hamilton, 1799.

———. *The Four Ages; together with Essays on Various Subjects.* London, 1798.

Jefferys, Thomas. *A Collection of the Dresses of Different Nations both Ancient and Modern.* London, 1757.

Johnson, Samuel. "The Idler." *Universal Chronicle* issue 45, February 24, 1758.

Lairesse, Gérard de. *The Art of Painting.* London, 1738.

Marriott, Thomas. *Female Conduct: being an Essay on the Art of Pleasing.* London: W. Owen, 1759.

Montagu, Lady Mary Wortley. "Constantinople To—." In *A New Miscellany,* edited by Anthony Hammond. London: Printed for T. Jauncy, 1720.

Nivelon, François. *The Rudiments of Genteel Behavior.* London, 1737.

An Old Rabi. "To Sir John Fielding." *Public Advertiser* (London), April 27, 1774.

Piles, Roger de. *The Art of Painting.* London, 1754.
———. *Cours de peinture par principes.* Paris, 1709.

Richardson, Jonathan. *An Essay on the Theory of Painting.* London, 1725.

Robinson, Mary. *Memoirs of the Late Mrs. Robinson, Written by Herself.* 2 vols. London: Printed for Richard Phillips by C. Mercier, 1803.

Rouquet, André. *The Present State of the Arts in England.* London: Printed for J. Nourse, 1755.

Stevens, George Alexander. "The Artists." In *Songs, Comic, and Satyrical,* 28–29. London, 1772.

Thicknesse, Ann (Ford). *The School for Fashion.* 2 vols. London: H. Reynell, 1800.
———. *Sketches of the Lives and Writings of the Ladies of France.* London: Dodsley and W. Brown, 1778–81.

Thicknesse, Philip. *Sketches and Characters of the most Eminent and most Singular persons now Living.* London: John Wheele, 1770.
———. *A Sketch of the Life and Paintings of Thomas Gainsborough, Esq.* London, 1788.

Villiers, William, Earl of Jersey. *Letter to Miss F—d.* London, 1761.

Webb, Daniel. *An Inquiry into the Beauties of Painting; and into the Merits of the most celebrated Painters, Ancient and Modern.* London, 1760.

Secondary Sources

Anonymous. *Letters to the Ladies on the Preservation of Health and Beauty.* London, 1770.

Asfour, Amal, and Paul Williamson. *Gainsborough's Vision.* Liverpool: Liverpool University Press, 1999.
———. "Gainsborough's Wit." *Journal of the History of Ideas* 58, no. 3 (July 1997): 479–501.

Asleson, Robyn, ed. *Notorious Muse: The Actress in British Art and Culture 1776–1812.* New Haven, CT: Yale University Press, 2003.

Asleson, Robyn, Shelley Bennett, Mark Leonard, and Shearer West, eds. *A Passion for Performance: Sarah Siddons and Her Portraitists.* Los Angeles: Getty Publications, 1999.

Asleson, Robyn, and Shelley M. Bennett. *British Paintings at the Huntington.* New Haven, CT: Yale University Press, 2001.

Barker, Hannah, and Elaine Chalus, eds. *Gender in Eighteenth-Century England: Roles, Representations and Responsibilities.* New York: Addison Wesley Longman, 1997.

Beauvoir, Simone de. *The Second Sex.* Translated and edited by H. M. Parshley. London: Jonathan Cape, 1953.

Bell, Mrs. Arthur. *Thomas Gainsborough: A Record of his Life and Works.* London: George Bell and Sons, 1897.

Bellamy, Joan, Anne Laurence, and Gill Perry, eds. *Women, Scholarship and Criticism: Gender Knowledge c. 1790–1900.* New York: Manchester University Press, 2000.

Belsey, Hugh. *Love's Prospect: Gainsborough's Byam Family and the Eighteenth Century Marriage Portrait.* Bath: Holburne Museum of Art, 2001. An exhibition catalogue.
———. "A Visit to the Studios of Gainsborough and Hoare." *Burlington Magazine* 129, no. 1007 (February 1987): 107–9.

Benton, Michael. "Visualizing Narrative: Bridging the 'Aesthetic Gap.' " *Journal of Aesthetic Education* 33, no. 2 (Summer 1999): 33–49.

Bermingham, Ann. "The Aesthetics of Ignorance: The Accomplished Woman and the Culture of Connoisseurship." *Oxford Art Journal* 16, no. 2 (1993): 3–20.

————. "Elegant Females and Gentlemen Connoisseurs: The Commerce in Culture and Self- image in Eighteenth-century England." In *The Consumption of Culture 1600–1800: Image, Object, Text*, edited by John Brewer and Ann Bermingham. London: Routledge, 1995.

————. "The Picturesque and Ready-to-wear Femininity." In *The Politics of the Picturesque*, edited by Stephen Copley and Peter Garside. Cambridge: Cambridge University Press, 1994.

————, ed. *Sensation and Sensibility: Viewing Gainsborough's "Cottage Door."* New Haven, CT: Yale University Press, 2005.

Black, Jeremy. *The British Abroad: The Grand Tour in the Eighteenth Century.* Stroud, England: Sutton, 2003.

————. *Italy and the Grand Tour.* New Haven, CT: Yale University Press, 2003.

Boime, Albert. *The Academy and French Painting in the Nineteenth Century.* New York: Phaidon, 1971.

Bowron, Edgar Peters, and Peter Björn Kerber. *Pompeo Batoni: Prince of Painters in Eighteenth-Century Rome.* New Haven, CT: Yale University Press, 2007.

Brant, Clare, and Diane Purkiss, eds. *Women, Texts and Histories 1575–1760.* New York: Routledge, Chapman and Hall, 1992.

Braunschneider, Theresa. *Our Coquettes: Capacious Desire in the Eighteenth Century.* Charlottesville: University of Virginia Press, 2009.

Brewer, John. " 'The Most Polite Age and the Most Vicious': Attitudes Towards Culture as a Commodity 1660–1800." In *The Consumption of Culture 1600–1800: Image, Object, Text*, edited by John Brewer and Ann Bermingham, 341–61. London: Routledge, 1995.

Bryant, Julius. *Kenwood: Catalogue of Paintings in the Iveagh Bequest.* New Haven, CT: Yale University Press, 2003.

Burney, Fanny. *Evelina, or A Young Lady's Entrance into the World.* Edited by Susan Kubica Howard. Peterborough, Ontario: Broadview Press, 2000.

Busch, Werner. *Emblematic or Expressive?: The Significance of the Garden Debate for Late 18th Century Painting.* Edited by Michael Rohde and Rainer Schomann. Leipzig: Edition Leipzig, 2004.

Butler, Judith. "Performative Acts and Gender Constitution: An Essay in Phenomenology and Feminist Theory." In *The Feminism and Visual Culture Reader*, edited by Amelia Jones, 392–402. New York: Routledge, 2003.

Byrne, Paula. *Perdita: The Life of Mary Robinson.* London: HarperCollins, 2004.

————. *Perdita: The Literary, Theatrical, Scandalous Life of Mary Robinson.* New York: Random House Trade Paperbacks, 2004.

Casteras, Susan P. Review of *Naked Authority: The Body in Western Painting 1830–1908* by Marcia Pointon, *Hanging the Head: Portraiture and Social Formation in Eighteenth-Century England* by Marcia Pointon, and *Painting Women: Victorian Women Artists* by Deborah Cherry. *Women's Art Journal* 17, no. 2 (1996–97): 32–35.

Cheek, Pamela. *Sexual Antipodes: Enlightenment Globalization and the Placing of Sex.* Stanford: Stanford University Press, 2003.

Cherry, Deborah, and Jennifer Harris. "Eighteenth-Century Portraiture and the Seventeenth-Century Past: Gainsborough and Van Dyck." *Art History* 5, no. 3 (1982): 287–309.

Clery, E. J. *The Feminization Debate in Eighteenth-Century England: Literature, Commerce and Luxury.* New York: Palgrave Macmillan, 2004.

Coggin, Philip. " 'This Easy and Agreeable Instrument': A History of the English Guittar." *Early Music* 15 (May 1987): 205–18.

Colley, Linda. *Britons: Forging the Nation 1707–1837.* New Haven, CT: Yale University Press, 1992.

Comstock, Helen. "Gainsborough's Portrait of the Ladies Erne and Dillon." *Connoisseur* 95 (March 1935): 157.

Cormack, Malcolm. *The Paintings of Thomas Gainsborough.* New York: Cambridge University Press, 1991.

Craft-Fairchild, Catherine. *Masquerade and Gender: Disguise and Female Identity in Eighteenth-Century Fictions by Women.* University Park: Pennsylvania State University Press, 1993.

Derrida, Jacques. "The Law of Genre." In *Glyph: Textual Studies,* edited by Samuel Weber, translated by Avital Ronell, 203–32. Baltimore: Johns Hopkins University Press, 1980.

Egerton, Judy. "William Hoare of Bath." *Burlington Magazine* 133, no. 1 (January 1991): 47–48.

Einberg, Elizabeth. *Gainsborough's "Giovanna Baccelli."* London: Tate Gallery Publications, 1976. An exhibition catalogue.

Ellis, Joyce. "On the Town: Women in Augustan England." *History Today* 45 (December 1995): 20–27.

Fiering, Norman S. "Irresistible Compassion: An Aspect of Eighteenth-Century Sympathy and Humanitarianism." *Journal of the History of Ideas* 37, no. 2 (April–June 1976): 195–218.

Flügel, John Carl. *The Psychology of Clothes.* London: Hogarth, 1930.

Fordham, Douglas. "New Directions in British Art History of the Eighteenth Century." *Literature Compass* 5, no. 5 (2008): 906–17.

Foreman, Amanda. *The Duchess.* New York: Random House Trade Paperbacks, 2008.

Fraser, Flora. *Beloved Emma: The Life of Emma, Lady Hamilton.* London: John Murray, 2003.

French, Anne, ed. *"The Earl and Countess Howe" by Gainsborough: A Bicentenary Exhibition.* London: English Heritage, 1988. An exhibition catalogue.

Gage, John. "Saving Faces," review of *The British Portrait 1660–1960* by Sir Roy Strong et al., *Family and Friends: A Regional Survey of British Portraiture* by Andrew Moore, *The Swagger Portrait: Grand Manner Portraiture in Britain from Van Dyck to Augustus John, 1630–1930* by Andrew Wilton, and *Hanging the Head: Portraiture and Social Formation in Eighteenth-Century England* by Marcia Pointon. *Art History* (December 1993): 663–68.

Gainsborough, Thomas. *The Letters of Thomas Gainsborough.* Edited by John Hayes. New Haven, CT: Yale University Press, 2001.

Garstang, Donald. *The British Face: A View of Portraiture 1625–1850.* London: P & D Colnaghi, 1986. An exhibition catalogue.

Gaunt, William. *Court Painting in England: From Tudor to Victorian Times.* London: Constable, 1980.
———. *The Great Century of British Painting: Hogarth to Turner.* New York: Phaidon, 1971.

Gigante, Denise, Malcolm Andrews, and Maureen Harkin. "Multidisciplinary Views of David Marshall's *The Frame of Art: Fictions of Aesthetic Experience, 1750–1815.*" *Eighteenth-Century Studies* 4, no. 4 (Summer 2007): 677–83.

Glanville, Helen. "Gainsborough as Artist and Artisan." In *A Nest of Nightingales: Thomas Gainsborough and the Linley Sisters,* edited by Giles Waterfield, 15–29. London: Dulwich Picture Gallery, 1988. An exhibition catalogue.

Gower, Ronald Sutherland. *Sir Joshua Reynolds: His Life and Art.* London: George Bell and Sons, 1902.

Grover, Danielle. " 'Partly Admired and Partly Laugh'd at at Every Tea Table': The Case for Ann Thicknesse (Née Ford) and *The School for Fashion (1800).*" *Female Spectator* 12, no. 3 (Summer 2008): 5–8.

Hallett, Mark. "On the Road." *Eighteenth-Century Studies* 36, no. 4 (Summer 2003): 564–70.
———. "Reading the Walls: Pictorial Dialogue at the British Royal Academy." *Eighteenth-Century Studies* 37, no. 4 (2004): 581–604.

Harari, Josué V., ed. *Textual Strategies: Perspectives in Post-Structuralist Criticism.* Ithaca, NY: Cornell University Press, 1989.

Hart, Gail. "Review of *Performance and Femininity in Eighteenth-Century German Women's Writing: The Impossible Act* by Wendy Arons." *Monatshefte* 99, no. 4 (2007): 556–58.

Harvey, Karen. *Reading Sex in the Eighteenth Century: Bodies and Gender in English Erotic Culture.* New York: Cambridge University Press, 2004.

Haye, de la, Amy, and Elizabeth Wilson, eds. *Defining Dress: Dress as Object, Meaning and Identity.* New York: Manchester University Press, 1999.

Hayes, John. *Gainsborough: Paintings and Drawings.* London: Phaidon, 1975.
———. *The Landscape Paintings of Thomas Gainsborough.* 2 vols. London: Sotheby's Publications, 1982.

Heil, Walter. "An Eighteenth-Century English Portrait: Charles Fredrick Abel by Gainsborough." *Art in America* 35 (October 1947): 319–23.

Hogarth, William. *The Analysis of Beauty.* Edited by Ronald Paulson. New Haven, CT: Yale University Press, 1997.

Holman, Peter. "Ann Ford Revisited." *Eighteenth-Century Music* 1, no. 2 (2004): 157–81.

Ingamells, John. *Mrs. Robinson and Her Portraits.* London: Trustees of the Wallace Collection, 1978.

Jaffé, Patricia. *Lady Hamilton in Relation to the Art of Her Time.* London: Arts Council of Great Britain and the Greater London Council, 1972. An exhibition catalogue.

Jenkins, Ian, and Kim Sloan. *Vases and Volcanoes: Sir William Hamilton and His Collection.* London: British Museum, 1996.

Jones, Vivien, ed. *Women and Literature in Britain: 1700–1800.* New York: Cambridge University Press, 2000.
———. *Women in the Eighteenth Century: Constructions of Femininity.* New York: Routledge, 1990.

King, Shelley, and Yaël Schlick, eds. *Refiguring the Coquette: Essays on Culture and Coquetry.* Lewisburg, PA: Bucknell University Press, 2008.

Knott, Sarah, and Barbara Taylor, eds. *Women, Gender and Enlightenment.* New York: Palgrave Macmillan, 2007.

Kriz, Kay Dian. *The Idea of the English Landscape Painter: Genius as Alibi in the Early Nineteenth Century.* New Haven, CT: Yale University Press, 1997.

Lajer-Burcharth, Ewa. "Fragonard in Detail." *Differences: A Journal of Feminist Cultural Studies* 14, no. 3 (Fall 2003): 34–56.
———. "Image Matters: The Case of Boucher." In *Dialogues in Art History from Mesopotamian to Modern: Readings for a New Century*, edited by Elizabeth Cropper, 277–300. New Haven, CT: Center for Advanced Study in the Visual Arts / Yale University Press, 2009.
———. "Pompadour's Touch: Difference in Representation." *Representations* 73 (Winter 2001): 54–88.

Langford, Paul. *Englishness Identified: Manners and Character 1650–1850.* Oxford: Oxford University Press, 2001.
———. *A Polite and Commercial People.* Oxford: Clarendon Press, 1989.

Lawrence, Cynthia, ed. *Women and Art in Early Modern Europe: Patrons, Collectors, and Connoisseurs.* University Park: Pennsylvania State University Press, 1996.

Leonard, Jonathan Norton, and the editors of Time-Life Books. *The World of Gainsborough 1727–1788.* New York: Time-Life Books, 1980.

Leppert, Richard. *Music and Image: Domesticity, Ideology and Socio-Cultural Formation in Eighteenth-Century England.* New York: Cambridge University Press, 1988.
———. *The Sight of Sound: Music, Representation, and the History of the Body.* Berkeley: University of California Press, 1995.

Levy, Martin. "Gainsborough's *Mrs. Robinson*: A Portrait and Its Context." *Apollo* 86 (September 1992): 153–54.

Lowenthal, Cynthia. *Lady Mary Wortley Montagu and the Eighteenth-Century Familiar Letter.* Athens: University of Georgia Press, 1994.

Mannings, David. "Gainsborough's Duke and Duchess of Cumberland with Lady Luttrell." *Connoisseur* 183 (June 1973): 85–93.
———. *Sir Joshua Reynolds: A Complete Catalogue of His Paintings.* New Haven, CT: Yale University Press, 2000.

Marsden, Jonathan, ed. *The Wisdom of George the Third: Papers from a Symposium at the Queen's Gallery, Buckingham Palace June 2004.* London: Royal Collection Publications, 2004.

Mazella, David. "Sensibility and Its Context: Two Recent Books," review of *Cato's Tears and the Making of Anglo-American Emotion* by Julie Ellison and *Characteristics of Men, Manners, Opinions, Times* by Shaftesbury (Anthony Ashley Cooper). *Eighteenth-Century Studies* 36, no. 3 (Spring 2003): 436–41.

McClintock, Anne. *Imperial Leather: Race, Gender, and Sexuality in the Colonial Conquest.* New York: Routledge, 1995.

McPherson, Heather. "Picturing Tragedy: Mrs. Siddons as the Tragic Muse Revisited." *Eighteenth-Century Studies* 33, no. 3 (Spring 2000): 401–30.

———. "Reconsidering Romney" (exhibition review). *Eighteenth-Century Studies* 36, no. 3 (Spring 2003): 411–22.

———. "Searching for Sarah Siddons: Portraiture and the Historiography of Fame" (exhibition review). *Eighteenth-Century Studies* 33, no. 2 (Winter 2000): 281–84.

McVeigh, Simon. *Concert Life in London from Mozart to Haydn*. New York: Cambridge University Press, 2004.

Miles, Ellen G. *The Portrait in Eighteenth-Century America*. Newark: University of Delaware Press, 1993.

Montagu, Lady Mary Wortley. *The Complete Letters of Lady Mary Wortley Montagu*. Edited by Robert Halsband. 3 vols. Oxford: Clarendon Press, 1966.

Moore, Andrew, with Charlotte Crawley. *Family and Friends: A Regional Survey of British Portraiture*. London: H.M.S.O., 1992.

Morris, Edward. *French Art in Nineteenth-Century Britain*. New Haven, CT: Yale University Press, 2005.

Mras, George P. *Eugène Delacroix's Theory of Art*. Princeton, NJ: Princeton University Press, 1966.

Paston, George. *Lady Mary Wortley Montagu and Her Times*. New York: Putnam, 1907.

Paulson, Ronald. "English Painting—One School or Two?" (review of David Solkin, *Painting for Money: The Visual and the Public Sphere in Eighteenth-Century England*, and Marcia Pointon, *Hanging the Head: Portraiture and Social Formation in Eighteenth-Century England*). *Eighteenth-Century Life* 17, no. 3 (1993): 104–19.

———. *Hogarth's Graphic Works*. New Haven, CT: Yale University Press, 1989.

Penny, Nicholas, ed. *Reynolds*. London: Royal Academy of Arts, 1986. An exhibition catalogue.

Perry, Gill. "Ambiguity and Desire: Metaphors of Sexuality in Late Eighteenth-Century Representations of the Actress." In *Notorious Muse: The Actress in British Art and Culture 1776–1812*, edited by Robyn Asleson, 57–80. New Haven, CT: Yale University Press, 2003.

———. *Spectacular Flirtations: Viewing the Actress in British Art and Theatre 1768–1820*. New Haven, CT: Yale University Press, 2007.

———. "Staging Gender and 'Hairy Signs': Representing Dorothy Jordan's Curls." *Eigtheenth-Century Studies* 38, no. 1 (2004): 145–63.

Perry, Gill, and Michael Rossington. *Femininity and Masculinity in Eighteenth-Century Art and Culture*. New York: Manchester University Press, 1994.

Pevsner, Nikolaus. *Academies of Art: Past and Present*. New York: Da Capo, 1973.

Piper, David. *The English Face*. Edited by Malcolm Rogers. London: National Portrait Gallery Publications, 1992.

Plumb, John Harold. *The Pursuit of Happiness: A View of Life in Georgian England*. New Haven, CT: Yale University Press, 1977.

Pointon, Marcia. *Hanging the Head: Portraiture and Social Formation in Eighteenth-Century England*. New Haven, CT: Yale University Press, 1993.

———. " 'Surrounded with Brilliants': Miniature Portraits in Eighteenth-Century England." *Art Bulletin* 83, no. 1 (2001): 48–71.

Porter, Roy. *Enlightenment: Britain and the Creation of the Modern World*. New York: Penguin Putnam Press, 2000.

———. "Review of *The Culture of Sensibility: Sex and Society in Eighteenth Century Britain* by G.J. Barker-Benfield." *Journal of Social History* 28 (Summer 1995): 894–97.

Postle, Martin, ed. *Joshua Reynolds: The Creation of Celebrity*. London: Tate Publishing, 2005. An exhibition catalogue.

———. " 'The Modern Apelles': Joshua Reynolds and the Creation of Celebrity." In *Joshua Reynolds: The Creation of Celebrity*, edited by Martin Postle, 17–34. London: Tate Publishing, 2005.

———. " 'Painted Women': Reynolds and the Cult of the Courtesan." In *Notorious Muse: The Actress in British Art and Culture 1776–1812*, edited by Robyn Asleson, 22–56. New Haven, CT: Yale University Press, 2003.

———. *Thomas Gainsborough*. Princeton, NJ: Princeton University Press, 2003.

———. "Thomas Gainsborough's 'Lost' Portrait of Auguste Vestris." *British Art Journal* 4, no. 1 (Spring 2003): 64–68.

Redford, Bruce. *Venice and the Grand Tour*. New Haven, CT: Yale University Press, 1996.

Retford, Kate. *The Art of Domestic Life: Family Portraiture in Eighteenth-Century England.* New Haven, CT: Yale University Press, 2006.

———. "Gender and the Marital Portrait in Eighteenth-Century England: 'A Sort of Sex in Souls.'" *British Journal for Eighteenth-Century Studies* 27 (2004): 99–120.

———. "Sensibility and Genealogy in the Eighteenth-Century Family Portrait: The Collection at Kedleston Hall." *Historical Journal* 46, no. 3 (2003): 533–60.

Reynolds, Sir Joshua. *Discourses on Art.* Edited by Robert R. Wark. San Marino, CA: Huntington Library Publications, 1959.

———. *Discourses on Art.* Edited by Stephen O. Mitchell, Library of Liberal Arts. New York: Bobbs-Merrill, 1965.

Ribeiro, Aileen. *The Art of Dress: Fashion in England and France 1750–1820.* New Haven, CT: Yale University Press, 1995.

———. *Dress and Morality.* Oxford: Berg, 2003. First published 1986 by B.T. Batsford, London.

———. *Dress in Eighteenth-Century Europe 1715–1789.* New Haven, CT: Yale University Press, 2002.

———. "Hussars in Masquerade." *Apollo* 105 (February 1977): 111–16.

———. "Turquerie: Turkish Dress and English Fashion in the Eighteenth Century," *Connoisseur* 201 (May 1979): 16–23.

Rogers, Katharine M. *Feminism in Eighteenth-Century England.* Urbana: University of Illinois Press, 1982.

Rosenthal, Angela. *Angelica Kauffman: Art and Sensibility.* New Haven, CT: Yale University Press, 2006.

Rosenthal, Michael. *The Art of Thomas Gainsborough.* New Haven, CT: Yale University Press, 1999.

———. "Gainsborough's *Diana and Actaeon.*" In *Painting and the Politics of Culture: New Essays on British Art, 1700–1850,* edited by John Barrell, 167–94. Oxford: Oxford University Press, 1992.

———. "Thomas Gainsborough's Ann Ford." *Art Bulletin* 80 (December 1998): 649–65.

Rosenthal, Michael, and Martin Myrone, eds. *Gainsborough.* London: Tate Publishing, 2002. An exhibition catalogue.

Saisselin, Rémy. *The Enlightenment Against the Baroque: Economics and Aesthetics in the Eighteenth Century.* Berkeley: University of California Press, 1992.

Shawe-Taylor, Desmond. *The Georgians: Eighteenth-Century Portraiture and Society.* London: Barrie & Jenkins, 1990.

Sheriff, Mary. *The Exceptional Woman: Elisabeth Vigée-Lebrun and the Cultural Politics of Art.* Chicago: University of Chicago Press, 1996.

Shesgreen, Sean, ed. *Engravings by Hogarth.* New York: Dover, 1973.

Siddons, Sarah. *Reminiscences of Sarah Kemble Siddons, 1773–1785.* Edited by William van Lennep. Cambridge, MA: Widener Library, 1942.

Silverman, Kaja. *The Threshold of the Visible World.* New York: Routledge, 1996.

Sloman, Susan. *Gainsborough in Bath.* New Haven, CT: Yale University Press, 2002.

Solkin, David. *Art on the Line: The Royal Academy Exhibitions at Somerset House 1780–1836.* New Haven, CT: Yale University Press, 2001. An exhibition catalogue.

———. "Gainsborough's Classically Virtuous Wife." *British Art Journal* 2, no. 2 (Winter 2000–01): 75–77.

Steward, James Christen. *The New Child: British Art and the Origins of Modern Childhood, 1730–1830.* Seattle: University of Washington Press, 1995.

Stewart, Mary Lynn. "The Politics and Spectacle of Fashion and Femininity." *Journal of Women's History* 17, no. 1 (Spring 2005): 192–200.

Straub, Kristina. *Sexual Suspects: Eighteenth-Century Players and Sexual Ideology.* Princeton, NJ: Princeton University Press, 1992.

Strong, Roy C. et al. *The British Portrait: 1660–1960.* Woodbridge, Suffolk, England: Antique Collectors' Club, 1991.

Timm, Annette F., and Joshua A. Sanborn. *Gender, Sex and the Shaping of Modern Europe: A History from the French Revolution to the Present Day.* New York: Berg, 2007.

Tours, Hugh. *The Life and Letters of Emma Hamilton.* London: Victor Gollancz, 1963.

Ty, Eleanor. "Engendering a Female Subject: Mary Robinson's (Re)presentations of the Self." *English Studies in Canada* 21, no. 4 (December 1995): 407–30.

Vaughan, William. *British Painting: The Golden Age.* New York: Thames & Hudson, 1999.
———. *Gainsborough.* New York: Thames & Hudson, 2002.

Wark, Robert R. "Thicknesse and Gainsborough: Some New Documents." *Art Bulletin* 40, no. 4 (1958): 331–34.

Waterhouse, Ellis. "Bath and Gainsborough." *Apollo* 98 (November 1973): 360–65.
———. *Gainsborough.* London: Edward Hulton, 1958.
———. *Painting in Britain 1530 to 1790.* Edited by Nikolaus Pevsner. New York: Viking Penguin, 1986.
———. *Three Decades of British Art 1740–1770.* Philadelphia: American Philosophical Society, 1965.

West, Shearer. "Libertinism and the Ideology of Male Friendship in the Portraits of the Society of Dilettanti." *Eighteenth-Century Life* 16 (May 1992): 76–104.
———. *Portraiture.* New York: Oxford University Press, 2004.

Whitley, William T. *Artists and Their Friends in England 1700–1799.* 2 vols. London: Medici Society, 1928.
———. *Thomas Gainsborough.* London: Smith, Elder, 1915.

Wilson, Kathleen. "Citizen, Empire, and Modernity in the English Provinces, c.1720–1790." *Eighteenth-Century Studies* 29, no. 1 (Fall 1995): 69–96.

Wilson, Michael I. "Gainsborough, Bath and Music." *Apollo* 105 (February 1977): 107–10.

Wilton, Andrew. *The Swagger Portrait: Grand Manner Portraiture in Britain from Van Dyck to Augustus John 1630–1930.* London: Tate Gallery, 1992. An exhibition catalogue.

Zimmermann, Michael, ed. *The Art Historian: National Traditions and Institutional Practices.* New Haven, CT: Yale University Press, 2003.

Photo Credits

Introduction
Cincinnati Art Museum, 12; Rob Deslong-
champs, 16

Plates
Scott Hisey, 19; Courtesy of the Huntington
Library, Art Collections, and Botanical
Gardens, San Marino, California, 23; © The
Metropolitan Museum of Art / Art Resource,
New York, 29; Image courtesy of the Board of
Trustees, National Gallery of Art, Washington,
37; Graydon Wood, 25; © Tate, London 2010, 31

**Benedict Leca, "A Favourite Among the
Demireps": Thomas Gainsborough and the
Modern Woman**
© The Trustees of the British Museum. All
rights reserved, 58; Scott Hisey, 41, 42, 47,
53, 59, 71, 75, 76, 108–9; Copyright The Frick
Collection, New York, 67; Courtesy of the Hun-
tington Library, Art Collections, and Botanical
Gardens, San Marino, California, 62; © The
Metropolitan Museum of Art, 104, 106–7; © The
Metropolitan Museum of Art / Art Resource,
New York, 60, 100; Reproduced by kind per-
mission of the Society of Dilettanti, London,
48; Bildarchiv Preussischer Kulturbesitz /
Art Resource, New York, 50; © Tate, London
2010, 77, 78, 80–81, 83, 84–85, 87, 88–89, 90,
94–95; © By kind permission of the Trustees of
The Wallace Collection, London, 54, 60

**Aileen Ribeiro, "A Most Extraordinary Figure,
Handsome and Bold": Gainsborough's Portrait
of Ann Ford**
© The Trustees of the British Museum. All
rights reserved, 112, 113, 117, 118; Scott Hisey,
110, 112, 142–43; © Courtauld Institute of
Art Gallery, London, 114, 115; Copyright The
Frick Collection, New York, 132, 136, 141;
Reproduced by the kind permission of the Earl
and Countess of Harewood and Trustees of
the Harewood House Trust, 131; © Hunterian
Museum & Art Gallery, University of Glasgow,
121; Courtesy of the Huntington Library, Art
Collections, and Botanical Gardens, San
Marino, California, 121; Erich Lessing / Art
Resource, New York, 125; © The Metropolitan
Museum of Art / Art Resource, New York,
132; Image courtesy of the Board of Trustees,
National Gallery of Art, Washington, 135; By
consent of the owners; photograph © National
Portrait Gallery, London, 139; © The National
Trust, Waddesdon Manor, photo: Eost and
MacDonald, 134; © Tate, London 2010, 116, 127,
138; V&A Images, London / Art Resource, New
York, 127; © National Museums Liverpool, 126;
© By kind permission of the Trustees of The
Wallace Collection, London, 124, 133

**Amber Ludwig, "Virtue in a Vicious Age":
Fashioning Feminine Identity in Eighteenth-
Century London**
Rick Hall, 165; Private Collection / Bridgeman
Art Library, 148, 179, 181; © The Trustees of
the British Museum. All rights reserved, 155,
158, 159; Scott Hisey, 144; License granted
courtesy of The Rt Hon The Earl of Derby, 163;
Copyright The Frick Collection, New York, 161;
Courtesy of the Huntington Library, Art Col-
lections, and Botanical Gardens, San Marino,
California, 156; © National Gallery, London /
Art Resource, New York, 169, 170; Image cour-
tesy of the Board of Trustees, National Gallery
of Art, Washington, 149; © National Portrait
Gallery, London, 150; © By kind permission
of the Trustees of The Wallace Collection,
London, 157

End Matter
Private Collection / Bridgeman Art Library,
181; Courtesy of the Huntington Library, Art
Collections, and Botanical Gardens, San
Marino, California, 194–95, 196.

Index

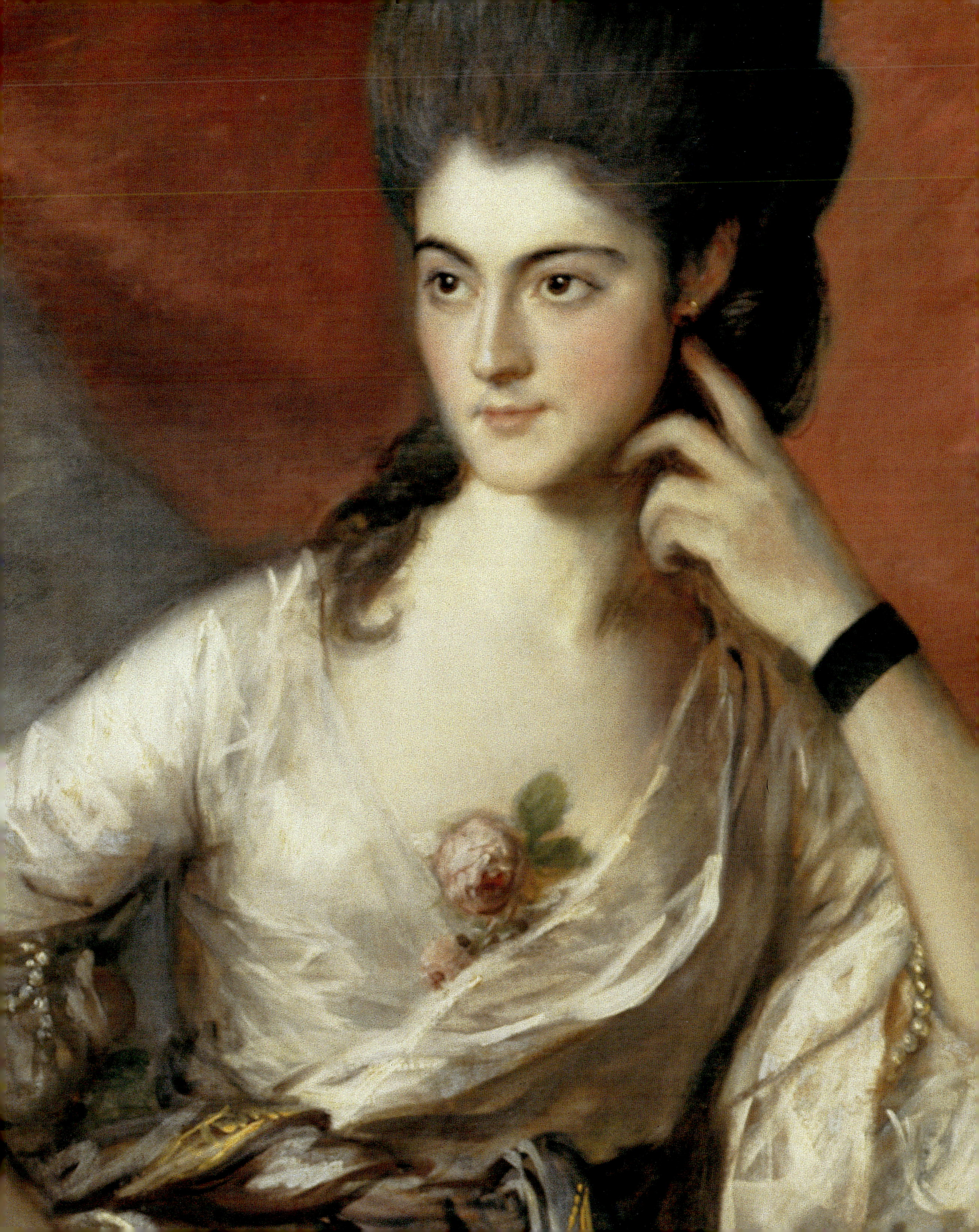

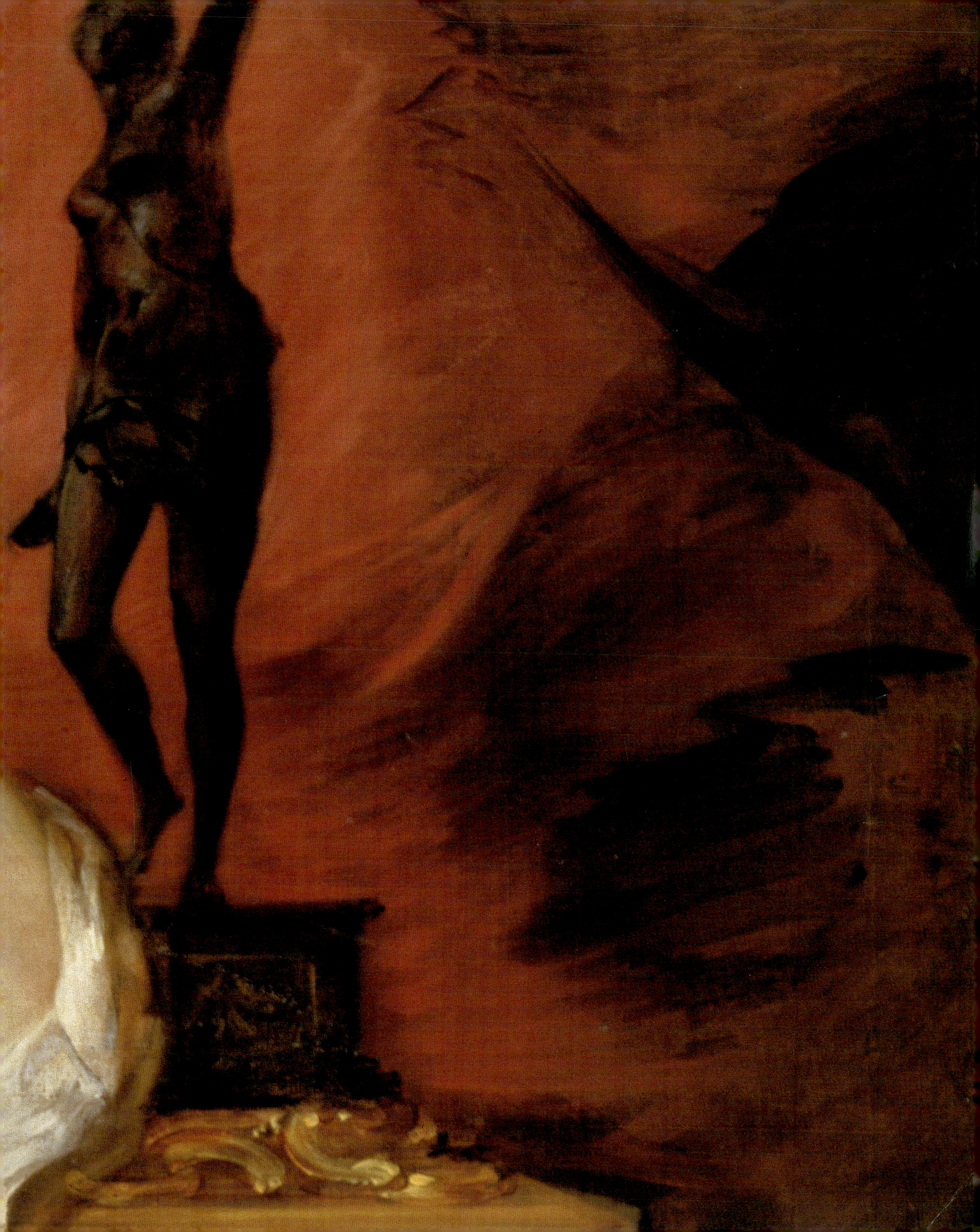